ACTON: THE FORMATIVE YEARS

John first Lord Acton.

DAVID MATHEW

ACTON

THE FORMATIVE YEARS

907.2024
A1883 Ma

GREENWOOD PRESS, PUBLISHERS
WESTPORT, CONNECTICUT

148542

Library of Congress Cataloging in Publication Data

Mathew, David, Abp., 1902-
  Acton, the formative years.

  Reprint of the 1946 ed. published by Eyre & Spottiswoode, London.
  1. Acton, John Emerich Edward Dalberg Acton, 1st Baron, 1834-1902.
D15.A25M3 1974   907'.2'024 [B]   73-19308
ISBN 0-8371-7323-X

First published in 1946 by Eyre & Spottiswoode, London

Reprinted with the permission of A. P. Watt & Son

Reprinted in 1974 by Greenwood Press,
a division of Williamhouse-Regency Inc.

Library of Congress Catalog Card Number 73-19308

ISBN 0-8371-7323-X

Printed in the United States of America

To

DOUGLAS WOODRUFF and to MIA WOODRUFF

in memory of Aldenham

CONTENTS

	PAGE
INTRODUCTION	1
A NOTE ON METHOD	8

PART I: BACKGROUND AND YOUTH

I. GENERAL ACTON	11
II. THE PALAZZO ACTON	20
III. DALBERG AND ALDENHAM	26
IV. OSCOTT	30
V. THE OLD CATHOLICS	38
VI. THE WHIG MARRIAGE	46

PART II: INFLUENCES OF EARLY MANHOOD

I. THE GERMAN SCENE	55
II. DR. DÖLLINGER	67
III. MOSCOW	76
IV. TOCQUEVILLE	86
V. FERMENT	99
VI. THE ENGLISH HISTORIANS	106
VII. DR. NEWMAN	114
VIII. THE "RAMBLER" PERIOD	123
IX. THE HOUSE OF COMMONS	131
X. VICTORIANA	140

PART III: THE FIRST ACHIEVEMENTS

I. ACTON AS A REVIEWER	148
II. THE LIBRARY AT ALDENHAM	159
III. THE EMERGENCE OF THE HISTORIAN	165
IV. THE INFLUENCE OF MR. GLADSTONE	174
V. CRYSTALLISATION	181

INDEX	189

LIST OF ILLUSTRATIONS

John first Lord Acton   *frontispiece*
    By *Franz von Lenbach*

Sir John Acton, sixth Baronet: Prime Minister of the
    Two Sicilies   *facing page* 48

Sir Richard Acton, seventh Baronet   64

Aldenham Park   80

Monument to Sir Richard Acton in Aldenham Chapel   96

Pope Gregory XVI, Tsar Nicholas I and Cardinal Acton   128

Marie Countess Granville   144
    By *Ary Scheffer*.

Special thanks are due to LORD *and* LADY ACTON *by whose courtesy all these portraits now at Aldenham Park are reproduced. The illustration of Aldenham Park is reproduced by the courtesy of the* Hon. Mrs. DOUGLAS WOODRUFF.

INTRODUCTION

THE STUDY of the formative years of the most learned of English historians has always come before my mind as one of the most entrancing of all subjects for research. The unique appeal has lain in contrast; the background Neapolitan, Russian, South German, French, at once rich, lavish and improbable, crossed with the old Catholic squirearchy of the West of England and set in the last serene days of the high Whig world. Out of these mixed contending ways of life there would issue the historian who was at once the governing factor in so much later study and a strong sustaining force in his own right.

The fame of Lord Acton as an historian has been growing steadily. We can now see more clearly than his contemporaries the penetrating quality of certain of his judgments and the grasp that he possessed of the essentials of European politics. He combined an experience of political machinery, which was much wider and more sensitive than his rigid principles would at first suggest, with an unparalleled array of knowledge. His Germanic style was marked by a conscious and heavy clarity; he was always lucid. In later life, especially, his writing was burdened with allusions. Still, once the context was made clear, his meaning was no more open to question than his praised integrity. The development of his thought fell into three stages; the first period was the explanation of the second, and both prepared the way for the golden assurance of his final years.

John Emerich Edward Dalberg Acton was born at Naples in 1834 and died at Tegernsee in Bavaria in 1902. His life was thus centred on those peaceful reaches of the nineteenth century in which the French Revolution and the Napoleonic struggles were fading memories. He was hardly concerned with any military upheaval and only one major conflict crossed his field of vision; from England he analysed the causes and the progress of the Franco-Prussian War. It was the civic effects of power which always engaged his mind. He had a unique appreciation of the consequences which would spring from the new unbridled nationalism. He was among the first to understand the evil latent in all racial theories. No man ever had a juster view of the perils inherent in a dynamic sovereignty when this is coextensive with a racially homogeneous State.

Naples and Paris, Russia and the United States in turn acted by attraction or repulsion in the development of Acton's ideas which were fortified by so extraordinary an erudition. Through his stepfather Lord Granville he imbibed the Whig ideals and he had a close and indeed instinctive knowledge of the politico-aristocratic world and of the chancelleries of Europe. It is a characteristic of his approach to nineteenth-century history that Acton's thought is penetrating in the measure in which his detailed information is accurate and deep. Döllinger and the Bavarian intellectual circle influenced him profoundly. It was from these years in Munich that he gained the power to absorb, but not always to synthesise, the most diverse impressions. Burke was a chosen and a safe ideal, for in reality the young historian reflected all that complex of mood and supposition which had gone to mould the European possessing class. It was perhaps this element which gave to him his strong initial sympathy with the thought of Alexis de Tocqueville. Both men throughout their studious lives were concentrated upon the problem of how to preserve an element of freedom in the new society.

The second period of Acton's life lasts from his first submission to the dominating and imperious thought of William Ewart Gladstone, a process which was completed about 1864. It includes his brief parliamentary career and his emergence as a Gladstonian Liberal, the first two decades of his married life and the last years in which he lived in his old home at Aldenham. To this phase belongs the Vatican Council and the grant of his peerage and his association with Döllinger's old age. Gladstone bestrides, and in a sense bestrides alone, the whole middle period of Acton's thought. The final period is marked by his recognition as an historian. This may be held to coincide with the foundation in 1886 of the *English Historical Review*, whose first volume contained that study of "German Schools of History" which was to prove one of Lord Acton's most massive contributions in his chosen field. His honorary doctorates at Oxford and Cambridge date from about this time; he became a Fellow of All Souls in 1890. For the last seven years before his death he held the Regius chair of Modern History at Cambridge. This book deals with the first period of his life, the formative years.

In many respects Lord Acton stands at the parting of the ways. More than any man of his time, except Tocqueville, he foresaw the actual nature of the development of world forces. Whatever may be thought of his constant search for factors of balance in the Constitution, his hatred of absolutism gave a point to each judgment upon politics.

Acton belonged, too, to the first great period of modern historical research. He was the heir of the generation which had founded the *Ecole des Chartes* in Paris and the School of Method in Berlin. The tools were ready to his hand, his bibliographical knowledge was immense and the whole was at the service of his zest for tracing the development of ideas. No man has surely ever known so much of the recondite printed sources. He was very swift to follow the bearing of every statement and the implication of each letter; his power of correlating data was most striking. He had an unrivalled understanding of the way that public business was conducted in the eighteenth and nineteenth centuries in Western Europe.

It was a consequence of these gifts that Acton could bring a form of inherited experience to bear on events in Europe which took place since the Revolution of 1688. He was by nature nothing of a mediaevalist and he never treated the politics even of the seventeenth century with that sureness of touch with which he would approach questions of modern government. A great deal in fact depended upon Acton's own background. It may safely be said that no great professor ever came from a world that was so completely unprofessorial. He had an hereditary and immense experience of the circles of privilege upon the Continent. He had pursued his way among the archaic extravagance and the immediate sophisticated simplicity of the Bavarian *haute monde* and past the elegant and dubious northern gentlemen who haunted the *purlieus* of the Court of Naples in the period of Alfred d'Orsay. In this study it is worth examining such points in concrete.

Sir John Acton's inheritance came to him in two parts, the paternal fortune when he succeeded his father in the baronetcy at the age of three and the German wealth when Lady Granville died in 1860. Apart from investments in the English funds these moneys came from many sources, ancestral Shropshire land, estates and *rentes* in the Electorate of Trier, Napoleonic subventions made to Dalbergs and that haul, not large by old Whig standards, which his grandfather General Acton had gouged out of the Crown of the Two Sicilies. This upbringing in a world from part of which he would recoil left a seal on him that was ineffaceable. In one sense he was very *grand seigneur*; he was surely not at all self-conscious and he had an assurance both in act and judgment which was to be in most respects a blessing. He early possessed a familiar intercourse with the great and a contemptuous knowledge of those who gained by devious paths the intimacy of politicians. The climber and political middleman was a type distasteful to him; he was not a man who reined in his contempt.

This was among the factors that created the great veneration which possessed him for the pure scholar. In any case the *minutiae* of scholarship would fascinate him. At the same time it seems clear that Acton's avid pleasure in study was heightened by the contrast provided between Döllinger's conservatism, which was so altruistic and remote, and the persistent deft intrigues of nineteenth-century politics. There was little that Acton did not know about the honeycomb of Austrian and Sardinian politics or those of France under the Second Empire. With English politics, except as seen through Lord Granville from the high Whig angle, he was less familiar. Through all his early life he was slowly but inexorably approaching Mr. Gladstone. In history he came to find a conception of *political sin*; he despised manœuvres and place-hunting. John Acton matured early; he had all the rich man's abhorrence of self-seeking. These elements played their part in forming judgments which even before thirty were very massive, based on the widest reading and contemporary experience, extremely poised and definite, but so severe.

With this there went a social ease and pleasure which was at once light and serious and Germanic; the wit of the mid-nineteenth-century breakfast table. For this reason it is necessary to consider the world of the great capitals, with its gay brittle custom and European *convenances*, in which he was immersed when free from study. He had all the marks of those who benefited by the politico-social fabric underpinned in the thirty years that followed the Congress of Vienna. Thus he was at ease with his equals; he valued the *bourgeoisie* as a solid buttress; he was uninterested in Legitimism. Closely associated with these conceptions was the influence which Catholicism had upon the temper of his mind. Hitherto this matter has not been examined; but there seems little doubt that to Acton his ancestral Faith was illuminating, disappointing, at times utterly exasperating, noble and inevitable. One thing is surely true, that to him Catholicism was always inescapable; it had been brought to him through many channels and in many guises. There were the hearty philistine English Catholic gentry who lived in their great houses spaced around him; there was the romantic intellectual selfconscious Munich group; in childhood there had been his mother's active, warm and cultivated piety; in boyhood there was Wiseman's influence which at first entranced and then repelled him. Perhaps more effective than all these was the whole vast complex background of the world of privilege in Catholic Europe. There is much here to be disentangled. Lord Acton's place as an historian is the result of the fruition of his unexampled reading crossed with a rare power of correlation and based upon a mixed and improbable inheritance.

In the field of ideas it was the thinkers of the seventeenth century, Leibnitz especially, with whom he was first at home; thenceforward he would trace each criss-cross line. In dealing with the mode of every change between the Peace of Utrecht in 1713 and the outbreak of the war of 1870, Acton always possessed that ease of treatment which had first been brought to bear on contemporary political events by Burke his master. Both men belonged essentially to the period of the secular unity of Europe and sought in the politics of their time for the norm of a political institution which would prove itself able to endure. Both master and disciple were in essence conservative believing Whigs nourished by a class supremacy which all along maintained its flanking *literati*. It is for this reason that every study of the formative influence on Acton must include a consideration of those Burkian doctrines on which the structure of this thought rested.

Edmund Burke was the one teacher whom Acton came to early and never left. It is remarkable that each one of the great historian's successive mentors sustained this influence. There were to be certain changes of direction in Acton's outlook, but through each variation he remained attached to this political philosopher. His feeling for Burke is as clear in the immaturity of his writings for the *Rambler* as in his final Cambridge lectures. From him he learned the need for ordered liberty.

It was a part of Acton's work to kindle reason with his moral fire. Thus in the cold dry air of the eighteenth century the Constitution had been set up where men of earlier times had placed far different mysteries. "We ought", wrote Burke [1] in the *Appeal from the New to the Old Whigs*, "to understand it according to our measure, and to venerate where we are not able presently to comprehend." It is essential to stress this religious note. One other sentence well describes so much that Acton valued. "The example", Burke explained,[2] "of a wise, moral, well-natured, and well-tempered spirit of freedom is that alone which can be useful to us, or in the least degree reputable or safe." In one of his letters to Mrs. Drew written in the winter of 1880 Acton described the effect produced on him by the literary remains of this great man. "You can hardly imagine", he explained,[3] "what Burke is for all of us who think about politics, and are not wrapped in the blaze and the whirlwind of Rousseau. Systems of scientific thought have been built up by famous scholars on the fragments that fell from his table. Great literary fortunes have been made by men who traded on the hundredth part of him." These phrases ring with that assured enthusiasm which would mark Acton's maturity. He was driven to them by many forces and not least by his strange background.

* * *

And now I come to my acknowledgments. In the first place I must express my gratitude to Lady Galway, whose impression of Lord Acton's personality first gave me a view of the great historian's character. I must thank the Master of Trinity and Sir Edmund Whittaker, the latter in particular for conveying the luminous quality of the historian's Cambridge years. Lady Oxford and Asquith described to me a visit to Hawarden in 1896 when Lord Acton was staying there. Lord FitzAlan has provided me with an account of the effect that he produced in his last years in Conservative and Catholic circles.

I am grateful to the Librarian to the University of Cambridge for his assistance and to the staff of the Library for their courtesy when I was working in the Acton Library and on the Acton Papers. I must also thank Fr. Vincent Reade for permission to study the Acton-Newman correspondence preserved among the Newman

---

[1] *Appeal from the New to the Old Whigs*, p. 213.
[2] *ibid.*, p. 209.
[3] *Letters of Lord Acton to Mary Gladstone*, pp. 56-7.

MSS. in the Oratory at Birmingham. I am grateful to Professor F. L. Woodward for information in regard to some of the sources for this book; I am indebted to his great knowledge of the English scene in the period that this work covers. Dame Una Pope-Hennessy has kindly assisted me through her intimate understanding of the Crimean period in English letters. I have been happy in the aid that I have received from Wilfrid Meynell and in the use of the fine Victorian library at Greatham.

I must express my thanks to Professor Hayek and Professor Butterfield for their views on different aspects of Lord Acton's thought. I am indebted to Professor Powicke and Sir Charles Oman for an evaluation of the Oxford history school during the period under discussion, and to the late A. J. Carlyle whose account of the Oxford teaching in his youth was at once so light and memorable.

I am especially grateful to my friends Douglas and Mia Woodruff, Alick Dru, Alfred Gilbey, Arnold Toynbee, Rose Macaulay, John Armstrong, Maurice Gorham, Brian Wormald and Robert Speaight who have borne with and assisted at my discussions of different aspects of this theme. With these names I would place that of R. A. L. Smith, who shortly before his death planned a study of Lord Acton's political ideas. I owe much to Graham Greene.

Finally, I must thank Lord and Lady Acton and Lady Throckmorton both for providing background detail and an opportunity to study Aldenham and Coughton. W. A. Pantin was my guide to Buckland. I must thank Fr. W. H. Munster for giving me access to the fine nineteenth-century library at the London Oratory, and I am grateful to the Librarian and staff of the London Library for their unfailing courtesy. Still, however much my friends have assisted me they are not responsible for my conclusions. It is only my brother Gervase with whom I have discussed this matter from each angle and then line by line as he amended and modified each draft. Such as it is, my work owes everything to him, and no book more than this study of a subject which is at once so intricate and fascinating.

DAVID MATHEW.

WOBURN SQUARE, *June* 1938.
CARLISLE PLACE, *January* 1945.

A NOTE ON METHOD

AS THE SCENES in this book are built up in such detail it seems desirable to give some explanation of the method used and the way in which each element is constructed. The fact that the footnotes are in general confined to providing the authority for quotations makes this more necessary. It is, perhaps, simplest to proceed by examining two matters in detail as typical of the rest, choosing for this purpose the description of Dr. Döllinger's house in Munich and Acton's visit to Moscow with Lord Granville. We can take first the account of the historian's stay in Russia during August and September 1856.

The many details of Lord Granville's mission to Moscow are for the most part found assembled in the ambassador's diary and in the correspondence which he maintained with his friend Lord Canning, at that time Governor-General of India. The whole body of these letters is printed in Lord Edmond Fitzmaurice's biography of the second Earl Granville. Some of these letters are in diary form. Thus the reference to the "Dog and Duck" appears under an entry made on 8 January 1856. The details in regard to the Chatsworth plate, the Minton vases, the episode of the Queen's portrait, the arrangement of the candles in the ballroom of the Graziani Palace and the names of Lord Granville's horses Marlborough and Woronzow all come from the same source. The notes on Morny's *équipage* are found in an entry made by Granville at Aschaffenburg on 23 June 1856 (i. p. 183) and the anecdote of the Prince de Ligne is related during the stay at Moscow (i. p. 200). A delay at St. Petersburg on 14 August recalled to the ambassador's mind the stand for Lord Ailesbury's State coach on which he commented. It was on his return from this mission that Granville ordered the *percherons* for his farm at Golder's Green (i. p. 228). The Russian officer was detected carrying off the pineapple in his helmet at the State ball on 25 September (i. p. 213). The statement as to the inability of the younger members of the mission to speak French occurs in a note under 2 September made after Lady Granville's first ball. These points include all the detail brought out in the account of Acton's journey with Lord Granville except that provided by quotations whose references are given in the footnotes to the chapter.

A NOTE ON METHOD

In the description of Döllinger's house in Munich something is due to Acton's letters of the period giving details of his room with its glass-fronted bookcase and the timetable that he followed. The account of Dr. Döllinger's favourite walks in the Bavarian capital is taken from Luise von Kobell's *Conversations* (ed. 1892), and the professor's favourite rhymes like the Brantôme jingle and the Thuringian verses come from the same source (pp. 36 and 23), so also do the details of Döllinger's views on tobacco and alcohol (p. 25). Acton's walks with the professor in the English Garden are described in his letters. The details of the furniture of the professor's rooms and of his favourite flowers are found in Luise von Kobell's volume. It is true that the placing of the furniture and pictures can only be traced back to Döllinger's old age, but it is specifically stated in the *Conversations* that the arrangement of his study was unchanged since he first took up residence in Munich. The episodes of the professor's early life and in particular the story of his taking the part of Dunois in the *Jungfrau von Orleans* come from this source. The letters of James Hope printed in Robert Ornsby's *Memoir* give an impression of Döllinger in 1840 and 1844; they also contain a fairly detailed account of Dr. Windischmann's apartment. John Hungerfold Pollen's *Diary*, printed in his biography by Anne Pollen, contains the single reference to the visit paid by Döllinger and Acton to Dr. Pusey.

A very similar account to the foregoing would cover each detail given of the Château of Tocqueville and the description of Alexis de Tocqueville's life in Paris and Normandy. These points are to be found in the two volumes of Nassau William Senior's letters and journals. The journal in Normandy 1850 and at Sorrento 1851 have especial value in this connection. One description in this book on Lord Acton comes, however, in a different category. The account of Cardinal Wiseman's visit to Lady Mostyn at Talacre was given to me by her son the late Archbishop of Cardiff. Among the stories current at Talacre in the Archbishop's childhood was that of the Ince apparition, which is also described in an MS. collection of ghost stories relating to English Catholic houses made by one of the Welds of Chideock.

Each detail of Dr. Weedall's life at Oscott down to the most minute particulars can be found in the biography published in 1860 by Provost Husenbeth. In this connection use has been made of the *Memoirs of Lady Mary Arundell*. For the earlier chapters the precise careful accounts are very numerous. Details of society in Naples during Sir Ferdinand Richard Acton's short married life can be built up from the journals of Henry Edward Fox and from *La Récit d'une sœur*. The memoirs of John Orlando Parry contribute their own point of interest, while the first volume of *The Greville Memoirs* has great value arising from its author's point of view which is so characteristic of the privileged world of English politics. Manuscripts at Aldenham have proved of value in describing the life of Sir Richard Acton. Certain memoranda of expenses contribute to establishing the picture of the life of the senior line of the family. The Fortescue and Dartmouth MSS. threw light upon the estimation in which General Acton was held by English travellers and diplomats. This comes out very clearly in Sir William Hamilton's letters bearing on Lord Lewisham's travels in the kingdom of the Two Sicilies.

Apart from the two detailed examinations, this note has merely brought together a number of the trails that were pursued. In the selection of material a responsibility always rests upon the author, since the interpretation of each period must depend in large measure upon the detail chosen. In Lord Acton's case there is an almost startling contrast between his massive knowledge and his grave high-minded thought and that European background from which he sprang that was at once so brittle and romantic, light, easy, shrewd.

PART I: BACKGROUND AND YOUTH

CHAPTER I
GENERAL ACTON

IN THE LATE SEPTEMBER of the year 1764, in the last heats of the malarial summer, a coach rolled out of Pisa along the old posting road to Leghorn, which led out by San Giovanni al Gatano towards the custom house maintained by the grand ducal government of Tuscany. The well-hung carriage with its three travellers moved easily on the good surface of the highway. Opposite the elderly and gout-ridden Commodore Acton sat John Acton, his slim careful nephew, and beside him their cousin, Edward Gibbon, fresh from England. This young man's over-elaborate brocade and velvet drew attention to his strange face, the nose like a potato and the eyes alert with a too-mastering intelligence; in his corner, leaning back against the insufficient upholstery, he sat with his unyouthful and composed alertness.

The project of a history was already with him, and within a month he would be embarked upon *The Decline and Fall of the Roman Empire*. They were now passing through a pleasant champaign country; the grasses coarse; the horizons wide; the way quite level. The range of the steep Pisan hills lay behind them beyond the Arno, and there was nothing to break the even prospect. Earlier in the summer Gibbon had made an entry in his diary. "These Mountains", he noted [1] of the enclosing Apennines, "are not high ... I know nothing more melancholy than their general view." Now he was indulging in one of those experiments in social intercourse which afforded him such constant pleasure.

In that careful valuation of his assets, which Gibbon began to make in his clear-sighted youth, a prime place was occupied by his cousins, the Actons, "that ancient and loyal family of Shropshire Baronets". He had always professed the liveliest respect for the head of the house, Sir Richard Acton of Aldenham House and Round Acton in the County of Salop, and it was a pleasure to extend a youthful patronage to the financially rickety members of that stock.

[1] Edward Gibbon's *Diary*, entry under 19 June 1764.

In his Journal for August 1762 Gibbon gives a series of impressions of these same relatives. He was at that time twenty-five, and the younger Acton a year his senior.

"I found", he relates [1] with some complacency in the course of a description of a visit to Mrs. Darrel at Southampton, "a relation whom I had never seen and scarce heard of before. His story is curious. When my father was upon his travels about thirty years ago, he was taken ill at Besançon and knowing that a young relation of his of the name of Acton studied surgery at Paris he sent over for him. After he was cured, Mr. Acton fell in love with a Lady of the place, married her, changed his religion and settled at Besançon. He had several children; two of them are in the French service, in FitzJames' horse; the third, as soon as he grew up, was sent for to Leghorn by his uncle Commodore Acton, who, having passed from the service of our East India Company to that of the Emperor, Great Duke of Tuscany, commanded his fleet.

"This young Gentleman, now Captain of Foot and Lieutenant of a man-of-war in the Austrian service, is the person I am speaking of. He is come over to England for a few months to see his friends. At first sight he appears a very pretty sensible young man." [2]

This was followed by two other entries bearing on the development of their intercourse.

"20th. Mr. Acton dined with us. Too much wine again." [3]

"29 August. Another drunken day." [4]

Now, as they drove on across the Via Aurelia, Gibbon composed those sentences, which he was to write in his French journal that same evening, describing the urbane compassion which he felt for his less-favoured relatives. He admitted, with a temperate satisfaction, that they had overwhelmed him with courtesies, and he gave expression to his sympathy with Commodore Acton, for he was crippled and very lonely since he had been abandoned by the English colony on account of his change of Faith, and was quite unable to speak Italian. "Dans l'univers entière", notes Gibbon,[5] "ne lui reste que son neveu dont la réputation a beaucoup souffert du changement de son oncle, qu'on attribue à son manège."

They came that evening into Leghorn, to the long quays of

---

[1] *Autobiography of Edward Gibbon*, ed. John Murray, p. 11.
[2] *Gibbon's Journal to January 28th*, 1763, ed. D. M. Low, pp. 121-2.
[3] *ibid.*, p. 131.
[4] *ibid.*, p. 132.
[5] Gibbon, *Miscellaneous Works*, i. p. 195.

the Porto Mediceo and the fine new piazzas, very light and modern, past the Annunciata dei Greci and the façade of the Cisterone in that classic style which was then so much valued by the great English houses. But at Leghorn the Commodore was in some embarrassment, for Parson Burnaby, the chaplain at the English factory, was acting consul, a man with "a lively and ardent zeal for his holy profession". He was to publish a sermon on the whole Duty of a Protestant, to be sold to the common people for a penny. With the well-to-do and established English merchants the Commodore and his nephew had but little in common. Gibbon left them and passed on to Rome.

Inevitably the English passed them, for the Actons only moved in alternate decades: Besançon, Leghorn, Naples. They were not Jacobites, but rather soldiers of fortune. Both had admirable manners, and the younger talent. At the moment their luck was out, for they were stranded in a niggardly provincial service whose revenues had been drained away in the calm that followed on the Peace of Paris. They were to live on the track of the Grand Tour, but their future was bound up with the dynasties of the peninsula. The grand duchy of Tuscany and the kingdom of the Two Sicilies were the scene of their profession, not their leisure. It is not surprising that the Commodore and his nephew appeared careworn to the young lords in their costly chariots. Their careers, unsupported by capital, depended on a profitable knowledge of the strange Bourbon *terrain*: their advancement was to turn on how far they could make their own its foreign idiom.

* * *

The house at Aldenham had a marked influence upon all the Actons. To those in Italy it was a symbol, and it was only in the historian's time that it became the home of the younger branch, but it was the seal of a contact that they never lost. The family, of great antiquity and settled for many centuries upon this land, had been Cavalier and resolutely Tory; High Churchmen; perhaps Non-jurors. A solid wealth, which had increased since they received their baronetcy in the Civil Wars, would have brought them earlier to a peerage but for their politics. The house itself dated in its eighteenth-century state from 1691, the period of the Acton prosperity when they were all "tall men and Tories". It was a long deep house, dignified and heavy, with high-pitched roofs and wooden corbelled[1] eaves above the stonework. The fruit gardens beyond the north-west angle of the building seem to have dated from this time with their wrought-iron gates and the stone urns spaced upon the wall. The long slope of the avenue stretching away from the main front of Aldenham House was probably planted during these years.

There was no park land and the house stood squarely on rising ground in the midst of its own territory in the south-eastern part of Shropshire to the west of the turnpike road which ran from Bridgnorth to Shrewsbury through Astley Abbots. For the greater part of the century, from 1716 until 1791, the estate was held in turn by a father and son, Sir Whitmore and Sir Richard Acton. At this date, 1764, Sir Richard, a man of fifty-two, was in possession.

His life was very different from that of the Commodore and his nephew. Clearly of sober character, a small pursy man, he had none of the presence of his father, Sir Whitmore Acton, whose portrait hung at Aldenham with the great wig and the calm eyes and the air of assurance as he stood in his reddish-orange coat and russet surcoat with the lace falling from his throat. Sir Richard was attached to his own acres; his turn as sheriff had been his only public service; he had married twenty years before Lady Anne Grey, the plain sister of his neighbour Lord Stamford who lived at Enville Hall in the next county.

Old-fashioned and Christian, he sat at Aldenham with his Livy and his philosophical essays of the older school, carrying on a decorous correspondence with the Warden of All Souls in regard to land which the College owned at Alderbury, settling down to the fine rural fare "the mutton stakes and pidgions". The memoranda that he has left enable us to picture him with his flaxen russia cloth and his fine yellow broadcloth lined with fustian for the pockets and on his head his new ratteen beaver. Two notes of expenditure [2] complete the impression of the life at Aldenham.

> "1777. For the Housekeeper and Maid Servants.
> Saffron, cochineal, powders,
> A lenitive mixture for Mrs. Shaw 2/-,
> A nervous tincture for the cook 1/6,
> A pint of sweet oil 1/3.

[1] These corbelled eaves still survive on the north and west fronts. The date 1691 appears on a stone medallion on the west wall. The house appears to have been a double one, composed of two main blocks separated by a small central court.

[2] These notes with the other memoranda are kept among the MSS. at Aldenham Park.

"1775. Mr. Boulton's Bill.
A jellybag,
diaper linen,
green persia,
yellow shalloon,
for the housekeeper 9 yards of Russian huccaback."

It was a far cry to Leghorn or to the Court of the Two Sicilies, but these two strains, the Aldenham tradition and the eighteenth-century cosmopolitan world, were mingled in the Actons and not least in the historian.

One other factor in relation to Sir Richard Acton has some significance. He had joined the Roman Church in the seventeen-fifties and now maintained a chaplain, while keeping aloof from the internal controversies of his new Communion. His action, so rare at this time, is worth noting, for it may have influenced young Edward Gibbon in his transient conversion. That kinsman very seldom embarked on any course of action which he considered from a worldly standpoint to be "impossible".

When Sir Richard lost his son in 1762 he showed an interest in young John Acton, his eventual heir, who came from Italy to Aldenham for a visit and was regarded as a possible husband for his only daughter. But the marriage project, if it ever existed, came to nothing. He went away and did not return, and Sir Richard settled down to his quiet pursuits.

* * *

Twenty years passed. The Commodore was now dead and John Acton had come south in 1778 to reorganise the Neapolitan naval force. He was minister of war, a hard-won post. Beset by rivals, he had earned the enmity of the Spanish court and was under a raking fire from their ambassador, who had the more influence since the King of Spain was the father of King Ferdinand of Naples. He was forty-eight and still unmarried, and indeed prudently a bachelor since he largely owed his favour to the affection he had aroused in the determined Queen of the Two Sicilies. The travelling English had only a faint interest in that kingdom, and Acton's position was in some respects equivocal; in these years he tended to be cold-shouldered.

By 1784 new interests had come into fashion with the travellers. There was a stress upon the natural sciences and art was seen in a fresh perspective. The English minister, Sir William Hamilton, who had a dilettante concern for all these things, could scarcely tolerate John Acton's labours. The twenty years of the latter's shrewd advancement had separated him from his carefree countrymen who were accustomed to the smooth working of their own great oligarchy. And there was little to link him with the young Whig lords or the members of Lord North's administration. Three letters from the Dartmouth Papers will give an impression of that English world in Naples, which pressed so close about him, and in which General Acton had such little part.

"There is at present", wrote Sir William Hamilton at Caserta to the Earl of Dartmouth, the lord privy seal,[1] "a slight eruption of Vesuvius. I have continued my remarks with constancy and assiduity. A new edition of my letters with additions and 50 coloured plates will, I flatter myself, show this wonderful operation of Almighty power." And then, while Lord Dartmouth was considering the views of a Gothic pile which Lord Hardwicke had erected to close one of the vistas from Wimpole Hall, another letter came from Naples. "Mr. Stevenson", Hamilton wrote of the travelling tutor to Dartmouth's son Lord Lewisham,[2] "seems to me as proper a companion for a young man as any I have ever seen in that situation." "The sensible and sedate", he continued later, "soon tired of the noisy Neapolitan conversations, take refuge with us, and indeed I know of no other true society in Naples."

To that "true society" Acton did not belong, for as they trifled he must still maintain himself by his tortuous and brave manœuvres. His English contacts were now fading and old Sir Richard with his marbled hose and jellybag would have felt little more at home than he himself did with Hamilton's sciences and nice perspectives. General Acton was free from the surface life of these English *milords*. He must play for position, dexterously and without support, in the weakest of those satellite systems which followed in the wake of the old regime. The pharaoh tables were for the moment out of favour and Pompei and Vesuvius were now the mode; but General Acton threw and threw.

* * *

[1] Cal. Dartmouth MSS., pp. 224-5.
[2] *ibid.*, pp. 238-9.

It was 1799, and in the last fifteen years the world of Aldenham had receded further. The Revolution had snuffed out the urbane travellers. The coaches with the calm English heraldry had vanished. Since the overthrow of the French monarchy no pains were taken to conceal suspicion. There was a new tension bred from fear, and Acton was prime minister of Naples. In this high post he weathered the storms more easily than in that deceptive peace before the Revolution. Now he was closely united to his sovereigns in their misfortunes. He was freed from those dangers arising from the light airs of drawing-room politics which assail the foreign favourite in an unchallenged monarchy.

It was twenty years since he had come from Leghorn, and he had never lost the advantage which he had acquired upon his first arrival. Very careful, with the pursed lips and those small blue eyes, he had improved upon his own dexterity. Much had come to him. Lord Nelson was at Palermo. Away in Gatchina the Emperor Paul, then planning for the Order of Malta of which he had become Grand Master, concerned himself with the affairs of Naples. And Acton gathered in each benefit which came from the transient interest of Europe in the Two Sicilies.

A portrait at Aldenham, dating from about this time, gives an impression of General Acton in his late maturity during his early sixties in his years of power. He was not tall and still slender; his powdered hair drawn back from his smooth forehead; the dominant feature those careful eyes. The star of St. Januarius, the Russian Orders and the Gold Cross of Malta on his breast showed against the wide pattern of the braiding, and below this were the stiff vermilion facings. On each gold button was stamped the Bourbon lilies. He is painted standing on a terrace and behind him are seen the cupolas of the churches and beyond them the roadstead of Palermo and a great ship riding smoothly on a pale blue sea below the cliffs of Monte Pellegrino.

He had indeed done well out of his admiralty. Money he loved. For this and for the exercise of power he could call to his service patience. Not apparently imaginative, he was easily satisfied with his own policies and could adhere to them. He was thus well qualified to turn to full account the possessive affection of the Queen of Naples. And his northern blood, perhaps the tenacious Burgundian strain, enabled him to assuage his sovereign's ravaging and proud ambition. He was worn now by the long struggle

B

against his rivals and by a constant watchfulness. For Acton's policy of hostility to France and alliance with Austria and England was calculated to unite his enemies if also to satisfy the Austrian Queen. Still that maturing talent which had built up his rule in Naples had left him unfitted to deal confidently with the English envoys. He could counter the bizarre manœuvres of Lady Hamilton, but Nelson he never won and for Arthur Paget he was at once over-friendly and by far too cautious.

To the English opinion there seems to have been something not only exotic but unreal about the personalities of the government of the Two Sicilies, an attitude which finds exact expression in a letter from Lord Elgin, then on his way to Constantinople, to the Foreign Secretary. At this time the King had retreated to Palermo and the short-lived Parthenopean Republic had been set up in Naples with French aid. "Cardinal Ruffo in Calabria, and the partisan called *Il Gran Diavolo* towards Rome," begins the measured statement,[1] "used no means to prevent the further progress of the enemy. Meanwhile the King has shown to his enemies a vindictive and unconciliatory disposition, and to his friends the utmost distrust and pusillanimity." By the terms of his foreign service it is clear that Acton himself was linked in the same smooth disapprobation with the King and the Roman Cardinal and the bandit *Fra Diavolo*.

General Acton was now sixty-three and he wished for marriage and an heir. The baronetcy had come to him in 1791 and he had also inherited the estates subject to the life-interest of Sir Richard's only daughter, the widowed and childless Mrs. Langdale. He chose as his bride his niece Marianna Acton, then in her eighteenth year, a little frightened pigeon of a girl. In addition to the Catholic ceremony an Anglican service was conducted at the English envoy's house by Lord Nelson's chaplain. After all his labours the General planned to pass his remaining days in England. For twenty years his powers had been exerted to provide within certain limits an adequate functioning of the governmental mechanism. He had borne King Ferdinand's recurrent jealousy and the long strain of the Queen's temperament. He had exhausted his own understanding of the old bureaucracy; but in this matter the English proved unfriendly.

"I have heard", wrote Arthur Paget in a private letter to Lord

[1] Letter from Lord Elgin to Lord Grenville, Cal. Fortescue MSS., pp. 17-18.

Grenville,[1] "a good deal lately about General Acton's retiring to England; at length he told me confidentially the other day that such was his intention. I know that his idea is in case of going to England to have credential letters with him, but as there appears to me to be a great degree of analogy between General Acton and Count Rumford's situation, I should feel it my duty not to allow the former to leave this country with the idea of appearing in England in a public character from this Court." In consequence he remained in Sicily.

Children were born to him, Sir Richard Acton (who succeeded him) in 1801, Charles Edward Januarius the future Cardinal, and a daughter Elizabeth. The French occupation kept him from the *Regno*. Living at Palermo he saw Austerlitz, Trafalgar, Tilsit and the entanglement of Napoleon's armies in Portugal and Spain. Acton's career was ending safely; his calculations had not played him false. He gave a staid regalian adherence to the received maxims of religion. He accepted decorously the Church's ministrations and in the spring of 1811 died, worn out. It is recorded [2] that a downpour wrecked his funeral procession at Palermo and that night fell on his hearse with the great shields left standing deserted in the roadway.

It is very natural that the General's character should have proved repugnant to Lord Acton's notions. Yet, with his acumen and the wide variety of methods through which he accumulated so respectable a fortune, it is not possible to deny to his achievement its own perfection. Twenty-three years after his death, his grandson the historian was born into a family whose background was conditioned by the General's efforts.

[1] Letter from Arthur Paget to Lord Grenville dated 13 May 1800, Cal. Fortescue MSS., p. 225.
[2] *Gentleman's Magazine*, obituary notice 1811.

CHAPTER II

THE PALAZZO ACTON

IT WAS A SETTING which was hardly likely to have yielded a great Liberal historian. For it was a far cry to the ethos of Hawarden from that extravagant and carefree circle with its own elegance and its raffish followers which centred upon the palaces of the Chiaja in Bourbon Naples. Legitimism; a rigid social sense; a piety intermittent and very brave and unaffected; a feeling for de Maistre and a cultivated sensibility; a complete assurance and a tolerance for rogues alike marked a society which was secure and buttressed by an ample credit. Their political outlook was inherited and came down to them without enthusiasm or illusion. The lackeys foamed about them; the lights burned in their domestic chapels; the lawyers sat at their desks by the barred windows. They were accustomed to the bending hierarchies.

On 10 January 1834 in the Palazzo Acton alla Chiaja there was born a son and heir to Lady Acton the young wife of Sir Ferdinand Richard Edward Acton and the only child and heiress of Emerich Josef Franz Heinrich Felix Dismas Kammerer von Worms, Baron and Duke of Dalberg, the nephew of Karl Theodor Anton Maria, Elector of Mainz and Primate of the Confederation of the Rhine. The child was christened John Emerich Edward in his father's palace, in the chapel where the family sat in their red velvet *fauteuils* with the gilded arms. Above them the wax lights rose in the candelabra. The *History of Liberty* was far away.

There are several impressions extant of the life in the Palazzo Acton at that time. The young John Orlando Parry had recently made his *début* as a vocalist and was then in Naples. "The whole of that part of the Chiaja", he wrote in an account of a fête on 1 March 1843,[1] "facing where Sir Richard Acton lives was all brilliantly illuminated by the wood fires which they make in iron baskets and place on poles. . . . Oh! What a magnificent house and what splendid style everything was in. The walls were covered with crimson and gold paper, every door was covered with gold leaf and the most splendid carving all embossed with gold. All the ottomans were covered with white satin and gold embroidery."

[1] Cf. *Victorian Swansdown:* extracts from the early travel diaries of John Orlando Parry, ed. Cyril Bruyn Andrews and J. A. Orr-Ewing, p. 197.

Other elements in the scene presented themselves to Mr. Greville's more accustomed eye. It was four years earlier that he had come to Naples in the late spring of 1830. Between watching the procession of carriages on the Via della Chiaja, and attending the Opera, "a very indifferent opera of Rossini's, ill sung, called [1] the *Siege of Corinth*", and sitting under the "treillage of vines" at Capo di Monte, Greville went to dine with Sir Richard Acton. And he had been taken by Acton, who was his junior by some seven years, to a ball at the Duchess of Eboli's. "Very few people," he entered in his diary with his neat acidity,[2] "and hardly any English, and those not the best; only four, I think: Sir Henry Lushington the Consul; a Mr. Grieve of whom I know nothing but . . . that he killed his brother at Eton by putting a cracker in his pocket on the 5th of November; Mr. Auldjo the man who made a very perilous ascent of Mont Blanc, of which he published a narrative; Mr. Arbuthnot, who levanted from Doncaster two years ago." This was surely very characteristic of the Naples of that time, the personable gentlemen without credentials.

For it was a world which retained a certain moral hardihood. The gathering sentiment did nothing to impair an unsurprised realism of outlook. Baron Ward, the Yorkshire jockey whom the Duke of Lucca had discovered, was already exercising his equivocal influence. It was to be expected that adventurers would flourish as the posts lengthened out from their own country. The air of enclosed remote safety which comes to us from some of the Memoirs of this period only serves to emphasise that fact. It was just because of these dangers that the life of the young heiresses was so guarded.

A rather tripping verse and a pretty sentiment; in fact, a fine sententious delicacy of approach characterised the elegant circles in each southern capital. This was the case in the polite *villeggiatura* around Naples. The orange groves and sunsets formed a back-stage setting for the soft uninteresting decoration, the blue satin and white silk of the Duchess of Floridia's apartments in the royal palace. It was a setting not splendid in the eighteenth-century sense but with a certain solid, rather *bourgeois* grandeur, the padded vacuous footmen and the thick looped curtains and the light slanting from the carriage lamps as they passed up slowly to the *porte*

[1] *The Greville Memoirs*, ed. Henry Reeve, i. p. 335.
[2] *ibid.*, i. pp. 335-6.

cochère. Against such a background moved the young men of sensibility, the sober pompous noblemen, the adventurers of disastrous character, the careful matrons and their daughters. While the delicate young men of fortune, like Albert de la Ferronays, would be translating Tom Moore's lyrics into French, swindlers of pretension would encounter the most devastating of exposures. No element of this society was yet possessed by that mid-nineteenth-century quality of respectability.

Another impression of that world is given by Mrs. Augustus Craven, *née* de la Ferronays, in her *Récit d'une sœur*. It is an approach from the religious angle written in later life by one who gave full rein to an emotional susceptibility; but it has this special value that the author was an intimate of the Acton household and pursued the historian's mother with a fond affection.[1] Many years later, when he retained but little sympathy for such early memories, Acton would only accuse Mrs. Craven of "want of serenity".[2] Her view, however, was specialised, conditioned by a devotional outlook and though not necessarily uncandid certainly very carefully composed.

The La Ferronays, Charles X's ambassador at Rome and his family, came driving down to Naples in the January after that July Revolution which had cost the Count his post. They settled in a house on the Chiaja next door to Sir Richard Acton's palace, and the scene is presented with a tranquil pastel melancholy. As a background there is the poverty of their villa at Castellamare, with great *saloni* bare and empty, their father's *calèche* standing ready for sale in the courtyard of the Casa Margherita and those obvious Roman memories of the nuns singing at the Trinità del Monte and the Coliseum in the moonlight.[3] Then the emphasis is shifted and there come the carefree vignettes of the *jeunes filles* gathering flowers in the garden of the Palazzo Acton, and going [4] to the opera to see the *Gazza Ladra*, and throwing sugar plums at the Carnival, and watching [5] the King of the Two Sicilies (the stiff young Bomba) go by in his illuminated car.

This is interesting quite apart from the guarded light that it

---

[1] To give the relevant dates: Pauline-Marie-Amande-Aglae de la Ferronays (there is an indication in the slightly luscious name), later Mrs. Craven, was born in 1808; Lady Acton was born in 1813; *La Récit d'une sœur* was published in 1866.
[2] Letter from Lord Acton to Mrs. Drew dated 1 September 1883.
[3] *La Récit d'une sœur*, pp. 16-20.
[4] *ibid.*, p. 28.
[5] *ibid.*, p. 44.

throws on life in Naples. For Mrs. Craven had much influence on Acton's childhood. "She was", he wrote later,[1] "almost my earliest friend." And Acton, who shook himself free from so many of his inherited experiences, was to react against that warm approach, "the orange blossoms on the road through Terracina".

In this connection two paragraphs should be read in close conjunction. Under the heading "Naples, March 1834" there is an entry[2] in the diary of Mrs. Craven's brother Albert. "Read Byron. Got up late; wrote a few lines to Montalembert; translated some of Moore." And later the author herself describes[3] the funerals passing along the country roads towards Salerno "with the face of the dead uncovered and a flower between the lips". Together these passages, and others similar, give evidence of a myrtle-wreathed thick sentiment which cloaked a preoccupation with a curious short-circuited morbidity; a cushioned air of mortal sadness.

But it was the implicit political faith of the La Ferronays which possessed a real significance; the preconceptions on which were based this wistful sentiment. Certainly a mild nostalgic Legitimism was not without its effect on Acton's upbringing as he grew to boyhood under the control of women. Thirty years later this Legitimism in its religious aspect was to rally to the support of Pio Nono warmly and loyally. But the historian's mind was to move out into its own austere channels. Perhaps his impatience with cosseted thought arose from the long contact in his early years with such easy and emotional approaches; for his own method was to be as little cosy as the iron pillars of the library at Aldenham.

It would probably be a mistaken view to consider this world as particularly monarchical. The reputation of the Bourbons was somewhat blown upon; it was the heyday of the Duchesse de Berry and Maria Cristina, and the young King Bomba had so little to commend him, censorious and heavy with the "snout of a Franciscan". Besides, some of the more elegant English travellers would always carry with them the salt of their Whig disapproval. Living out at Frascati at the Villa Muti the little delicate bitter Henry Fox, Lord Holland's heir, commented on the Bourbon

---

[1] Letter from Lord Acton to Mrs. Drew dated 1 September 1883.
[2] *La Récit d'une sœur*, p. 94.
[3] *ibid.*, p. 111.

idiosyncrasies. Discussing the story of the *Enfants de France* being shown savages whom they were told eat little children, he noted [1] that the Duc de Bordeaux had said "'Donnez lui Louis' (meaning one of his playmates), 'voyons s'il le mangera.' This", remarked Mr. Fox, "is the best proof I have heard of his very doubtful legitimacy."

For the Whigs the veneration for birth stopped well short of the throne. Their life could go forward neglectful of the royalty and buttressed in the strong framework of their system. In Naples the position was not dissimilar. They did not look to the Bourbons for their status, as the *cabriolets* passed swiftly up the Toledo and the *laquais de place* would cluster in the long cold stone corridors and the gentlemen went through to their *écarté*. To the Neapolitan circle with its changing personnel Caserta was irrelevant: it was Vienna and perhaps above all St. Petersburg that guaranteed them.

The atmosphere of the society of the Actons, La Ferronays and Dalbergs had in so many ways the character of a closed world. And it is curious that at Naples in the day-to-day social life it was perhaps not so much the influence of Metternich that was felt as the shadow of the Court of St. Petersburg. The names of the foreign residents suggest Russia and the Baltic Provinces and that interlocked, secure and unimaginative landlordism which stretched from the interior of Russia to beyond Königsberg and the Masurian Lakes: Count Putbus; Monsieur d'Alopeus; Prince Lapoukhyn. It was not Legitimism in the old-fashioned sense that made appeal so much as a confidence in the impregnable structure of the great powers on the Neva and in Vienna. The Conservative sentiment was realist without enthusiasm and taken for granted in the daily happenings. As a small point it was necessary even across Europe for those who had ever been in any way connected with the Russian Court to receive the imperial permission for their marriages. Thus the wedding of Albert de la Ferronays and Alexandrine d'Alopeus in the chapel of the Palazzo Acton was delayed on this account. The permission came and the bridal procession got under way with Mlle d'Alopeus "in white satin with lace and a wreath of white roses and myrtle and a diamond cross". (They are interesting, these details like the diamond cross, which suggest a later fashion and also indicate the religious and *bourgeois* element in the Russian world.) But it was all bound up

[1] *Journal of the Hon. Henry Edward Fox*, p. 243.

with the conception of Russia as a Mediterranean power; it was from Gatchina that the Emperor Paul had laid his designs on Malta.

In that day the detail of the Tsardom seemed very close; the Winter Palace with the pilasters and the corniced windows against that great wash of orange stucco, the work of Rastrelli calmed by age, the interior with the lavender marble pillars and the heavy gilded mahogany of the swinging doors and beside them the Preobajensky Guards. The chimneys of the palace showed very clearly against the northern sky laden with snow. The administration of the Autocrat of all the Russias was a factor present to each member of that cosmopolitan generation as it grew to manhood; the ministries across the square from the Winter Palace, the wide semicircle and the quadriga above the archway to the city. At this core was lodged that armoured bureaucracy which appeared to the possessing classes to be inevitable. Through Europe, from Stockholm down to Naples, one took for granted the permanence of all that anchored stonework with those endless façades and the gilded spires as the light fell on the ranged sealing-wax and the silver and the parchment and through the windows lay the Petersburg of the Tsar Nicholas, that balanced and immense perspective.

CHAPTER III
DALBERG AND ALDENHAM

A VERY DEFINITE ATTITUDE to rank coloured these years of Acton's infancy. The genealogical and heraldic *minutiae* of the eighteenth century had passed from fashion and were now replaced by a massive respect for the social hierarchy which was only apparently lightened by the sometimes playful character of the approach. As an illustration of the lighter vein there is a nice story told by Henry Fox of the ancestors of the Cardinal Gustave Maximilian Juste de Croy-Dülmen with whom he had been dining in his Roman villa. Noah is supposed to be seen struggling with a load towards the Ark when the following exchange takes place with the *Bon Dieu*. " Que faites-vous avec ce sac-là ? " " Mon Seigneur, je sauve le Prince de Croy."

To this tradition belonged the Dalbergs. The last representatives of a great Rhineland family, they were cosmopolitan in effect if not in intention. They valued the political *nuances* and their decorous extravagant progresses radiated from their house in Paris. Occasional notices give details of them: the Duchess with her very fair hair in the slightly forced gaiety of a Balzac world, and again, later, professing her belief in the liquefaction of the blood of San Gennaro; the Duke "a clever man but a great projector and speculator",[1] spending his fortune in following up his plans and theories.

In the background was the square *Schloss* at Herrnsheim; the high *Konversazions-saal* with the formality of the German style of the post-Congress of Vienna period; the chapel overcrowded with silver lamps and candlesticks, a rather messy ecclesiasticism; out on the lower wall of the castle terrace the black figs ripening. It was the whole complex of the Dalberg inheritance that influenced Lord Acton, and not that family. These he never knew, for the Duke died in 1833, the year before his birth, and his mother had been an only child. His father, Sir Richard, had taken the additional name of Dalberg-Acton in December 1833, and it is well not to forget this counterpoise to Aldenham.

[1] Passage from an account of a dinner with the " D. and Dss Dalberg at Mme Rumford's 18 June 1821 ", *Journal of the Hon. Henry Edward Fox*, pp. 73-4.

A letter written by an English friend to Sir Richard Acton at the time of his courtship of Mlle Dalberg suggests the atmosphere of her family background. "With regard to the Duke [of Dalberg]," runs the letter,[1] "he consulted me as to the possibility of your being created a peer and suggested his writing ... to ask Lord Grey about it." The quarterings were eminently satisfactory, but it was part of the conception of the Dalberg world that statesmen would be prepared to make these reasonable adjustments.

The Duke himself had been for twenty years a privileged spectator, ever since the Restoration when Louis XVIII had rewarded his opportune devotion by creating him a *pair de France*. As a young man, in some ways Liberal, he had been carried forward into the Napoleonic orbit and then drawn out again with the receding tide. It was an asset to be the nephew of the Primate Dalberg and to be so confidential and discipular with Talleyrand. Yet his technical diplomatic rank as envoy in Paris from the grand ducal Court of Baden enabled him to maintain his independence. Intimate in his relations with the old Germanic dynasties, he had had his share in promoting the marriage with Marie-Louise. The French Emperor's dukedom could not hold him and he allowed himself to follow the line of action which Talleyrand prescribed with so much foresight. It was a balanced career, culminating in a reasoned but voluntary withdrawal from the turmoil of public life about the time he reached his fortieth year.

Compared to the historian's two grandfathers, Sir Richard Acton's life was notably devoid of serious effort. He had passed through various educational phases: a spell at Westminster; then a private tutor; a period at Cambridge at Magdalene College, travels with "Monsieur le docteur Quin". Naples was his home. At Aldenham and Herrnsheim he only visited. After his marriage he had a house in Paris also, 25 Rue d'Anjou in the Faubourg St. Honoré. There seems to be only scanty evidence which bears upon his powers and character. Certain qualities can be discerned, a gaiety which perhaps came from his mother, a taste for sumptuous living and for a seemly patronage of literature. It is worth noting that he cared, at least superficially, about his library. He had no political life; he was an exquisite. His father-in-law's hope was

---

[1] This letter is among the papers at Aldenham and appears to have been written by Mr. St. John, who with his wife, Lady Isabella *née* Fitzroy, stood in a confidential relationship with the young baronet.

never realised; his only office was some minor post about the King of the Two Sicilies.

On the staircase at Aldenham there is a great picture of Sir Richard painted in the period of his brief marriage. He is represented at the summit of a craggy path on horseback, a delicate figure with his fair hair and those neat side-whiskers and a fine wide choker. His top-hat is in his hand and the cloak billows out behind him. In the background and away down below his horse's hoofs the smoke foams from Mount Vesuvius. He died in Paris of pneumonia very unexpectedly in the early part of 1837, and these seem almost all the facts that we are ever likely to discover about Sir Ferdinand Richard Edward Acton.

* * *

On his father's death the boy John, a child then three years old, succeeded to the baronetcy, to Aldenham which would be his in 1855 at that distant date when he should come of age, and to the prospects of Herrnsheim and the Rhenish lands. His mother was his guardian and there is a small portrait of her dating from about this time with erect careful carriage and elaborate piled hair. She was a young widow, only twenty-three, and both her mother and her mother-in-law were living—the Duchess, by birth a Genoese, a Brignole-Sala, now increasingly *dévote*, and Marianna Lady Acton, very tiny, with a brown wig settled low upon her forehead and her gay nature and soft eyes. There was one set of English relatives, the young family of Sir Richard's sister Elizabeth Throckmorton. All the rest were foreigners, on the Acton side Aunt Dachenhausen and on the Dalberg Aunt Marescalchi, and then the Carlo Actons and their children, and in the background the Prince of Monaco [1] of the house of Goyon-de-Matignon-Grimaldi and the Berg de Trips and the Landgravine of Hesse-Philippsthal.

The most important individual in the family circle was certainly the child's uncle Monsignor Acton, a young prelate of self-effacing

[1] The Duchess de Dalberg was *née* Marie-Pelline-Thérèse-Catherine de Brignole-Sala and her sister Anna had married Count Marescalchi, who had played an important role in the affairs of the Cisalpine Republic. The latter's daughter Anna-Margarethe-Marie-Juliane-Pelline was to marry Count Johann Maximilian von Arco-Valley and was eventually to become Lord Acton's mother-in-law. Through Marie-Catherine de Brignole-Sala, who was the wife of the Prince of Monaco and then the mistress and subsequently the wife of the Prince of Condé, it is curious to note that Acton was a cousin of that unsuccessful potentate Tancrède-Florestan-Roger-Louis, Prince of Monaco, who lost Mentone and Villefranche to the Sardinian Government through his intransigence.

tenacity who had recently been appointed to the great Roman office of Auditor of the Apostolic Camera. Delicate in his health, a fragile figure with hollow cheeks and those meek unsmiling eyes which veiled a swift intelligence, Monsignor Acton held to a permanent interest in the affairs of England. His views were large and clearly formed; his relations with the Pope were intimate; a Cardinal's Hat awaited him. He was a true ecclesiastic of the reign of Gregory XVI—that period of much activity in the Church and sanguine hopes, with new congregations and fresh missionary endeavours and the great prelates lying anchored in a Metternichian world. The Monsignor was anxious that his nephew should receive a wholly English education. At a later stage and in different ways he himself was to exercise a certain influence upon him; but for the moment he merely added his support to his sister-in-law's project that Aldenham should be his nephew's home.

This return to Aldenham, which took place after Sir Richard's death, resembled in some ways the coming of Prince Albert; for Lady Acton brought to the English countryside a taste in building which suggested a very different age and climate. The chapel with its light lines and the smooth white surface appears inspired by the classical taste of the Italy of the eighteen-thirties, as does the monument to Sir Richard Acton with his son and widow mourning beneath the lintel. They both suggest the South and that delicacy of execution which marks the Stacpoole medallions in San Bernardo alle Terme. But the changes made in the house itself were very different. They were apparently later in date and have that heaviness that came from Coburg: the front of the house was modelled in a thick smoothed grey stone with rounded window-dressings which set off the new plate-glass. A formal garden, geometrical and gravelled, was laid out between the chapel and the house. Still, the drawing-room was lovely with the air of the early 'thirties and a great chandelier and mirrors. From under the chandelier the little boy looked out upon the English countryside through plate-glass windows.

CHAPTER IV
OSCOTT

"I NEVER", SAID LORD ACTON in later life, "had any contemporaries."[1] This is a fact, stated with perfect accuracy, which has a bearing on the whole of the historian's boyhood and education. In the Throckmorton family, with whom the Actons were in constant contact, the eldest son, Richard, was three years his senior, the second, Nicholas, four years his junior; unbridgeable distances in childhood. Thus isolated, and subject to Lady Acton's very imperfect knowledge of Catholic education, John Acton grew up speaking both French and English, living apparently mainly at Aldenham, until it was decided to find a school for him.

It was the last period of the old rotund expressions in school advertisement, and a new technique of efficient statement was replacing those broader claims which had been made by the men who depended on the attracting of the private pupil. "M. l'Abbé Latouche,"[2] so runs an advertisement of the French College at No. 24, Foley Place, Cavendish Square, inserted in the year that Acton's schooling was under consideration, "Canon of Angers and Preacher of the French Chapel, George Street, London, has opened a College where French will be the only language spoken between the masters and élèves. The subject of instruction will be Hebrew for a few weeks, in the first instance, as a preparation for subsequent studies. Particular attention will be paid to the Oriental, European and Classic languages. He will teach Simultaneously with these, Arithmetic, Mathematics, Chemistry, Physics and the Natural Sciences. Pupils, above the age of eight years, are received on terms which may be learned on application at this establishment. M. Latouche proposes to receive a few additional pensioners, who will enjoy, with every domestic comfort, a religious, moral, literary and scientific education. A lecture is given every Tuesday evening, at seven o'clock, explanatory of his method, which will be found truly luminous, in harmony with our wants, and capable of realizing immense advantages." This was a vanish-

---
[1] *Lord Acton's Correspondence*, introduction, p. ix.
[2] *The Catholic Directory and Annual Register*, 1840, p. 83.

ing tradition, and the brave old gentleman was in no position to insert an advertisement in the following year.

Two notices from the period give an account of St. Mary's, Oscott. "The new College", begins the first of these two announcements, "has been built expressly for its present purpose, in a most healthy and cheerful situation, and is provided with everything requisite for a place of education. The system pursued in it embraces, besides the classical languages, French, Italian and German, which are taught to all who pursue the ordinary course of studies, Mathematics and Natural Philosophy, assisted by very complete apparatus, as well as History, Geography, Elocution and other branches of learning, becoming either a scholar or a gentleman." "The course of education",[1] runs a rather earlier advertisement of the same college, "comprehends every species of instruction which is necessary for those who are destined to independence, in or out of Parliament, for any of the learned professions, or for business. Arrangements are in progress by which the students of this College will have the opportunity of obtaining degrees in Arts or Law, and the other advantages held out by the newly-created University of London. . . . Students are admitted at any age from eight to fourteen." It was to Oscott that the young Sir John Acton was despatched.

The situation at Oscott at the time of his arrival in 1843 had a considerable effect on the development of this new student and the formation of his later lines of thought. It is perhaps therefore as well to give a brief account of the circumstances which led to the installation of the Right Reverend Nicholas Patrick Stephen Wiseman, Bishop of Melipotamus *in partibus infidelium* and Coadjutor of the Midland District, as president of the College, and to the uneasy residence of his predecessor Dr. Weedall in temporary charge of the preparatory school. For these two men, Weedall and Wiseman, gave to the historian those impressions of the intellectual approach of the Catholic Church which influenced him so profoundly. Weedall was the family friend; an intimate and former master of Sir Robert Throckmorton; old Catholic; full of simplicity; too unassuming. Over the hoar frost of this sober landscape in which Mr. Weedall kept his "two cows, half a dozen pigs, a stock of poultry" the personality of Dr. Wiseman rose like the

---

[1] This second notice appeared in *The Catholic Directory and Annual Register* for 1840, while the first notice came from the 1848 edition of the same publication.

sun. It was inevitable that he should have produced a deep effect on a youthful mind, quick and in some sense solitary through absence of companionship. The Bishop dazzled his privileged pupil and gained from him a form of intimacy conditioned by respect. But how was it that Acton came in time to view much that Wiseman stood for in that cold hostile light against which the mind was to move so unrelentingly? There was nothing unrelenting about Wiseman as he went forward so warm and glorious. The Ushaw portrait shows him tripping with contented dignity, a mitre on his head and his full cope billowing, nervous, assured and very sanguine. Over against him Acton was to stand with the iron laws that he had come to and his detached integrity.

For many years now the name of Oscott College had been inseparable from that of Mr., later Dr., Weedall. He was so typical of his generation of quiet security that a description of his outlook may explain the approach of the old serene Catholics to their Faith, so different in its *tempo* from that of the cosmopolitan worlds whether indifferent or *dévote*. It is a simple matter to picture Mr. Weedall, as he is drawn for us by his friend and biographer Provost Husenbeth, in the "old house" at Oscott of which he was in turn pupil, vice-president and president. A small man, five foot two in height, he wore in his early days a plain black coat, white stockings and a black leghorn hat with a broad brim, lined with green silk. His eyes were light and large but always weak. Even with the aid of spectacles his sight was too poor to enable him to read by candlelight. "His hair was light, and had that remarkable growth over his right temple, which is familiarly called a *calf-lick*."

"He was", wrote Husenbeth,[1] "remarkably fond of birds. He would come and pull your ear in the same good-natured manner which he retained all his life, and ask you to help him to carry out his cages." And again,[2] "he dearly loved a joke, and his laugh was hearty and contagious. No one told an anecdote better, though they might relate it in less time, for he was rather long over a story." Few men had a better "store of puns" or could equal his heavy rolling humour in its simple Latin. "When speaking on any grave subject, his manner was slow and sententious;

---

[1] *The Life of the Right Rev. Monsignor Weedall, D.D.*, by F. C. Husenbeth, D.D., V.G., published in 1860, contains all the very descriptive details of Mr. Weedall's habits which are set down here.

[2] *ibid.*, p. 305.

he chose the very words to produce the greatest effect and uttered them with strong emphasis and powerful expression. He gave a boy a shilling for promising not to bait with worms."[1]

He was fond of riding and devoted to his dog, "a large and fierce looking animal called Rose" which he kept chained up at the door of Holdford Farm. "Afterwards at Oscott he kept a bullfinch; and he spent a good part of one midsummer vacation in whistling to it in hopes of teaching it to sing the tune of the *Siege of Belle-Isle*."[2]

In architecture he was attached to Mr. Pugin's Gothic and he had a feeling for a seemly service. He was accustomed to sing[3] with taste and spirit "Mr. Webbe's expressive motette, *super flumina Babylonis*". During the daytime he would sit and work over that collection of some fifty sermons on which his quiet fame had been established. The theology of Collet was the ordinary textbook which he had studied. "This author", relates Provost Husenbeth,[4] "was chosen by Bishop Milner, because, as he used to observe, although he was often rigid and starch he was always safe." Very safe, oaken in his piety, a little ingenuous, very certain and determined was Mr. Weedall.

His happy forties had been passed during the contented decade which followed on the granting of Emancipation in 1829. He had enjoyed those quiet days, coming in splashed from the road to dinner at the Throckmortons' house at Weston Underwood, listening to the solid pursy jokes of Bishop Bramston, the seemly jesting about Newport Pagnell, the decanter circulating quietly, the candlelight falling on his host's silver buttons, the peace and confidence.

At Oscott he had built the "grandest church and college".[5] A practical man, compact and nimble, Dr. Weedall climbed about the scaffolding admiring the growth of Mr. Pugin's pinnacles. He had installed in the new sacristy "the white satin vestment with galoon lace" and the green brocade chasuble "beautifully diversified with flowers and ornaments"[6] which had been purchased for

---

[1] *The Life of the Right Rev. Monsignor Weedall, D.D.*, p. 307.
[2] *ibid.*, p. 8.
[3] *ibid.*, p. 55.
[4] *ibid.*, p. 55.
[5] Letter from Mary Lady Arundell of Wardour to Ambrose de Lisle dated 4 May 1838, *Memoirs and Letters of Lady Mary Arundell*, ed. Rev. Joseph Hirst, p. 117.
[6] Husenbeth's *Life of Weedall*, p. 51.

the college by Bishop Milner. Now everything was well completed.

But, when Acton came in 1843, Weedall had no contact with the new college. He was back, through the sacrifice of his friend Mr. Foley, in charge of the preparatory school now housed in the building which had been the college before he had undertaken the great new fabric. There, a man of fifty-five and quite dispirited, he was once more established. "Dr. Weedall", wrote Provost Husenbeth, "sat down thus in a very low place, compared with his former dignity and elevation. He was the pastor of a small flock of poor country people, and the president of a small school of young boys." For he had suffered a disaster.

The episode that follows has a definite bearing on the development of Lord Acton's outlook. It was only a small matter ot ecclesiastical politics, but it clearly foreshadows the historian's hatred of the adroit solution. Monsignor Acton was busying himself with the affairs of England. The episcopal "districts" of the Catholic community, which possessed four vicars apostolic, were to be increased to eight. In May 1840 Dr. Weedall heard to his surprise that both he and his vice-president Mr. Wareing were to be promoted to the newly created Northern and Eastern Districts. He hurried to Rome and begged to be excused from the episcopate on the score of his weak sight and his general ill-health. His own bishop expressed surprise at this appointment as he had already informed Propaganda that Dr. Weedall was too delicate for such a labour.

At Rome Bishop Baines came to his assistance and broached this relatively unimportant matter to the Pope in person as he and Gregory XVI sat side by side on the hard ecclesiastical sofas of Castel Gandolfo. Meanwhile Dr. Baggs at the English college put into Italian the President's simple statements as to the constant pains he suffered in his head. But Weedall, standing with his *calf-lick* pulling people by the ear, was no match for Monsignor Acton. He was received gently and reasonably and his request was granted. Then he set out for England to find that he had lost his home. Dr. Wiseman had been appointed President of Oscott. The fine college was at the disposal of the new coadjutor, ready for the deployment of his grand ideas. Poor Naboth had taken no thought to his vineyard.

*   *   *

From the moment of his arrival Bishop Wiseman imposed himself upon the imagination: very tall, a great dignified, rather disordered presence, he fostered projects of the widest scope. "We were proud of him," wrote Lord Acton at the end of the century to Wilfrid Ward,[1] "we were not afraid of him; he was approachable and generous, and no great friend of discipline." His was an intermittent but a lasting influence. "He was", declared one of his pupils, Canon Smith,[2] "much away from the College visiting at great houses, Protestant and Catholic." There was much in him to inspire a child of quick intelligence. "He was ... looking far afield," wrote Lord Acton,[3] "and these other things were what characterised him. We used to see him with Lord Shrewsbury, with O'Connell, with Father Mathew, with a Mesopotamian patriarch, with Newman, with Pugin, and we had a feeling that Oscott, next to Pekin, was a centre of the world." With the boys, too, Wiseman would shake off that sensitiveness veiled by a pompous manner which so much hampered him. His difficulties with his colleagues were concealed from the children and his sanguine plans enveloped them. "How seldom", we read in one of the Bishop's *memoranda*,[4] "has a word been spoken which intimated that those who entered the College considered it as more than a mere place of boys' education, or [saw in it] a great engine employed in England's conversion and regeneration."

Upstairs in his study on the first floor Dr. Wiseman would sit tracing plans with his swift easy pen for the employment of this great engine. Downstairs young John Acton wrote to his mother:[5] "I have had a pound taken out of my dormitory so I have no money scarcely left."

Yet the child was soon writing generously:[6] "I am very happy here, and perfectly reconciled to the thoughts of stopping here some more years." The strange involved adult vocabulary is very remarkable in a boy of his age; a child fitted by his training to respond to the Bishop's panoramic visions.

[1] It seems clear that Acton's statements on this subject are entirely sincere, but composed with care in view of the official character of the biography in which they were to be published. Cf. *Life and Times of Cardinal Wiseman*, by Wilfrid Ward, i. p. 348.
[2] *ibid.*, i. p. 350.
[3] *ibid.*, i. p. 349.
[4] Memorandum printed in Ward's *Life of Cardinal Wiseman*, i. p. 448.
[5] *Selections from the Correspondence of the First Lord Acton*, vol. i., ed. J. N. Figgis and R. V. Lawrence, p. 1.
[6] *ibid.*, i. p. 1.

It was during these years that the Oxford Movement was developing and that Newman made his submission. He and a number of his companions came to Old Oscott in the winter of 1845, and Acton, now twelve, duly noted their arrival:[1] "There are so many new converts here that I do not know half their names." Still, it was not these conversions that then or later seem to have appealed to him. It was rather Wiseman's encyclopaedic approach to history.

It is perhaps as well to indicate here how remote Acton was to remain from the impact of the Oxford Movement. He came from a world in which, until the Tractarian secessions, the notion of conversion was relatively unfamiliar. The changes of allegiance among the Acton-Dalberg circle were occasioned primarily by marriage, whether they were of the character of the romantic conversion of Alexandrine d'Alopeus or of that meek acceptance of a more complex Faith which was required of Lutheran princesses before they could come forward to receive the bridal crown of a Russian marriage.

The Tractarian converts were Acton's seniors by twenty years, the space that separated him from Faber. The warming friendships and the shared emotions were always to be foreign to his temperament. The brand of English Tory politics which so many of these converts maintained was likewise profoundly unappealing. Those explicit Liberal doctrines to which Acton came would inevitably constitute a barrier.

A very few of his contemporaries, who belonged to the party to which he gave himself, were to become Catholics in later life. Still, much was to happen before 1870 and the events of these years would divide him from Granard and Ripon. For the rest, few men were more remote from the historian's outlook than those fox-hunting Tory peers of the western Midlands who came to Rome from their Tractarian nurseries. On the other hand, the rather grand mediaeval ecclesiasticism which was to mark Lord Bute's approach [2] would also lie outside his field of interest. The processes of conversion as such would always appear to him unsympathetic.

[1] *Selections*, i. p. 2.
[2] Acton was born in 1834 and the convert peers in question were as far as age went grouped around him. Lord Ripon was born in 1827, Lords Albemarle and Louth in 1832, Lords North, Abingdon and Granard in 1836, Lord Ashburnham in 1840 and Lord Bute, the youngest, in 1847. Sir Francis Burnand, who was received in the 'fifties, was born in 1836, and St. George Mivart, the youngest of the converts of the Newman period, in 1827. Richard Simpson, who was to be so closely associated with Acton, was born in 1820.

It was history of a very different kind which brought out all his single-minded zeal.

With Wiseman's ultramontane views there also went an attitude to world history which could not fail to be encouraging to a developing mind like that of the young Acton, a mind awakened but of course uncritical. In Wiseman's view all history was a paean to the Church's progress. "What struck me most", wrote Lord Acton of the Bishop in later years,[1] "was his extraordinary facility." Certainly no writer could marshal his facts more rapidly or with such an assiduous *empressement*. "And he secured", went on the historian in the same letter, "a very great library—Marini's or Garampi's, I forget which—and sent for a monk of Monte Cassino, who pasted little coloured patches in the books and perhaps arranged them." The grandeur of Wiseman's whole conception found a ready response in young John Acton. "I am going", he wrote,[2] aged thirteen, to his mother with that strange vocabulary which makes one ponder, "to write a compendium of the chief facts, in history, for my own occasional reference." The attractive taste for the construction of such a compendium is surely a major factor in the historian's development.

Out in Rome, Monsignor Acton's quiet career was moving forward. Since 1842 he had been a Cardinal-Priest of the title of Santa Maria della Pace. In his edifying little volume of the *Last Four Popes* Wiseman penned a tribute to him. "So gentle," we read, "so modest, so humble was he, so little in his own esteem, that his solid judgments, extensive acquirements, and even more ornamental accomplishments, were not easily elicited by a mere visitor or casual guest. Certainly his countenance seemed to have retained the impression of a natural humour that could have been easily brought into play. But this was over-ruled by the presence of more serious occupations, and the adoption of a more spiritual life."

A letter written by Wiseman some years later will explain how he dazzled the young Acton as well as how he failed to hold the adult Liberal. "It",[3] he is referring to his novel *Fabiola*, "had one good effect. It is undoing some of the mediaeval frostwork which late years have deposited round English Catholic affections to the forgetfulness of Rome and its primeval glories."

---

[1] Letter quoted in Ward's *Life of Cardinal Wiseman*, i. pp. 352-3.
[2] *Selections*, p. 2.
[3] Ward, *op. cit.*, ii. p. 191.

CHAPTER V
THE OLD CATHOLICS

THE old Catholic landowners were courteous to, if uninterested in, Bishop Wiseman. They were not much concerned with "glories", primeval or otherwise, and they could not know how much the work of that prelate was to affect them. It was in this circle that the heir to the Acton-Dalberg inheritance found himself as he grew up at Aldenham. Around him there stood those old rooted squires who held so firmly to their Faith and to their Tory principles. Little as the boy or indeed his mother had in common with these country neighbours, they yet conditioned his upbringing once it had been decided to provide Sir John Acton with an English Catholic education.

Newman in his *Second Spring* sermon was to fail to appreciate the strong position of these stocks with which his delicate and academic mind had little contact. For the 'thirties and the 'fifties were periods of prosperity for the landed interest. The agricultural depression was not yet upon them; the early returns of mining royalties and way-leaves were well established; the industrial revolution had come to increase, if not to consolidate, the former rent roll. One tradition in particular had led to the accumulation of substantial properties in Catholic hands. For generations a Catholic heiress had very seldom been permitted to carry an estate away from the network of that established cousinage. "Mixed marriages" were looked upon with cold disfavour, and especially those in which the husband was a Protestant. It was held that the bride would have only a slender hope, in the then state of public opinion, of maintaining her principles. Each knot of cousins had its story of such weakness, like that of the Miss Haggerston who abandoned her religion and carried the great inheritance of Ladykirk to the Marjoribanks family.

The Catholic estates nearest to Aldenham, Acton Burnell and Shiffnal Manor, both illustrate the working of this system. Sir Edward Smythe took his full share in county life. He had been sheriff the year after Emancipation; he was Tory, insular, staunchly Benedictine in his sympathies. In addition to a compact estate of rather over five thousand acres in his own county, he owned the

Wootton Wawen property in Warwickshire, which had come from the Lords Carrington, and the long-disused house at Eshe in the new Durham coalfield. Acton Burnell had been modelled in its present form by Sir Edward's father. It was a comfortable mansion exhibiting[1] "a noble elevation, constructed of fine white stone, having in the centre a boldly projecting Ionic portico of four columns, surmounted by a pediment under (which) is the carriage entrance with niches for statues". Like all that Catholic world on which the Oxford Movement broke, it was very real. There was no room in that rather grand untidy hall for Mr. Pugin.

About the same distance from Aldenham but some fifteen miles to the north lay Shiffnal Manor, the property of Sir Edward Smythe's cousin the eighth Lord Stafford. Here the Jerninghams controlled a considerable accretion of landed wealth. Besides Shiffnal, which had come through the Earls of Stafford from the Norfolk Howards, they held estates in Staffordshire, and the Jerningham manors in East Anglia centred on the vast and straggling house at Costessey. In this case also the conditions of the time were favourable, for the Shiffnal valley was yielding to the new industrialism. The Shrewsbury and Birmingham railway line was now constructed; the trucks from Ironbridge and Coalbrookdale rolled by on their heavy flanges into the area of the new Black Country.

The old Catholic landowning family was thus often supported by great wealth, not usually carefully harvested and looked after in a patriarchal fashion by a conveyancing firm of sound repute. Contact with Rome and sometimes with Vienna was well maintained. There was usually one period of foreign travel. A rather Continental sense of *noblesse* and of the value of quarterings was at times apparent.

Evidence of the prosperity of this *milieu* is provided by the immense sums expended on church building in the Midlands by John sixteenth Earl of Shrewsbury, who was at that time the leading Catholic layman owing to the religious eclipse of the then Duke of Norfolk.[2] In this circle there was a relationship with the

---

[1] The following description comes from the text of Neale's *Views of Seats*, vol. ii., second series.

[2] Bernard twelfth Duke of Norfolk, who held the title from 1815 until 1842, was an old man, Catholic, quiet and measuredly eccentric, while his son, who died in 1856, was a great Whig peer almost without religious affiliations.

vicars apostolic which was very close and sometimes difficult. Shrewsbury was himself the grand-nephew of the two Talbot bishops. The Cisalpine storms had passed, and the peers and their spiritual leaders exacted respect from one another. There was formality and friendship but little ceremony. The leading laity had a very deep-rooted distaste for the savour of the Wiseman purple and for what they considered as undignified and foreign gestures of respect.

The recognition of an equality between their spiritual and temporal leaders bore a little hardly upon the clergy, for there were still special trials in the position of chaplain to a noble lord. Nevertheless this was only to be expected in the draughty corridors of Alton Abbey, which was then the apex of the Catholic world. "The Mansion", so begins an account [1] of this brittle flaking building in the manner of the later Strawberry Hill, "owes much of its splendour to its proprietor, who employed great taste in the erection. On ascending the hill by a serpentine road the eye is frequently relieved with a view of a square embattled tower, built by his Lordship as an observatory. The form of the house is irregular, having in the centre a gable with a large pointed window, under which is the principal entrance to the Hall; the front extends on each side by embattled towers.

"The gardens and pleasure grounds are truly romantic. Art is here sweetly united to nature, and the hand of taste is profusely displayed in every part. A light iron bridge cast in imitation of the Southwark Bridge, London, erected under the superintendence of Mr. Gardner, crosses a canal. Upon a pedestal in the grounds is a colossal head of the late Premier, Mr. Pitt." Within the chapel a decent and ordered ceremonial was observed. The vicars apostolic clustered under the groined roof of the noble staircase. Outside the rain of Staffordshire fell heavily upon "the colossal head of Mr. Pitt".

Still, this Gothic atmosphere was in no way typical. Pugin was to come to Lord Shrewsbury's aid and would transform his abbey into Alton Towers, but at this date the Pugin influence was for the most part confined to church design. The old Catholic landowners were not then architecturally adventurous. They gave no thought to such affairs as they lived in their great square Georgian houses with the heavy porticos, riding to hounds and

[1] Neale's *Views of Seats*, vol. iv.

entertaining. It was their grandparents who had in so many cases been the builders,[1] and now they left construction to the converts like Ambrose de Lisle, who created Grace Dieu Manor with its Gothic charm, so delicate and fussy.

In spite of the very special character which marked the squirearchy of the Old Religion it is a misconception to regard their way of life as either withdrawn or austere. Their tastes were frequently adventurous, as in the very different cases of Charles Waterton and Roger Tichborne. Yet there was a certain stiffness in their reactions. They prided themselves both on their foreign contacts and their insularity. Their patriotism was manifest; they readily bought Commissions in an age which was primarily civilian; they had a curious outmoded veneration for the Hanoverians.

In a world which was profoundly moved by politics they were almost without contact with such issues. For this reason they could never enter into the system of values of the great Whig houses. This has a bearing on Acton's future. Nothing could really make the Smythes and Plowdens comprehensible to the Leveson-Gowers. The links of the old Catholics were with the country Tory peers and solid baronets. In the eighteenth century their leaders had been familiar with the idea of splendour which was now quite lost to them. In its place they kept up a domestic and staid magnificence. The ladies of the family were for the most part at home; they worked at their embroidery in the firelight; they were esteemed and much respected. An account of Burton Constable, written in 1840, will give an impression of such a Catholic interior on the largest scale.

"In the entrance hall. A billiard table. Two beautiful tables in imitation porphyry. One scagliola. Stuffed birds. A dog of the name of Wolf, of the arctic breed, introduced into England by Captain Parry, prized for his sagacity and fidelity, which occasioned a wound from the stiletto of an assassin at Rome, and ultimately his being poisoned in Paris; preserved and brought over to England, he is now stationed in the hall of his master, and still appears the

---

[1] The characteristic date of the normal large Catholic country houses is worth examining. It is of interest to record some examples. Apart from the great Payne mansions Thorndon and Wardour, there were the fine square houses of the early eighteenth century like Ince or Swynnerton or Foxcote and the George II houses like Burton Park and Tixall or on a smaller scale Rotherwas. Hooton Hall was by Wyatt. Later Georgian examples would include Llanarth and Hesleyside and Spetchley. These instances suggest at what an early date the landowners had wealth at their disposal.

mimic guardian of the property of him whose life he once defended, and perhaps preserved. Chartists' pikes."

The chapel is described as being "in the Ionic style", and in the morning drawing-room reference is made to "two splendid screens of needlework, one a giraffe by Lady Constable; the other a macaw by Miss Chichester". The library was furnished suitably with two alabaster vases from Florence, placed upon two tables of Verd antique, and two small figures, excellent likenesses of Rousseau and Voltaire.

The breakfast-room can be examined in more detail. "The mouldings", so runs the account,[1] "of the doors, pillars, pilasters, their capitals and bases, the bordering of the paper, all ornamented with dead and burnished gold. The furniture a costly specimen of green and gold. The chimney-piece of marble; over the mantelpiece a beautiful French clock, in or. molu., supported by finely moulded and highly finished full length figures. The walls hung with valuable paintings: 1. The Holy Family; 2. Neapolitan fête by Fabricius; 3. Satyr and Nymph by Reubens; 4. Naples, its inhabitants eating maccaroni, ibid." This rather naïve description brings back clearly the whole composed scene, so friendly and pleasant; "the boudoir with a carpet after a design by Lady Constable, made at Axminster" and a screen which Miss Chichester worked in the winter evenings with a border and the flowers of the pink rose. It was a far cry to the gaieties of Lady Acton's circle as Miss Chichester slowly stitched at her macaw.

There went with this quiet life and its tamed and specialised concerns an interest in the religious state. The daughters of the old Catholic houses entered in considerable numbers into those grey stone steep-roofed convents, built in a new constricted Gothic, which had been established since Emancipation. Their aunts and great-aunts had been received into these same communities, then in exile in the Low Countries or in France. About such matters, as in all that touched religion, the Catholics maintained a close reserve in the presence of those who did not share their Faith. This applied not only to the women but also to the men. The latter had an interest in sport which was in many cases deeper than that of their neighbours; they had the feeling for the countryside natural to squires whom politics did not call to London; they took their share in each activity in their county; they had a relationship with their equals which was sound and not intimate.

[1] *History and Antiquities of the Seignory of Holderness*, ii. pp. 242-8.

Towards the Protestants they were friendly but unaccommodating. With the Anglican episcopate relations were more distant than in the days of the Jerningham Letters at the opening of the century. The cordial and mundane respect which had coloured the attitude of the Bedingfelds and Jerninghams to the Bishop of Norwich is not found in this later generation. And from the Anglican side the evangelical clergy and members of the episcopate of strict views were not drawn to that social intercourse with Papists which had marked their predecessors.

The rich landowners of the Old Religion had a high sense of dignity and, as far as their *terrain* was concerned, were conscious of their own supremacy. A curious extract in a letter written by Mary Lady Arundell of Wardour brings out this fact. "No heretics", she is writing[1] of the situation at Tunbridge Wells in 1839, "ever attend, and though I would always have them kept in the background and behind the Christians, still I like them *to be there* and to be kept quiet as they used to be at Wardour." It is a novel picture and one worth pondering, the Protestant tenants and domestics kept herded at the back beneath the gilded cornices and gallery at the west end of Wardour Chapel. A little stiff and with a solidity of thought and diction the old Catholics moved on into the Victorian Age maintaining their own observances; loyal; assured; wholly incurious.

In each of these respects the family of Acton's uncle, Sir Robert Throckmorton, typified this long tradition. They had held the leadership among those calm and stringent Cisalpine laymen who had desired a definite share in the government of their community. The more aggressive members of the episcopate aroused in them a strong distaste which was only partially masked by their good breeding. They had supported the foundation of Oscott where they sent their sons for education.

The Throckmorton property was very considerable in extent and widely scattered. The family resided principally at Coughton Court near Alcester, which had been their seat since the fifteenth century, and in the quiet and rambling house at Weston Underwood. They also owned Buckland House, a fine square Georgian pile above the Vale of the White Horse, which had come to them with the heiress of the Yates, who had also brought in Harvington

---

[1] Letter from the Dowager Lady Arundell of Wardour to Ambrose de Lisle dated 13 February 1839, *Memoirs and Letters of Lady Mary Arundell*, ed. Rev. Joseph Hirst.

and the rich farming lands near Kidderminster. The last of the Courtenays of Molland had bequeathed to them a wide and poor estate in Devon under Exmoor. In addition, Sir Robert's aunt Lady Throckmorton possessed in her own right Carlton House in the East Riding.

It was Coughton which bore the stamp of the Throckmortons. Set in the fields beyond the Arrow, the long Tudor house was dominated by the square stone tower in the centre of the spreading wings. Below the old roof line, which stretched away on either side of the stone parapet, were the rows of new sash windows set in the yellow stucco. Within this ancient solid house was an unexpected range of family portraits which contrasted with the absence of eighteenth-century pictures and *objets d'art*. There were portraits of two lines of the Throckmortons and of the Fairfax children and the strange Yate heads with their withdrawn and wearied smile shielded by the elaborated Stuart lace. Over the fireplace in the hall there stood the great portrait of Sir Robert Throckmorton, a contemporary of the Chevalier de St. George. This had all the enamelled manner of Largillière, the boy standing with his powdered hair, slim and posed and elegant, with the staring whiteness of the soft kid gauntlets and the hard bright worked gilding and the fur caught back with negligence to show the purple lining. There was no repetition of this luxury. The present generations were represented by the Stapleton miniatures and by a miniature of Cardinal Acton as a boy in a dark blue cloak and a soutane and by a small dull painting of the then Lady Throckmorton, who was his sister.

The early Victorian proprietors of Coughton were little interested in their histories and freed from antiquarian tastes, an unselfconscious family. To the young Acton whose uncle the Cardinal was dead since 1847, the Throckmortons represented the English adherents of the Catholic Faith in his own circle. They held to the Conservatism of the squirearchy and to the values of that life of Warwickshire which it was not in John Acton to appreciate.

On the religious side, Dr. Weedall, who here reappears, was the priest of their predilection. They belonged to those whose piety was of a solid type unsympathetic to the new devotions. In these matters they would have echoed the sentiments of Dr. Lingard, who was so much respected by all that world. "Decidedly", wrote that priest¹ in reference to *les petites dévotions*, "they give an air of novelty to Catholicism. They were unknown to its first professors."

It was this atmosphere that Acton found at Coughton in the holidays. Dr. Weedall at Leamington, for he had soon left the preparatory college at Old Oscott, was the head of the nearest considerable congregation. It was to this church that they would go on the great feasts. "A good part of it", wrote Provost Husenbeth ² of the Catholic flock of Leamington, "was composed of highly respectable residents with occasional visitors, being generally persons of superior education, capable of appreciating his [Dr. Weedall's] talents, and relishing his eloquent and learned discourses. The town was genteel and pleasant, and the neighbourhood on all sides interesting." The state of the church itself is well expressed. "It is", the account continues,³ "a handsome building in the Grecian style; but Dr. Weedall soon after he came to Leamington, being quite enamoured of everything Gothic, had a great wish to *gothicise* the interior, so far as this could be done in a building of a widely different character." Carefully the narrative records the results that he achieved in this endeavour. "He did this, however, successfully by adopting that style of transition, or Oriental Gothic, usually termed Byzantine; and the chapel was superbly decorated in that style."

It was close in the church with no air coming through the tastefully coloured window erected by Mr. Croster's "meritorious exertions". Full of substance, the long discourse wound forward. It was rational and not unexpected. In the reserved front pews sat the Throckmortons and young Johnny Acton; on those red cushions with the feet upon the red cloth hassocks. This was the presentation of religion to which they, but not he, were long accustomed.

[1] *Life and Letters of John Lingard*, by Martin Haile and Edwin Bonney, letter to Mrs. Maxwell, p. 308.
[2] *Life of Weedall*, p. 231.
[3] *ibid.*, p. 235.

CHAPTER VI
THE WHIG MARRIAGE

WITH THE EXCEPTION of the lasting influence that Döllinger was to exercise over Lord Acton's mind, the chief ties of his youth with the Catholic Church have been described. There was much that must have appealed to him in the old English Catholics: their profound and workaday integrity; their devotional practices, a little stiff but very cool and moderate; their robust common sense fortified by a calm recognition of their own position; their discomfort in the presence of the warm emotions when these invaded the religious field. Nevertheless there was a barrier between them and him which could not be surmounted. For Acton, who was so much the intellectual, never seems to have been able to reach to interior sympathy with men to whom such a conception had no meaning. With women, on the other hand, he would sometimes prove quite unexacting.

His mind was to move forward slowly according to its ordered principles, which were as glistening and secure as piston rods. He would see, and appears to have required that others also should see, all the premises and the conclusions. It was not the old English Catholics who could cope with this too-clear mind and those principles which moved it, so Liberal and crystalline. To them he seemed solitary and in consequence intimidating.

Wiseman's influence on him was very different. There was nothing intimidated in the bold sweep of the Cardinal's processes. Wiseman's effect on the historian was great; but it was an inevitable factor in the latter's development that in time this influence curdled.

In many respects one of the most crucial events in Acton's formation was his mother's second marriage. For in 1840 Lady Acton had married Lord Leveson, the eldest son of the first Earl Granville, then ambassador in Paris. There were no children of this union, and although Leveson succeeded his father in 1846, he continued to use Aldenham as his country house throughout the long period of his new stepson's minority. Thus there was brought home to John Acton an understanding of that great world which still took its political doctrine and its privileges for granted.

It seems that he was confronted in Lord Granville's circle by everything except discussion. There was a certain faintness in this stepfather's influence, for, like so many of the Leveson-Gowers, his character was marked by an anchored sceptical assurance and by a gift of indolence. Both those qualities were incomprehensible to one who possessed the strange Acton-Dalberg heredity.

Nevertheless it was this marriage that brought the historian into contact with the secular values of the Age and with the last generation of the Whig political hegemony. Alone among English Catholics John Acton was the stepchild of those great clans the Leveson-Gowers and Cavendishes. From the terraces of Trentham and the new glass-houses the dilapidated English Catholic world receded and appeared to lack reality. And Dr. Wiseman, too, was seen in new perspective. In his own apartments in the Granvilles' town house in Bruton Street lived old Charles Greville, turning over the volumes of his diaries, polishing and re-phrasing. He had come across the prelate "in full episcopal costume, purple stockings, tunic and gold chain", and had passed upon him what was surely the judgment of his world. "The day before yesterday", he noted,[1] "I met Dr. Wiseman at dinner, a smooth, oily, agreeable Priest." It is worth observing that there was no period at which Acton was unaware of the Protestant estimation of his pastors.

Yet it would be a mistake to overstress the antithesis between this novel Whig background and that of his richer Oscott fellow-students. The dividing line was not so much religious as political and social. Within that secure oligarchy, buttressed by a rationalism which was diluted and very civil, the provincial note of the Tory squires was seldom heard. The Whigs had never lost their cosmopolitan affinities, and it was these in fact that had brought about the Granville-Acton marriage.

Further, there was by this time a cleavage between the outlook of the men and women in the great Whig houses. Half a century earlier there had been an identity of view between Lord Granville's grandmother, Georgiana Duchess of Devonshire, and the men of her immediate circle. In the interval that had elapsed the political views had maintained themselves with more success than had the *insouciance* of their easy Deism. That happy, extravagant, Voltairean detachment which had marked the Devonshire House circle had now vanished. Everything had become more serious.

[1] *The Greville Memoirs*, ed. Lytton Strachey and Roger Fulford, iv. p. 397.

The men retained a notion of their privileged leadership which was by this time conditioned by a sense of duty; the women had recovered a vocabulary which was almost as religious as the Evangelicals. Children received a Christian education such as would fit them for their great place. And it was through the side of the women and the children that little Johnny Acton had come to this new world. Theirs was the first influence; the effect of the Whig noblemen came later and was more permanent.

Lady Acton's marriage had been arranged in Paris and the cosmopolitan element was at first much in evidence. There was a good deal of leisurely expensive travel, and in 1843 a Roman winter. Acton was then nine years old and his mother and stepfather took an apartment in the Palazzo Simonetti on the Corso. At this stage there came into his life an association which was for a time very close. John Acton is described in Mrs. Oldfield's recollections [1] as "the intimate boy companion" of Granville Fullerton, a sensitive and moon-faced only child, who was Lord Granville's nephew. Fullerton was the younger by six months, constantly delicate, a little spoiled, fond of Macaulay's *Lays of Ancient Rome*. Later he followed his friend to Oscott and went into the Army and died at twenty-one. His cousin declares [2] that "he was bright and cheerful . . . and had nice intellectual tastes". Nothing remains to remind us of him except a marble bust by Matthew Noble.

Lord Granville, who was devoted to children, cared for his nephew with a warmth of feeling much deeper than that friendly cordial interest with which he approached his own wife's little boy. There seems no reason to suppose that Granville Fullerton meant anything in Acton's life or that he came to mitigate his sometimes startling loneliness. Much more significant was Granville's sister. Lady Georgiana Fullerton renewed an aspect of Mrs. Craven's influence.

She was a contemporary and close friend of Acton's mother and was a literary and romantic woman with a religious sentiment which in its early stages found support in the chivalric setting of the Eglinton Tournament. Later she was an intimate of Mrs. Craven's. She wrote poor verse and well-considered burdened novels, and in 1846 became a Catholic. Lady Georgiana was constantly at Herrnsheim and Aldenham.

---

[1] Recollections of Susan Pitt printed in Mrs. Augustus Craven's *Life of Lady Georgiana Fullerton*, p. 230. [2] Susan Pitt's recollections, *ibid.*, p. 233.

Sir John Acton, 6th Baronet, Prime Minister of the Two Sicilies.

It is, however, her political views that have more interest, for here her Whig ancestry became apparent. A letter that she wrote [1] on French affairs when Acton was seventeen is worth recalling. She believed in "the reign of the *Classes moyennes* through a representative government". She dreaded in 1851 both the Bourbons and the Orleanists. "The last would oppress [the Church], the former protect her, and I do not know which would be worse." She rejoiced that the new ministry in Paris was composed of "respectable men and friends of *order*".

Lady Georgiana was to pass out of Acton's life away into her mourning weeds and the control of confessors. Later she would refuse to contribute to the *Rambler*. Still, her influence was something of a bridge. Her views as to the position of the Church were closer to Lord Acton's final judgment than what he was so soon to learn from Dr. Döllinger.

Yet these were only points of detail, and behind them spread that old Whig spirit which still contrived to exercise an influence which was at once mature and ineradicable. It is not here a question of Whig doctrine; that, and in particular the thought of Burke, Acton would come to in his young manhood. It is the impact of the tradition which would affect his boyhood and his youth. This tradition was made up of many elements and was conditioned by the exercise of power conceived of as inherent. The Whigs shared one characteristic which is often manifested in a driving oligarchy; alike in their heyday and their decline their approach was profoundly unhistorical. They lived in the present and easily adopted current modes. It was in keeping with this trait that Granville himself should have accepted the politico-economic views of Bright and Cobden.

The Whig mood was essentially receptive, a character which this class has shared with all the world's great patrons. At the same time a philistine quality entered into their patronage. They had a self-assured almost rugged *insouciance*. In thought and expression and in taste they were the reverse of delicate. They had loved splendour and ostentation and self-criticism. It is no wonder that Prince Albert led his bride away from them so firmly.

It seems possible to maintain, and this would be a part of their philistine approach, that the Whigs were without any standards of self-expression. This and the curious receptivity for the current

---

[1] Susan Pitt's recollections, *ibid.*, p. 233.

mood explains how they became tied up with Lord Macaulay. About all affairs of secondary consequence they were both generous and adaptable; thus their moral standards were the fruits of class convention. No group, and this is an important point in Acton's moulding, was ever more completely free from any clerical influence. In spite of several apparent exceptions it is doubtful if there was ever such a being as a Whig prelate really integral to their class and taken seriously by them. When in office they purveyed ecclesiastical preferment with a care for their own clients and a solid unillumined common sense. Away below the level of their interests their bishops swam.

The outlook of the Whig families in this last matter had a powerful influence on their relations with political classes upon the Continent. In Sir Spencer Walpole's *Life of Lord John Russell* there is an account by the statesman's widow of his standpoint on religious questions. This is the more significant because Lord John was the traditional exponent of the old Whiggism throughout Acton's youth and early manhood. "His religion", wrote Lady Russell, "was as simple and true as everything else about him. His thoughts and opinions were not to be bounded or cramped by the regulations of any one sect built up by men. He looked forward to a day when there would be no priests." This will serve to explain how much the Whig tradition would commend itself to Monsieur Thiers and Monsieur Guizot.

Accustomed as they were to the recruitment of their own political supporters from the middle classes, the manner of the Whig oligarchs with the foreign *bourgeois* was very perfect. Their sound French, expressed against the background of an easy social habit, charmed and gave confidence. Abroad they were always ready for the new solution, and their interest was concentrated on the practical problems which had been set by this new century. It was this last quality, together with their strong sense of property, which gained them the support of the hard-headed group of English manufacturers.

In addition, the old high Whigs possessed a flexibility of mood which came to them from so many years of patronage. Their way of life was founded on the expert management of great wealth and on an understanding of the use of leisure. They knew they had no equals, and in this their final stage a delightful ease would flicker over all their social intercourse like summer lightning. They had an absence of pretension that would spring from their unapproachable and intact pride. They were the heirs of the Revolution of 1688 and the ark of a secular covenant had been entrusted to them. To defend the civic liberties of man was second nature.

It is sometimes difficult to remember how very short a space of time still separated them from their great period. The sixth Duke of Devonshire and his two sisters Lady Carlisle and Lady Granville all survived until after John Acton came of age; they had been brought up in the world of Fox and Sheridan. In this connection it is worth noting that as their party lost political effectiveness the character of privacy became more marked in the Whig ducal families. They were intimate and patriarchal and held to their own proud sufficiency. In one respect their outlook suffered change. The Whig oligarchy had retained a mood of casualness, aloofness and disdain in regard to the dynasty they had created. Now, and more particularly after the eighteen-fifties, they gave an allegiance to Queen Victoria which they would never have offered to the House of Brunswick. A Protestant-dynastic element was distilled as a consequence of their long ascendancy.

By this time, however, the impact of the way of life described had had its full effect upon John Acton. There were no children by his mother's second marriage, and this made Lord Granville's influence at once stronger and more evanescent. Until he came of age in 1855 the historian was under the guardianship of his mother and stepfather. For the next few years their house in Bruton Street was still his home in London. This situation lasted until Lady Granville's death in 1860. Thereafter the intimacy of that old oligarchic world receded and the young man would pass beneath the dominating influence of Mr. Gladstone.

Nevertheless John Acton was to owe much to the Whig connection. It was from this quarter, and also to some extent from the Herrnsheim tradition, that he gained that aptitude for the role of patron. The conception of a Maecenas of the world of scholarship had nothing in common with the outlook either of the Neapolitan cousins or of the Tory Catholic squires. Again, no man was to work with more industry than Acton; but he knew, with the assurance that the Whigs alone among his countrymen possessed, that all doors would be open to him. It seems, too, that he had an attitude towards money which is rarely found save among those who have lived in a circle of the most lavish expenditure without ever having been called upon to probe its detail. His high and carefree mind was not attuned to any economic problem, and it is no surprise to find that in his writings the economic motive is consistently ignored. It was surely the Whig influence, not Oscott and not Döllinger, which gave to him that singularly equable approach to the phases of negation and assent with which his contemporaries would meet the questions of religious creed. The same influence had also much to do with his surprising and early maturity both in standpoint and in expression. Perhaps it is not unreasonable to say that the Whigs were seldom adolescent nor was Acton. The Arcos, his Bavarian cousins, would certainly play a major part in forming him. The Granville-Dalberg-Arco influence combined to ensure that he should be cosmopolitan. He could never be as insular as the old Catholic squires nor as provincial as the Hawarden circle. It seems probable that Acton knew more than he understood. As far as England was concerned, the knowledge of the world that he possessed came filtered from the accustomed social practice of the great Whig house that sheltered him.

John Acton's education was pursued against this background. The framework of his upbringing was not as unusual as might at first sight appear. It was the use that he made of these opportunities that was so exceptional. One point had a marked effect on his development; his schooldays ended when he was fourteen. After a short stay in Edinburgh, he went in 1848 to Munich to reside with Professor von Döllinger and attend his lectures at the University. Already at this early age the idea of Cambridge had been mooted and set aside on account of the difficulties anticipated from the colleges who might be unwilling to accept a Roman Catholic undergraduate. "S'il faut", Acton wrote to his mother,[1] "que cela [Munich] me serve au lieu de Cambridge, j'y resterai volontiers jusqu'à ce que j'aurai fini toutes mes études." Apart from holidays he was to stay at Munich for six years.

The course on which he was now embarked was one that had found favour with several of the richer English Catholics. Dr. Döllinger had been warmly recommended by Sir Edward Vavasour. The room Acton was to occupy had been just vacated by John Herbert of Llanarth. His neighbour Augustus Jerningham, who

[1] *Selections*, p. 6.

had been in the same class at Oscott although four years his senior, travelled out with him to Bavaria.

At this point it is worth gathering together such details as are obtainable in regard to John Acton's experience of the Continent at the time when he set out for his Munich studies. Between Sir Richard's death and the beginning of the Oscott schooldays his mother divided her year between Paris and Aldenham. Beyond this our information comes in fragments. Thus Acton mentioned in later life that he had assisted at the uncontested election at which his stepfather, then Lord Leveson, was returned for Lichfield in 1841. It was one of those quiet, arranged successions, Anson giving place to Leveson-Gower. "I began my political life in 1841," he explained once to his friends,[1] "I canvassed at that election." No doubt the child of seven would produce a nice effect. Lady Grant Duff on reading over Lady Granville's letters said that his mother was clearly devoted to "her beautiful boy".

It is to a rather later period that the detail of his Parisian education, vouched for by Sir Mountstuart Grant Duff, must belong. In a study written after Lord Acton's death this friend stated categorically that he had been for some months prior to his arrival at Oscott at school at Saint-Nicolas du Chardonnet. This appears to be linked with a conversation with Ernest Renan noted by Sir Mountstuart in his diary under 24 March 1877. He had returned from visiting the author of *La Vie de Jésus* in his apartment on the upper floor of the Prince of Monaco's *hôtel* in the Rue Saint-Guillaume. "I never knew before", noted the diarist,[2] "that he [Renan] had just missed being at school with Acton, and had actually been at school with my Banffshire neighbour, Sir Robert Gordon of Letterfourie. All three were, like Albert de la Ferronays, under Dupanloup." This matter requires a brief examination.

Renan was born in 1823 and Sir Robert Gordon in 1824; they were thus ten years older than John Acton. Further, the seminary, which under Dupanloup began to accept lay boys not destined for the priesthood, was normally reserved for those of fifteen years of age and upwards. In the *Souvenirs d'Enfance* Renan speaks of Dupanloup with that penetrating, gentle, half-exacerbated regret which tends to underlie his lovely prose. "La réussite de la diffi-

---

[1] *Notes from a Diary*, 1892-95, ii. p. 124.
[2] *ibid.*, 1873-81, i. p. 242.

cile affaire de la rue Saint-Florentin", he explains[1] in relation to the deathbed reconciliation of Talleyrand, "l'avait mis à la mode dans le monde légitimiste; quelques relations avec le monde orléaniste lui assuraient une autre clientèle dont il n'était pas bon de se priver." The Dalberg connections with this world were clear enough; but if John Acton was ever at this house it was probably as a private pupil, since he was then only nine years old. There was certainly no contact with the Breton and Savoyard students, at least six years his seniors, who came to the *petit séminaire* of the diocese of Paris. Before leaving this subject one point made by Renan may be recalled. He is speaking of that background of the classics and of an assured dogmatic teaching within the social framework which was held to characterise the Church under the Orleans monarchy. "Certes la tentation est grande pour le prêtre qui abandonne l'Église de se faire démocrate. . . . Telle fut la destinée de Lamennais."[2] If Acton was ever taught by Dupanloup, he does not seem to have referred to it. Wiseman's is the name which held his childhood before he came to know Ignaz von Döllinger.

John Acton's acquaintance with Germany was at this time slight. He had passed some summers at Herrnsheim, which he would inherit after his mother's death. In the *Katharinenkirche* near by there stood the great array of Dalberg effigies, the primitive and elaborate life-size figures, the Gothic detail and the mantlings, the grave heraldic stone. His knowledge of German was rudimentary, for French had been his mother's favourite tongue. He was already very free from nationalism; boundaries conveyed but little to him. He went to Munich with a determination to make most extensive studies in a centre of European culture. This will seem an unusual approach for any boy of fourteen, but John Acton's lines of thought were all his own. His seriousness was very formidable. "M. Döllinger", he wrote to his mother on reaching the Professor's house, "me plait infiniment." With this phrase in mind it seems appropriate to consider the influences that were to mould the great historian.

[1] *Souvenirs d'enfance*, p. 168.
[2] *ibid.*, p. 194.

PART II: INFLUENCES OF EARLY MANHOOD

CHAPTER I

THE GERMAN SCENE

THE SITUATION in the German States in these middle years of the nineteenth century has often been described, but there are certain cardinal elements, especially in the Catholic South, which have not received attention. In the first place, there was a great interflow and mingling of opposing currents of thought and mood. In this network of sovereignties political and religious institutions had crumbled and suffered restoration; they had never been destroyed. The German lands had never undergone those swift destructive changes which had passed over France at the Revolution. Above all, the sovereign princes and such remnants of ancestral feudal custom as their presence guaranteed had not come to destruction at the hands of an insurgent *bourgeoisie*. The changes, and they had been many, were all completed in the form of compromise. Thus in 1803 and the succeeding years the ecclesiastical electorates of Cologne, Mainz and Trier and the prince bishoprics with their territorial jurisdiction had been swept away and incorporated in the neighbouring States. This was one section of established power absorbing another. It was a conflict wholly within the closed citadel of the princely rights.

A keynote of the life in Germany at this period was the sense of dynasty. In the Prussian world there had developed a sober and assured devotion to the House of Hohenzollern. Methodical in its unimpassioned emphasis and prosaic in expression, this attachment extended wherever there was the vestige of a Prussian interest. In the South there was a consciousness of the Wittelsbachs who approached the world of learning on more equal terms than did the Prussian princes. The full sovereignty of the many States and the private law, which regulated the affairs of royal and princely houses, preserved a structure which was monarchic and ancestral. The whole period was marked by the gradual supersession of long-rooted custom. The stream of German history came down through ancient and unbroken conduits.

The dislocation of life had been caused by the passage of foreign armies and not by the uprising of the German poor. The lords of all these lands had always been successful in dealing with their own *jacquerie*, and since the Peasants' Revolt in 1525 there had been quietude. The armies of the Thirty Years War, the forces of Marlborough and Prince Eugene in the campaign of Blenheim, and now more recently Napoleon's hybrid forces, had crossed and fought over and sometimes pillaged the German lands. Still, they had left behind them only the normal wreck made by professional soldiery, burning and wanton damage.

As the pennons of the French lancers disappeared westward for the last time along those elm-lined roads which crossed Franconia the accustomed round went forward undisturbed. Even as late as the mid-century an air of recovered peace still marked South German life. In such intellectual ferment as arose there was always a sense of measure, nor did the Bavarians ever lose an aptitude for somnolence. The thought of the time must be interpreted against a background which saw only easy changes and knew a vast security. There was a *bourgeoisie* with small resources which yet never felt want. The professional classes, university teachers, doctors, lawyers, were closely bound to the town merchants, and both in turn were linked to a strong farming stock. Behind them lay shared tastes and pleasures, the vineyards of that Southern country, the long pipes and the beer gardens.

Munich in the mid-nineteenth century was a symbol of this quiet and unselfconscious world of most secure experiment. The neo-classical buildings of the Bavarian capital bore the heat better than the new *Residenz* which had been copied from the Pitti Palace. Throughout those lazy summers the sunlight glanced from the expensive and raw marble. Around the Chinese temple in the *Englischer Garten* the dusty trees stood erect in the warm air.

This was a way of living which was not to receive its solvent for many years, for the thought values of German life were steeped in traditionalism layer on layer. Only external wars would shake the German structure, and these lay far ahead. The matter of religion is a good example, whether we consider Lutheranism, with its local patriotism and restrained observances, or the Catholicism of the German South. Many converging or disparate conceptions had gone to make up the attitude to Catholicism among the educated classes. There were indeed many points of view and romantic

elements which were often facile, but behind them all there stood
a class mood which was found across the territorial boundaries.
It was a legacy from one of the last of the Holy Roman Emperors,
Joseph II, to the Germanies. Difficult as it is to define, this mood
can be recognised as a standpoint which was at once mellow and
drained from all enthusiasm and curiously arid. The Tridentine
world had run its course.

Certain fundamental postulates must be examined to indicate the
outlook of the *milieu* in which John Acton found himself and against
which he and his immediate teachers had in part reacted. In the
first place, the State had long been regarded as both necessary and
beneficent. The institution of monarchy appeared to possess an
unbreakable strength reposing in the legal system; much was still
hoped from the reign of law. As a consequence of these views the
advancement of the human race was seen as operating through the
legal processes of the royal courts or through the royal ordinances.
Whatever power representative institutions should attain, it was
the law-making function which was conceived as significant. Conservatives would find in such ideas a bulwark, and Liberals had
not yet come to fear the modern State. The shadow of finance
capitalism had not fallen and men of small substance would join
all those of position in defending the sacredness of property.

In regard to the outlook on the Catholic Church many trends
of cultivated South German opinion at this time were still regalian,
that is to say that they granted to the State a controlling power;
implicitly it was considered that the new realms of knowledge
opened up since the *Encyclopédistes* would be worked by the
secular administration. The State was seen as the regulator of the
expanding universe. It is worth noting that the rule of the Wittelsbachs had lasted without interruption for six hundred years.
Bavarian intellectual circles thus conceived that their ancestral
State-form could absorb such ideas as might spring up in the
liberated centuries. The religious outlook of this class was tired
and somewhat formal, since it seems accurate to maintain that it
was the exhaustion of the Counter-Reformation which had given
birth to the Josephist form of *Étatisme*. This last position was so
important as a frame of mind in ecclesiastical and learned circles
that it requires some definition. The fact that Acton's own teachers
were arrayed against it only serves to emphasise its wide subcon-
scious hold upon the general mood.

This point of view derives its name from the Emperor Joseph II, who was the first sovereign to apply its principles. It was practical rather than theoretic and was under one aspect a German or rather a Central European variant of Gallicanism. But Gallicanism was an earlier phenomenon and implied a very strong, if national, ecclesiastical organisation over against the sovereign State. In the Josephist period the emphasis was placed on that secular power which was seen as covering each useful activity and as the wellspring of all human philanthropy. Gallicanism had had great Churchmen, like Bossuet, as its protagonists. The Josephist prelates, on the other hand, were in general men of little character, nerveless and hesitant. Their role as *philosophes* sometimes implied an interest that was fresh and vital but always kept quite distinct from their fatigued hereditary Churchmanship. The eighteenth-century Church seemed pale beside the virile monarchy.

The actual expression of the Josephist or Febronian theory, for it is known by both these names, dates from 1763. This was the year of the publication of *De statu praesenti Ecclesiae et legitima potestate romani pontificis*, a work written by the coadjutor of Trier, Johann-Chrysostom-Niklaus von Hontheim, Bishop of Myriophita *in partibus*, and issued under the pseudonym of Justinus Febronius. Behind this mood there lay the fact of Jansenism considered not as a doctrine but as a temper of mind. It is perhaps this that accounts for that note of aridity which dominates all this thought and its many variants. Port-Royal des Champs, that convent which fulfilled the role of the cool fortress of Parisian Jansenism, had been a purely seventeenth-century phenomenon, beautiful, unorthodox, not lasting; but once the spiritual element had been drained out of this tradition a temptation remained to the virtues of the Pharisee. This last characteristic went easily with the approach of the *philosophes*, which involved a high-minded seriousness of purpose and a standard of strict, but not specifically Christian, morality. Through this period admiration for the Stoics was increasing, and this led to an ethical severity which excluded humour.

The character of Febronius' work, as a recast of the Jansenist regalian position dealing with the subject of practical reforms, derived its significance from the passages in which reliance on the secular arm was recommended as a safeguard against "exaggerated foreign doctrine". A national feeling was gradually making headway and the patriot was seen as defending his nation inspired by the motives that were held appropriate to the Greek or Roman. The characteristic features of the world of the high Renaissance and its baroque succession were now being stripped away. The cultural values of the Counter-Reformation, including the whole Catholic-European solidarity, were by this time felt as alien.

At the instance of the Bourbon Crowns, Pope Clement XIV had in 1773 suppressed the Society of Jesus by the brief *Dominus ac Redemptor*. This was an event which ushered in, or more accurately recorded, a profound change in the climate of the thought of Europe. In the South German cities the Jesuit churches of the baroque tradition still reared themselves like waves above the old town squares; they were often a triumph of rococo, the angels on the monuments with their gilded trumpets, the careful massive drapery, the proud inscriptions. Along the side streets there lay the grey stone flanks of the great Jesuit colleges. But the fathers had left their pulpits with their guide rails and canopies, and the grapes and vine leaves carved upon the weathered oak. Their lecture-rooms and academic chairs were also empty. Expressed devotion to Rome was closely bound up with the dead Society.

In the Germanies the old conception of a theocratic monarchy as seen in the seventeenth-century sovereigns of the House of Austria and the first Bavarian electors had likewise vanished. The lavish use of metaphor and epigram, a decorous spiritual life constructed against an opulent backcloth, and a graded hierarchic concept of the social pyramid, were now seen as outmoded. Successive generations were growing weary of that formal education with its heavy and unbarbed Latinity.

Upon this scene there came the powerful and united influences of the Emperor Joseph II and his chancellor Prince Kaunitz. The minister had served the sovereign's mother Maria Theresa. During her reign his attitude towards the Church had been disdainfully correct. Later he was to show himself cold and barely placable; he had every hostility which can be seeded in intimacy, and he had begun life as a boy Canon of Münster. In certain respects the chancellor personified the extreme distaste of his age and class for any warm emotional expression in religion and their chilled avoidance of religious persons. All this was conveyed at least implicitly and by long contact to the heir to the throne.

Joseph II had reacted from his earlier orthodox religious teaching. He was determined to follow "a road through the dominions of superstition which was trodden centuries ago by Zoroaster and Confucius". He was isolated, nervous, a traveller, with a mind receptive within the limits of a rather narrow rigid swing. Phrases had power with him. "I shall have removed", he wrote, "from the chairs of my universities Andromache's web of the Ascetic doctrine." Another sentence indicates the same approach. "Posterity", declared the Emperor in reference to the successful campaign against the Jesuits, "will do justice to these ministers' efforts and will build them altars in the Temple of Fame."

This is only another aspect in a stronger, eccentric and more Germanic form of the influence of the *philosophes* which is considered to date from Montesquieu's publication in 1721 of the *Lettres Persanes*. High principles were drawn from classic sources. The tendency of the privileged classes in the mid-eighteenth century was to regard the future life as dim; nothing was as certain as the beneficent memory that their upright conduct might leave to enlightened mankind. The equable prospect from the windows of a nobleman's library led through the spaced cypresses to a pantheon in the middle distance.

In Germany the development of the rococo style, seen in such Benedictine houses as Ottobeuren and Niederaltisch, was contemporary with the new restrained classicism of the secular princes. The artificial quality of rococo, the light-hearted invention and the mannered stucco, soon seemed repellent to the generation which submitted itself to the Voltairean influence. The newly-serious mind could but recoil from those clashing perspectives and all the veiled elaborate artifice. On reaching manhood, men of birth laid aside the marionettes which had delighted them in the toy theatres of their expensive childhood; so too did they lay down the old religion.

In what may be called the governing classes sacramental life reached a low ebb. The rigorist Jansenist theories had in the first place discouraged approach to Communion save after a most searching preparation. In the chilled atmosphere an emotional element in worship was doubly suspect. The Lutheran Pietism of an earlier time had fallen into clear discredit, and within the Catholic Church the reaction against Quietism had carried far. There was moreover nothing "fashionable" in any nook or cranny of religious practice; the day was gone when Saint-Simon would detail dukes who followed "the gnosis of the Archbishop of Cambrai".

By the mid-eighteenth century it was becoming rare for a man of established rank to receive the sacraments while in good health. Such a nobleman when dwelling on his country properties would sit in his own pew or show himself within the family tribune. His gold-headed cane would be set in its place and the footman left standing in attendance. Behind or below him the peasants would crowd in to the Mass in those costumes which the nineteenth century was to find so delightful. There was a suitable outlook which the *Aufklärung* had given to its votaries. As the personage of quality settled to the arranging of his cuffs and the easing of his wig he would recognise that religious observances performed a certain useful social function.

This last phrase was at the kernel of the whole position, for it was precisely the work of the parochial clergy considered as a social function that the laws of Joseph II were intended to augment. At least, in the mind of the imperial legislator the Josephist decrees were conceived as building up the pastoral ministry. Teaching Orders, with the exception of the Society of Jesus, were not discouraged; Nursing Orders were warmly applauded. These were held to be elements of that civic well-being which the clergy were called upon to promote.

On the other hand, the organised *vita contemplativa*, that is to say the withdrawn life of the enclosed Religious, was attacked by name. In consequence, Carthusian monasteries were closed by the Emperor's order during 1782-83, not only in the Crown lands of Austria and Bohemia and in the Breisgau but also throughout the Austrian Netherlands and in Lombardy. The series of Bavarian charterhouses were suppressed by electoral decree in 1803. The old Benedictine abbeys with their princely courts and buildings and their wide estates went forward with some yielding to the times; but it is significant that in Acton's day neither the German charterhouses nor the Benedictine customs modelled on Beuron or Solesmes had yet been re-established. In all his thoughts the corporate liturgical life of the Church plays little part.

Yet the main purpose and consequence of these Josephist changes was to stress the position of the priests as a public functionary maintained by and answerable to the sovereign State. The matter in regard to which the royal *placet* was required extended constantly, and a sharp dislike was manifested in regard to each recourse to Rome. Yet this opposition to foreign influences was quite distinct from that nationalism which was beginning to make it palatable. In this case it was the far-flung Hapsburg lands which formed the unit; a determination had arisen that no Churchman should seek aid beyond the frontiers of the State structure which functioned under the rule of his own sovereign. It was sovereignty, not nationalism, that was thus exalted.

Such were the currents of thought in Southern Germany upon this matter of organised religion on the eve of the French Revolution. They ran deep and were in later generations almost imperceptible. Still, their remote action can be traced. Henceforward, to German Catholics interested in such subjects the idea of a Church establishment was fundamental. They might press for greater freedom, but they would never wish to break away from their allotted place in the State structure. Disestablishment was a conception that lay beyond the rim of their own world.

Among the ruling classes the custom of religious practice could founder slowly. With the coming in of the nineteenth century the "social duty" to support the Church became less urgent, while at the same time there were few who would wish actually to separate themselves from an immemorial expression of religious values. Catholicism had been an inextricable part of their family tradition now for many centuries; it was always available for them to reach towards. At the same time it was not conceivable that one from this *milieu* should avow himself a *libre penseur*, a term which carried with itself conscious middle-class associations. To men of lineage Catholicism as a part of the furniture of a carefree and a neglecting mind was in the climate of their long inheritance. This was the background of so many of John Acton's friends and relatives.

Another factor contributed to the strength of the Josephist influence. It was predominantly non-intellectual; it bore fruit in bureaucratic measures and in a certain social and civic attitude; it could persist for very long as a frame of mind. For this reason the Romantic school of which Acton was the immediate inheritor did not really conquer the old regalian influence. They existed at different levels and to some extent in different classes. The Romantic school, considered as operating within the Catholic culture and with Munich as its geographical centre, was active, self-laudatory, urban and *bourgeois*. The Josephist influence in its final phase was aristocratic and political, hardly formulated, a dislike, a tendency. The clergy who came out from the seminary at Freiburg-im-Breisgau even as late as 1840 supported Febronian ideas; it was such men who were for so long the chaplains in the schoolrooms of the princely families in Baden, Würtemberg and Old Bavaria as well as in the Austrian provinces.

It is always difficult to place ideas in immediate opposition to one another, because so many movements imbibe elements from the thought of those whom they themselves denounce most hotly. Thus at this date we can see that the Romantic school in so far as it centred upon Munich had its own regalian element. The shadow of Louis XIV fell, so to speak, on the just and on the unjust. From 1825 until his abdication in 1848 Bavaria was ruled by King Ludwig I. The Romantic school personified for this purpose in Josef von Görres and, anxious to replace the tired Bavarian *Étatisme* of King Ludwig's father by a very different spirit, called on one king to balance another and concentrated on Ludwig I.

This was the sovereign whom Görres summoned to be a "Christian prince, a pillar of the Faith". It is worth quoting what his physician Dr. Ringseis was to say of him:[1] "Love and enthusiasm for Christendom and for the Fatherland are for Ludwig I the noblest impulses of the artistic spirit." As these words imply, the King of Bavaria, like his brother-in-law the King of Prussia and the latter's minister General von Radowitz, was among the few who retained and were possessed by the dream of a Romantic kingship. In Munich this meant a concept of Catholic sovereignty seen in terms of a Gothic spirit. De Maistre in an earlier age had outlined a position which had been clouded by this transient Romanticism, a period fashion which took many forms.

On the one side there was that flowering of the Munich style to which the King devoted his first regal years, the *Propyläen* and the swift creation of an architecture which was Graeco-Germanic in inspiration. The senses were stunned by its raw and innocent magnificence. And then there came the later Gothic phase, the care for the restoration and completion of Cologne Cathedral, the purchase of Boisserée's collection, the patronage of Reichensperger. The transfer of the University from Landshut to Munich, the patronage of exiled scholars, the intense susceptibility to German verse, were all part of an enthusiasm for the German past which had the

[1] Ringseis, *Erinnerungen*, i. p. 468.

buoyancy of Walter Scott. It seems fair to link it with Melrose and Deloraine, that easy, sonorous idealisation of the Middle Ages, in this case charged with sentiment, which was at once haunting and so evanescent. This spirit is in part reflected in that assembly of Görres's friends the Round Table, whose very name denotes an atmosphere inimical to sharp cold thinking. These features in the situation were, however, not the most important for John Acton, who was never to be given to Gothic dreams. In its political aspect and in the relations between the Wittelsbach King and the Catholic grouping the reign had a different significance.

It may be seen as the tendency towards the creation of a modified nineteenth-century absolutism at once technically "constitutional", Catholic, *bourgeois* and pacific, all carried out in the Maecenas-spirit. In so far as this involved the reliance of a politically Catholic body upon an individual sovereign, it was a movement towards another form of royal control. Such dependence when entered into by a religious party has always an air of unreality, for it must so often hinge upon a ruler who, however strong his faith, does not maintain a sacramental practice; in this case, it was to end in the rather absurd catastrophe of King Ludwig's infatuation for the dancer Lola Montes.

The King was generous to the endowed Catholic body, but also to the Old Lutherans. He had a royal view of the privileges of his own family; his mind oscillated as to contacts with Rome and the value of sending students to the German College. He had a distaste for the Jesuits and disapproved of "rigorist" confessors. In spite of all that has been written about Joseph II and successive Kings of Prussia, it was not these sovereigns only who deserved the title of *rois sacristains*.

If this situation had elements on the religious side from which Acton was to recoil, it also carried political implications no less distasteful to the future Liberal. The Abel Ministry, which was the political expression of this idea, represented a bureaucratic-professorial outlook grateful to the conservative mind of François Guizot. It was in tune with all those ministries drawn from the doctrinaire circles of the State service through which the sovereigns of Europe governed while the *bourgeois* interest propped up the thrones. The *bürger* world, as Acton was to find, was very loyal, but the old South German aristocracy looked tranquilly upon the Wittelsbachs. It was only a generation since the mediatised families

Sir Richard Acton, 7th Baronet.

had lost their status as rulers. In 1803 their little sovereignties had been engulfed by Würtemberg, Bavaria or Baden. It was natural that they and their friends and cousinage should be a little guarded, a trifle patronising and disdainful in their attitude towards these royal stocks. Two sets of influences were now to play upon John Acton; on the one hand there was Dr. Döllinger, but on the other Count Arco.

Meanwhile, at Munich one could not forget the ultimate guidance of the Tsar of Russia. Thus Baader, who was associated with Görres in the Round Table, claimed to have suggested the idea of the Holy Alliance when in Russia. Like Görres, Baader exercised a powerful influence on Döllinger. Nevertheless, it was just this link-up with Russia which in time would make Acton turn from the political presuppositions that he would find among the inheritors of Görres's circle.

The Bavarian dynasty would never, no more than other German royal houses, dissociate itself from that world-view which the Court of St. Petersburg presented. The Tsar would intervene in all the royal marriages in Würtemberg, whose rulers were bound to him by so many ties. Among the monuments of this age is the Greek tomb that the Duke of Nassau built on the Neroberg at Wiesbaden for the Russian grand duchess who had been his wife. A comment in Prince Bülow's *Memoirs* is very striking in this connection. "If", he wrote of his childhood days at the Court of Strelitz,[1] "the Grand Duke of Mecklenburg-Strelitz said that the Tsar would have wished this or that, it was as if God Himself had spoken."

These factors make it understandable that the opposition should link together autocracy and clericalism, and a certain irresponsibility devoid of humour in the presentation of Wittelsbach ideas was most inviting to attack. As long as Nicholas I of Russia lived, no great gulf would separate the royal German picture from the Legitimist world of Charles X. Three snatches from the verse of Béranger are worth recalling:

> Curé, fais ton devoir,
> Remplis pour moi ton encensoir.[2]

And then that cry from 1826:

---

[1] Prince von Bülow, *Memoirs*, i. p. 8.
[2] From the "Marquis de Carabas", Béranger, *Des Familles*, p. 68.

> L'homme rouge apparait encore.
> Riant d'un air moqueur,
> Il chant comme au chœur,
> Baise la terre, et puis ensuite
> Met un grand chapeau de jésuite.
> Saints du Paradis,
> Priez pour Charles Dix.[1]

Finally comes the very comprehensive attack on the Holy Alliance of the Christian sovereigns:

> Qu'un jour Stamboul contemple avec ivresse
> Les derniers Grecs suspendus à nos mâts:
> Dans son tombeau faisons rentrer la Grèce:
> Les rois chrétiens ne la vengeront pas.[2]

Heinrich Heine, with the suppleness of thought and swiftness of transition which so marked him, put the contention in another way:

> Der Deutsche wird die Majestät
> Behandeln stets mit Pietät,
> In einer sechsspännigen Hofkarosse.

Here is all the irritation with the German deference for kingship, the feeling for its trappings, the old State coaches of the German crowns. And then with a change of mood it is the same State coach with black-plumed horses decked with crape which will carry the sovereign when his people bring him, still obsequiously, to that end which it requires no knowledge of German to understand:

> In einer sechsspännigen Hofkarosse,
> Schwarz panachiert und beflort die Rosse,
> Monarch einst nach dem Richtplatz kutschiert
> Und untertänigst guillotiniert.

---

[1] From the "Petit Homme Rouge", *ibid.*, p. 219.
[2] From "Psara ou chant de victoire des Ottomans", *ibid.*, p. 194.

CHAPTER II
DR. DÖLLINGER

DR. VON DÖLLINGER presented a marked contrast to Dr. Wiseman. He was almost as far removed from Lord Granville. His untempered quick sympathy and his ramifying sleepless scholarship were both calculated to win John Acton. These and his *anglomanie* also drew him towards the serious and ardent boy. "J'ai lu", the latter wrote to his mother in 1848,[1] "la lettre du prof. Döllinger avec la plus grande joie. Elle me prouve qu'il propose me faire suivre mes études dans la manière même que je désirais, seulement il se prépare à me donner beaucoup plus de liberté qui je ne désirerais avoir chez lui. Je vois que c'est un homme dans lequel je pourrai avoir la plus parfaite confiance, et je mettrai avec plaisir toute la direction de mes études et de ma conduite entre ses mains."

"He is unquestionably", young Acton wrote from Munich in what appears to be his first letter from his new home,[2] "the most cool-headed man I ever knew, and probably the most dispassionate. His judgment is singularly original and independent—he prefers Byron, and probably Dryden and Moore, to Milton, and thinks Wellington the greatest of modern generals. He is minutely conversant with English literature." There the boy sat, only fourteen but yet so self-possessed, in his room with its fine glass-fronted bookcase and "a unique set of historical maps".[3] After writing home he would turn to reading German, for he was not yet acquainted with that language. This was followed by an hour for Plutarch and another hour for Tacitus. At two o'clock came dinner and converse with the professor. "I see him then for the first time in the day."[4] It is worth examining what the young Acton would find when he went down to the drawing-room, as it was called, in which Dr. Döllinger and his young guests took their midday meal.

It was not a large room, but from the accounts which have come down to us it seems congested. There were vases of yellow wallflowers if in season, a dark green velvet sofa in the style of

---
[1] *Lord Acton's Correspondence*, p. 6. [2] *ibid.*, p. 7.
[3] *ibid.*, p. 8. [4] *ibid.*, p. 8.

Louis-Philippe, every available space crowded with pictures. Arranged between distant views of Rome and Paris was a lithograph of the members of the Frankfort Diet of 1848. Copies of the portraits of Bossuet and Fénelon from the old *Pinakothek* balanced each other and were flanked by a reproduction of Giotto's Dante. There was a head of Christ in oils.

The professor, sitting at the head of the table, had the water-carafe beside him. A preciseness of manner and of taste survived from the early days at Würzburg. Some of the older articles of furniture had come, like his cook, from his father's house. He was forty-nine years of age and very settled. We can picture from the many photographs that slender figure with the careful bearing, the wrinkled priestly face, the bony hands. Dr. Döllinger had a distaste for beer unusual in a Bavarian, and he found the taking of tobacco painful. He would not permit it in his presence. In the evenings the water was replaced by a tall jug of lemonade. Items of autobiography fell from him. "Perhaps had I gone to Berlin and heard Savigny and Eichhorn I might not have forsaken the study of law." He had a great feeling for painting, and especially for Van Eyck; he would consider the elements which charmed him in each composition.

In the big library, to which the young John Acton went to borrow books but did not sit, there were more pictures, including engravings of Raphael's portraits of Julius II and Leo X. There the boy could stand and marvel at the thirty penholders in their cardboard case, at the massive black inkstand and the sandbox. In the late afternoon the professor would on occasion invite him as his companion on that daily walk to the English Garden past the ornamental water to the Chinese Tower. Döllinger had a townsman's love of birds and flowers and sunshine. This was how he envisaged Tegernsee and the repose of a Bavarian summer. Master and pupil would speak English when together. "M. Döllinger", we read, "me plaît infiniment. Il a les connaissances les plus étendues dans l'histoire et la littérature de tous les pays et de tous les temps." The next phrase is worth noting: "Je ne sais pas s'il est fort dans les sciences physiques."

With all this there went a very simple ease of disposition. The professor was fond of quoting homely verses, the friendly jingles of a nursery history:

Quand le Pasque-Dieu décéda,
Par-le-jour-Dieu lui succéda,
Le diable m'en porte s'en tint après,
Foi-de-gentilhomme vint après.

He would thus render from Brantôme the list of the favourite oaths of Francis I and his three predecessors. He was also fond of the old Thuringian rhyme:

Oh! gracious God, we pray,
Grant fruit and rain and sun to shine,
On Reuss, Greiz, Schleiss, and Lobenstein.

"Il est excessivement simple", wrote Johnny Acton.

In such an atmosphere Acton grew to manhood, reading with that copious enthusiasm which never left him. He could not only borrow from the professor's own great store, but the whole of the Royal Library was open to him. The other students in the house were often young men debarred by the then statutes from attending an English University. It may be hazarded that their principal gain from this sojourn in Munich was a knowledge of German. It would seem that neither Döllinger nor Acton had much in common with such co-religionists. Among all those who came and went, Acton was the only boy and Döllinger would mould him.

In considering the formation of the historian it is essential to consider this priest's outlook. He was a man of simple tastes and preconceptions and of a wide discursive scholarship. Nothing that came within the scope of literary history and mythology was remote from Döllinger's concern. He had always a high grand simplicity, and the romantic mood of early nineteenth-century German writing had marked him deeply; his standards would remain those of the frugal contented *bourgeoisie* from which he sprang. In his father's house at Würzburg, as the son of the professor of anatomy in that University, he had imbibed the political and social axioms which he never questioned. It was a tranquil and protected world with the Napoleonic wars a memory and the young Ignaz von Döllinger shyly and unsuccessfully playing Dunois in Schiller's *Jungfrau von Orleans*.

The professor's attachment to the House of Bavaria was very strong and his links were perhaps closest with Maximilian II. He was royal chaplain to this sovereign and to his son. In a sedate fashion the Wittelsbachs would flatter him. It was the custom to ask him for explanations of the Scriptures. "Louis II", we are told,[1] "seemed to be especially interested in passages of the Bible having reference to the Kingly office, and in portions of the Song of Solomon." In spite of his enthusiasm for English customs Döllinger was insistent that ministers should be responsible not to Parliament but to the Crown. Two expressions of opinion, which belong to a later stage of the professor's life, seem worth recording here for the bearing that they have upon his outlook. He is found speaking of General Gordon as a figure of heroic proportions. "Second to none", so runs the telling sentence,[2] "in moral grandeur, and worthy to be placed by the side of Bismarck and of Moltke." He had, too, his own romantic vision. "Out of all the nations of the modern world, the German people, like the Greeks of old, have been called to an intellectual priesthood, and to this high vocation they have done no dishonour."[3] It was always what he conceived of as the Germanic nations which appealed to Döllinger. "Vanity", he observed tartly,[4] "is an accepted characteristic of the French." In simplicity he would roll out his unflagging and long quotations from Shakespeare and Walter Scott, Goethe and Schiller.

There was much that was appealing to the professor in Shakespeare's country, and it is not always appreciated that Dr. Döllinger had been for so long familiar with certain specialised ingredients of the English scene. There was the contact with the Catholics and the translation of his *Church History* by Dr. Cox of St. Edmund's College; but it was the earnest Protestants who really drew him. Writing much later, in 1890, in an account of Döllinger's historical work which he contributed to the *English Historical Review*, Lord Acton was to make a comment which rather tends to place his teacher's English contacts in a false perspective. "Early acquaintance with Sir Edward Vavasour and Lord Clifford", he explained,[5] "had planted a lasting prejudice in favour of the English Catholic families, which sometimes tinged his judgments." It was, however, not to the Catholics but to the Tractarian element in the Established Church that Dr. Döllinger made most appeal. This matter, which has its importance for John Acton, is worth a cursory examination.

Döllinger was essentially a scholar, simple and self-contained,

---

[1] *Conversations of Dr. Döllinger*, by Luise von Kobell, p. 45.
[2] *ibid.*, p. 172.   [3] *ibid.*, p. 206.   [4] *ibid.*, p. 121.
[5] *Essays on Liberty*, p. 388.

with a part reverent, wholly friendly approach to the private life of the upper classes. He saw England as a conservative, monarchic land based on a privileged society which was increasingly Christian. What could be more congenial than Dr. Pusey? In support of this view we can quote the journal of James Hope, a young Tractarian who had one of the most acute and balanced minds of his generation: "There is about him [Dr. Döllinger] a simplicity of thought and manner which is most agreeable and which suits well with his great learning." [1]

This was in 1840, and four years later, on the occasion of a second visit, Dr. Pusey himself wrote to the professor: [2] "Perhaps also Dr. Döllinger could give you some information as to St. Ignatius Loyola's *Exercitia Spiritualia*, for they seem to have been so often re-moulded that there is some difficulty to ascertain (1) what is ye genuine form, or at least to obtain a copy, (2) whether any other re-casting of it be found easier to use." Dr. Pusey was forming at Christ Church "a little shelf of R. Catholic books". James Hope was staying at the Austrian Legation and left to visit his close friends the Thun und Hohensteins at Tetschen; this was that Arco setting which the professor loved.

In its own way James Hope's background had something of the same attraction with a more obtrusively religious influence. For a natural affinity subsisted between the easy South German kindliness and that protected Christian life with its decorous chaste sentiment, faintly romantic, which had grown up in the enclosed gardens of the vicarages of England. The shadow of Mr. Keble's principles fell on those lawns. Thus in the rectory at Dittisham, looking down through the plum blossoms to the Dart by the horse-ferry above the Anchor Stone, Hope's sister Dorothea lived with her husband, Lord Henry Kerr. There the rector and his wife ministered with a practical charity, their days as easy as a Devon summer. Lord Henry's cousin the Earl of Mount Edgcumbe had brought him south to this family living.

In his talks with Dr. Döllinger and his friend Dr. Windischmann, James Hope was shrewd and the priests kindly. "They said that most of the clergy have something of the Fathers upon their shelves." [3] To the quick Scotsman with his intimate know-

---

[1] *Memoir of J. H. Hope-Scott, Q.C.*, by Robert Ornsby, i. p. 237.
[2] Letter dated 9 September 1844, *ibid.*, ii. p. 51.
[3] *ibid.*, i. p. 235.

ledge of civil law the professor stood out as most impressive. "I am", he wrote on his second visit,[1] "more struck with him than ever." "Notanda,"[2] so runs one of the headings in Hope's journal, "the R. Catholic Church is not in a very flourishing condition in Bavaria. There is, moreover, a great want of clergy, the profession not being popular, though chiefly supplied from the lower orders."

It was a consequence of this relation that, after Newman's submission to Rome in 1845, Döllinger kept contact with both sides. From Munich he would equally maintain touch with the Tractarians and the Catholic converts. In 1851 he came to England and in the distribution of his visits this trend is marked. A note in the diary of John Hungerford Pollen,[3] then still an Anglican and Fellow of Merton, makes this clear: "May 2, 1851. Came, with letters to me from Hope, Döllinger, the German historian, and Sir John Acton, his pupil. I was greatly pleased with Döllinger, a good English scholar; he thinks that foreign Protestants face fairly, if externally, the question of the Middle Ages: not so the English historians, who, he thought, had never appreciated or judged truly of those times." The last sentence of this entry is significant: "Döllinger, after seeing Pusey, left for Newman." Very early he sowed in his pupil's mind that appreciation of the Church of England as an anchored conservative religious entity, an impression which Mr. Gladstone would seize hold of and transmute.

It would seem probable that it was during this visit that the project of a spell at Cambridge was seriously mooted. In the inaugural lecture which Lord Acton delivered in June 1895 on entering upon his professorship he was to refer [4] to the time "when I was reading at Edinburgh and fervently wishing to come to this University. At three colleges I applied for admission and as things then were I was refused by all." A difficulty at once arises from the fact that John Acton's stay at Edinburgh occurred during 1848 when he was only fourteen years old, so that any approach then must have been tentative. A letter to Mr. Gladstone written in January 1896 puts the matter rather differently. "My little Captatio", explained Acton [5] in reference to the passage which has just

---

[1] Letter dated 9th September 1844, *ibid.*, ii. p. 50.
[2] *ibid.*, i. pp. 233 and 238.
[3] *Life of John Hungerford Pollen*, by Anne Pollen, p. 37.
[4] *Lectures on Modern History*, p. 1.
[5] *Lord Acton's Correspondence*, p. 157.

been quoted, "meant that, late in '49 or early in '50, I attempted through John Lefevre, to obtain admission as an undergraduate. But Magdalene, and two other Colleges, refused to have me. There is nobody there who remembers the circumstance, but they conjecture that Papal aggression had to do with it. I have not verified dates." The Ecclesiastical Titles Bill was introduced in February 1851 following on the creation of the archbishopric of Westminster, and this may be taken as the high-water mark of anti-Catholic feeling at that period. In every way it seems most likely that the last and most serious attempt to enter Cambridge was made in 1851 when Acton had reached seventeen. John Shaw-Lefevre was at that time deputy clerk of the Parliaments; Magdalene had been Cardinal Acton's college.

At whatever date it was finally abandoned, the Cambridge project was soon definitely laid aside and replaced by the continuance of the courses at the University of Munich, varied by holidays abroad with Dr. Döllinger, who thus acted as a most superior kind of travelling tutor. Finally, in 1853 John Acton was to make with Lord Ellesmere that journey to the United States which would be his first independent venture and which was destined to leave so strong a mark on his ideas.

In this connection it is worth considering how far the schools of German scholarship affected the young historian's development. In the first place, his knowledge of German soon became perfect, and to his death he retained an ease with that language and a tendency to fall back upon a German idiom. This was to stand him in good stead with the academic scholarship of an English century which possessed a particular reverence for German thought. At the same time, all such influences were for many years only to come to Acton through conversations with Döllinger and through the latter's comments on his reading. During the long period of his training the German writers in especial would thus reach John Acton at second hand. Their work had first to pass the filter of Döllinger's specialised consideration.

Writing in later life, Lord Acton was to stress the profoundly ecclesiastical character of the professor's interests. "In early life", explained Acton in that study of Döllinger's historical work which was the only completed chapter in the biography of his master that he projected,[1] "he had picked up chance copies of Baronius

[1] "Döllinger's Historical Work", *Essays on Liberty*, p. 379.

and Petavius, the pillars of historic theology; but the motives of his choice lay deeper. Church history had long been the weakest point and the cause of weakness among the Catholics, and it was the rising strength of the German Protestants." In the same connection a litany of the old high names in ecclesiastical archaeology will by itself suffice to show how far Döllinger's interests ever lay from that new German learning which was to exercise so deep an influence upon Great Britain. "In this immense world of patient, accurate, devoted research," wrote Acton [1] of the beginning of the professor's training, "Döllinger laid the deep foundations of his historical knowledge. Beginning like everybody with Baronius and Muratori, he gave a large portion of his life to Noris, and to the solid and enlightened scholarship that surrounded Benedict XIV, down to the compilers, Borgia, Fantuzzi, Marini, with whom, in the evil days of regeneration by the French, the grand tradition died away. He has put on record his judgment that Orsi and Saccarelli were the best writers on the general history of the Church. Afterwards, when other layers had been superposed, and the course he took was his own, he relied much on the Canonists, Ballerini and Berardi; and he commended Bianchi, De Bennettis, and the author of the anonymous *Confutazione*..." The names roll on, an ordered sequence of northern baroque. The shadow of Trent lay on such studies. It was a far cry to Göttingen.

The next paragraph also bears on this point. "He seldom", continues Acton,[2] "quotes contemporary Germans, unless to dispute with them, prefers old books to new, and speaks of the necessary revision and renovation of history." The statement that follows [3] is the obvious sequel to this position. "Hegel remained, in his eyes, the strongest of all the enemies of religion, the guide of Tübingen in its aberrations, the reasoner whose abstract dialectics made a generation of clever men incapable of facing facts." These sentences lead up to that peroration in which with a touch of rhetoric characteristic of his generation Acton [4] sums up the influences that acted on the professor and therefore through his training on himself. "The men to whom Döllinger owed his historic insight and who mainly helped to develop and strengthen and direct his special faculty, were not all of his own cast, or remarkable in the common description of literary talent. The assistants were count-

---

[1] "Döllinger's Historical Work", *Essays on Liberty*, p. 387.
[2] *ibid.*, p. 389.   [3] *ibid.*, p. 381.   [4] *ibid.*, p. 393.

less, but the masters were few, and he looked up with extraordinary gratitude to men like Sigonius, Antonius, Augustinus, Blondel, Petavius, Leibnitz, Burke, and Niebuhr, who had opened the passes for him as he struggled and groped in the illimitable forest."

CHAPTER III

MOSCOW

THE ASSOCIATIONS OF MUNICH and the life with Dr. Döllinger at once enlarged and narrowed John Acton's horizon. It is clear that these influences brought him into a world of scholarship and enquiry to which he would otherwise have been completely foreign, but at the same time it is necessary to examine briefly the many tides of German thought which passed him by. The example of the Prince Consort had encouraged the tendency of the English academic world to look towards Germany, but students from England always turned to a section of that country quite remote from the world of Ignaz von Döllinger. The Universities to which the English went were normally Lutheran in origin, often rationalist in emphasis and frequently within the Prussian orbit. Some of the earlier British contacts had been made with the Georgia Augusta University at Göttingen, where George Finlay, the historian of Greece, had studied, and where Acton's own grandfather, the Duke of Dalberg, had sat on the seats with the *hochwohlgeboren*.

At Munich, Acton was cut off absolutely from the German military tradition. The remnants of the Romantic school had a form of Catholic internationalism based on an aesthetic feeling for an unreal Middle Ages which had nothing in common with the bearing of arms. It was the dark Gothic religious mystery and the world of monk and palmer to which they turned, not the knight's vigil. Bavaria was never to possess that cavalry and grenadier tradition which would make the Prussian landowner so comprehensible to the English class which at that date officered the Brigade of Guards. Ludwig I in particular had starved his army, and in so far as the South Germans were drawn to the military life, it was towards Vienna that they tended. The world of arms that they understood was that old imperial Austrian tradition which Marshal Radetzky represented.

On the other hand, in England the philistine cast of mind was swiftly led to admire the Prussian army. Queen Victoria's appreciation was widely shared. A class-consciousness, which was quite unspectacular and absolutely rigid, was nowhere maintained with the same purity as in the old Mark of Brandenburg and on the manors which stretched away towards the Baltic beneath the skies of the North German land. This strong confidence was allied with a military devotion to and a readiness for self-sacrifice for the House of Hohenzollern. A sense of duty was rooted in a form of dynastic Lutheran faith freed from Pietism and entirely undemonstrative. The whole could not fail to make appeal to the last sovereign of the House of Brunswick and to those who had reaped the benefits of the Hanoverian century.

With this there went that nationalism rooted in the militarist spirit which was always to be foreign to Lord Acton's world. The Bavarian-German feeling, which the historian experienced in all its variants, had almost nothing in common with the rigid and devoted doctrine that marked the Prussian military caste. Thus few men were more antipathetic to John Acton than the rising Prussian politician Count von Bismarck-Schönhausen. The conception of political *drilling* and the storm tactics of the marshalled vote were alike anathema to all his cherished thought on liberty.

Political constitutions had now gained in his eyes the almost sacred quality which they drew from that basis of the fundamental laws on which they rested. Bismarck's determination to manipulate the Prussian Constitution sprang from a "realist" approach which Acton found peculiarly abhorrent. Much of the clarity of the latter's thought developed from the sharp character of this dislike.

A similar element can be observed in Acton's comment on the Prussian historian von Sybel, whom King Maximilian II brought to Munich. He was always in immediate opposition to the mechanised forces of Prussian nationalism as they moved forward. It is, perhaps, only fair to say that it was not in John Acton's nature to appreciate soldiers. A more serious obstacle in the way of the development of the historian's chosen life was the difficulty that he found in appreciating North German scholarship. Only in his maturity did he come to see the richness of this field.

The memory of Niebuhr was still green and he was inevitably a venerated figure; but he had died in 1830. In Munich the next generation was apt to be judged by their reactions to the Catholic Church. Thus von Sybel's position was still further undermined on account of his distaste for Catholicism as an anti-national force. The position may be summed up in the comment made when Heinrich von Treitschke, who was Acton's exact contemporary, was elected very young to a professorship at Freiburg. All the feeling of the old German South is made clear in his description as the "Bismarck of the Chair".

It seems increasingly evident that Acton's understanding of von Ranke belonged to a very much later day. At this time there was the earlier Döllinger to come between them. In reference to these two scholars Acton was eventually to write [1] that in hot youth there was much to part them. Döllinger had pronounced the theology of Ranke's *Deutsche Reformation* both slack and trivial. The field of contemporary German scholarship was one which, for all his massive learning, John Acton in his early years had not yet ploughed.

It was inevitable that at this time there should be a disparity between the young historian's grasp of the historical apparatus which Döllinger had taught him and the fluid concepts of thought on politics which in his maturity would set so fast. In the end these concepts in politics and morals would come to dominate the immense technical erudition which in Lord Acton's later life existed mainly for their service. At twenty-two, however, he was still seeking. The projects connected with the Catholic quarterly review, the *Rambler*, and its successor the *Home and Foreign*, had not yet broken in his hands. He hoped with an illuminated seriousness for the most improbable of syntheses; there were no contemporaries to check his hopes.

At this stage John Acton was passed back from Dr. Döllinger's tutelage to that of his stepfather, a man whose indolent generosity would never flinch from any task which family loyalty placed in his way. Their first journey abroad together on official business would take them to Moscow, a city which lacked all the appeal that Munich held for the young Acton. In parenthesis his reactions were never primarily aesthetic.

The similarity of mood pervading European institutions, the strong ties binding the Russian and the German Courts, the natural conservatism of Döllinger's circle have all been stressed. Still, at Moscow the historian was to see the unified polity of Europe at what was to him its weakest point. This instinct was reinforced by the fact that everything in his background made Russia familiar. No more than Mr. Burke had Sir John Acton a fear of judging. The mission that we are about to consider had an important conse-

[1] " Döllinger's Historical Work ", *Essays on Liberty*, p. 396.

quence for his outlook. He was young, solitary, rather difficult at the Court of Russia. If Granville was the Whig *milord* of easy manners, preferring an hereditary political atmosphere to explicit doctrine, Acton was a searcher who would probe and query. Much reading had brought him to the Court of Russia; he would find his hatred of absolutism there.

In 1856 Acton, who had already made one journey to that country, accompanied his stepfather as private secretary on the elaborate special mission which Lord Granville headed as Queen Victoria's representative at the coronation of the Tsar Alexander II. This is a point at which we can pause to estimate Granville's influence upon his stepson and observe how it operated, attracting and repelling him. Unconsciously that background of high European privilege which they shared was a uniting bond, and the older man was always able to put a just value upon his junior's assets. Still, at the more conscious levels Acton's young seriousness was outraged at almost every turn.

In the first place, there was an air of levity about the ambassador's approach which could not fail to exacerbate. Never very far away from all that he said and did lay an equable and kindly cynicism which would recall the eighteenth century. He mocked playfully at his posts in politics—never, of course, at his place in English life. A quotation will serve to indicate this native quality. "The house beautiful, the China of the softest paste, the wine excellent, the Lord President", Granville wrote of himself,[1] "rather drunk." Beyond the Rhine in Döllinger's circle with its gentle fun they would not understand that indolent and barbed self-mockery.

Unfortunately the opinion which he held of foreigners in general was not a high one. And then he had a frivolous literary taste which it must have been hard for Acton to condone.

"I have begun", Granville wrote about this time to his friend Lord Canning,[2] "a Life of Madame de Chevreuse in the *Revue des Deux Mondes* by Cousin. It seems very amusing." This was not John Acton's approach. The elder man found Macaulay "charming reading", but such comment was *de rigueur* with his school of thought. At Mr. Gladstone he was inclined to mock.

---

[1] Letter dated 28 November 1855, printed in *Life of the Second Earl Granville*, by Lord Edmond Fitzmaurice, i. p. 128.
[2] Letter dated 9 December 1855, in the Granville-Canning correspondence, *ibid.*, i. p. 129.

"He is devoted to Homer. He is going to *réhabiliter* Helen, whom he has discovered to be a much injured woman." [1] This was the vein of humour of a less serious epoch. There was a Corinthian element in Lord Granville's amusements. He would ride to view his farm at Golder's Green, enjoyed a dinner at the "Dog and Duck" and sat with his friends chaffing "Poodle" Byng. On the other hand, his attitude to the world of fashion was irksome in its half-charmed lightness. "Coventry House", he would exclaim [2] in the days of the coming of the crinoline, "too gay and pretty. The society the refined essence of cream, with a beautiful buffet laid out. Some of the women could hardly get into the doorways." There was almost too much sunshine in the life of "Pussy" Granville.

There was present throughout a certain strain of French influence from which the old Whig circle would never really free itself. Inevitably this entailed a lack of interest in the German world into which Acton and the Liberals were bound to plunge. "I have been reading to Marie", Granville explained,[3] "the Duc de Broglie's speech on his reception at the Academy. It is clever, as only a French speech is when spoken by a gentleman and a master of that extraordinary language for conveying shades of opinion." He was now Lord President of the Council and leader of the Government in the House of Lords. His age was forty-one. He was in the easy prime of his career, a little troubled by the gout and needing Vichy water. Such was the background to the Moscow mission.

The party was very large and characteristic of that vanished world, the Staffords, Lichfields, the Robert Peels, the George Byngs and the Freddy Byngs, Lords Burghersh, Seymour, Cavendish, Lincoln, Dalkeith and Gerald Ponsonby. The sixth Duke of Devonshire, who had been on a similar complimentary embassy for the coronation of Nicholas I in 1825, lent the Chatsworth plate. The carriages and English horses were sent ahead by sea; from his stable Lord Granville kept for his own use Woronzow and Marlborough. There were vases brought out from Minton; the only omission was a portrait of the Queen. One was hastily prepared on the spot in Moscow by an honorary attaché. This was the final period of wig and candlelight. For the official ball

---

[1] Letter dated 9 December 1855, in the Granville-Canning correspondence, *ibid.*, i. p. 135.
[2] *ibid.*, i. p. 179.   [3] *ibid.*, i. p. 176.

Aldenham Park, Shropshire.

forty extra candles were fixed upon the cornices above the doors, while others were secured in the semicircular brass hanging stands brought out from England. The wigs for the postillions were thought an antiquated pretty affectation. The ambassador described his English coachman [1] as "worth his weight in gold. If you had pricked his cheek a gallon of porter would have rushed out." Lady Granville had her diamonds re-set. The Tsar would lead the *polonaise* through those high white Moscow rooms of the Graziani Palace against a background of uniforms and stars and the elaborate and shimmering trains.

The same small talk and episodes brought back that generation which had danced with a similar absence of conviction through the decades overshadowed by the Congress of Vienna. They spoke of the carriages of Morny the French ambassador, "gala and very pretty" with their shiny canting heraldry, a Hortensia and an eagle, and of the Prince de Ligne's refusal of the St. Alexander on the grounds that with his name and as a chevalier of the *Toison d'Or* he could not take a secondary Order. Lord Granville would reminisce about the late Lord Ailesbury's State coach which he remembered in the stand by Devonshire House and speak of the *percherons* he bought in France for use on the farm at Golder's Green. Away from the ambassadorial circle the conversation volleyed uneasily, for few of the English mission spoke any French. A Russian officer was detected carrying off a fine pineapple in his upturned helmet.

The diplomatic consequences of this special embassy were very slight. All business was transacted through the permanent staff working under the third Lord Kimberley, then ambassador to the Court of Russia. The stay on Russian soil was brief and only lasted through the months of August and September. The Canning correspondence well conveys the substance of the special envoy's talks with Gortchakoff and the effect produced by audiences with the new Tsar. The Russian complaint and *innuendo* would be countered by dignified rebuttal intended to be tranquillising. This form of careful amelioration of relations between the Tsar and the imperial ministers on the one hand and the Court of St. James's on the other was what Lord Granville practised and John Acton understood. It was part of the latter's background, a conventional and uninteresting heritage.

[1] Letter dated 9 December 1855, in the Granville-Canning correspondence, *ibid.*, i. p. 194.

F

In certain ways, however, the older man could influence his stepson. A curious example is the growing flexibility of the historian's vocabulary, which is manifest even in his early writings. A description given by Lord Granville of the Tsar's sister the Grand Duchess Marie Nicolaievna, who was then living at the Leuchtenberg Palace as the widow of Maximilien de Beauharnais, is a case in point. After describing this princess as "very handsome, grown fat and rather like the pictures of Catherine II", the ambassador continued:[1] "The only one (member of the Imperial family) I thought really pleasant was the Grande Duchesse Marie; so easy, so *grande dame*, so clever, so insolent, so civil." The use of the meditated and unexpected epithet as in the case of the word "insolent" is found again in very different contexts in John Acton's writings.

Nevertheless the difference of outlook between Lord Granville and Professor Döllinger was too wide to admit of an attempt at synthesis. It was certainly not possible for Acton to evade that light-hearted approach to a grave situation which was intimately chilling to the serious student. Far removed from the concerns of the young peers of his stepfather's entourage, there was nothing in that set-up which might soothe the historian's immature and nettled pride. It was not the members of the English mission who, to quote the article in the *Edinburgh Review*,[2] were astonished "by the vastness of his knowledge and his mode of exposition". Acton was twenty-two and already so learned; around him his compatriots laid their bets.

A contrast was already discernible between this new Russian scene and the old world of the Austro-Russian ascendancy before the fall of Metternich. It was, indeed, the Holy Alliance which was a uniting factor from Naples to St. Petersburg, and the papal monarchy and the Romanoff empire were perhaps never less distant than in the second half of the conservative reigns of Gregory XVI and Nicholas I. Now they were drawing apart from one another with the inter-planetary distances opening between them as they swung away each on its own course.

Philistinism alone could build a bridge between eastern and western Europe. Besides, those few Russians who became Catholics and thus entered upon the western cultural heritage, the Galitzins,

---

[1] Letter dated 9 December 1855, in the Granville-Canning correspondence, *ibid.*, i. p. 205.
[2] *Edinburgh Review*, No. 404, p. 502.

Schuvaloff and above all Madame Swetchine, by this very act became *déracinés*. It was only on a purely political level remote from religious and aesthetic implications that such a woman as Princess Lieven could move freely in the mental life of eastern and western capitals, and Dorothea Christophorovna Lieven, *née* Benckendorff, came from the Baltic Provinces and was Germanic in each instinct and tradition.

In any case, there is little evidence that John Acton was interested in Russian roots, keen as was his concern with the political development of the great empire. Though he seldom discusses the point, it seems that he appreciated clearly the powerful German elements in the Russian imperial policies which had developed so strongly under Catherine II and would remain until the fall of the Romanoff dynasty. Throughout his life he could grasp swiftly the type of contact that is formed on the level of the landed or bureaucratic ruling class. He had, too, at least in his earlier years, a marked affinity with those types of society which possessed an ecclesiastical wing. Perhaps, if we consider his future Anglican associations, he never wholly moved away from this conception. This Moscow visit found him at his most *polite*, and he certainly understood the springs of action of the Abbé de Lamennais much more clearly than ever he did those of the Abbé Migne.

An article contributed to the *Rambler* in 1859 by the Danish convert Baron Eckstein has an especial value in this connection. It brings forward very clearly the mandarin element in Acton's outlook and the presuppositions among which his thought would take its rise. It is what one can perhaps best call the mandarin element, in part reflected in his style, which was to make his detailed appreciation of contemporary politics of so much less value than his survey of general principles. When dealing with the events of his own and the preceding generation Acton could never escape from the tyranny of the social *nuance*, nor did he wish to. Some quotations will convey Eckstein's approach.

"Lamennais", he wrote,[1] "did not enter the Faubourg St. Germain through the *salons* or the court or literature or fashion; he approached it on the political side, by his connection with Chateaubriand and Bonald. None of these three men took absolutely the same line; their partnership was only in their antipathies and their dislikes." "Bonald", he went on,[2] "wanted to syste-

---

[1] *Rambler*, new series, i. p. 47.   [2] *ibid.*, i. pp. 47-8.

matise the old French monarchy, borrowing from Montesquieu what he says about the Germans and the feudal system, and from Bossuet a theocratic element, which would result in a Louis XIV. In rejecting Condillac's philosophy he retained the *tabula rasa*, though it was no longer nature but God who drew the lines upon it." Lamennais's hold on the royalists of the Faubourg St. Germain was, we are informed,[1] "his ability to make himself the mouthpiece of a vindictive aristocracy. Chateaubriand's only weapon was the pamphlet, Bonald's the spirit of system. It was thought at one time that Lamennais might become the Mirabeau of a counter-revolution. The power of his dialectics encouraged this hope. He resolutely put himself at the head of the religious, social and political indignation of the Faubourg St. Germain." It is, however, the passage dealing with the priest's European contacts[2] which is most revealing. "In gaining the *entrée* of the Faubourg St. Germain, Lamennais at the same time came into contact with a portion of the Catholic aristocracy of Europe, which brought him into relations with Italy and Germany. For this he was indebted to the family of Senft, which he attached to himself in the beginning of his political and religious career. The Count de Senft-Pilsach was ambassador of Saxony during the Empire and was in high favour at Paris. The family was originally Protestant but had become Catholic under the Empire. Their aristocratic and feudal pride was at home with Bonald, though they had no monarchical enthusiasm *à la* Louis XIV. In fact, they were much more aristocratic than monarchical. They belonged to that Catholic German school of which Count Frederick Leopold de Stolberg was the head, and Frederick Schlegel the brains."

James Hope stayed with the younger Count Senft when he first visited Döllinger in Munich. From Naples to the Rhineland and from La Vendée to Silesia, but not beyond, there spread that webbed cat's cradle. Certain postulates were accepted by the old world in *palazzo*, *schloss* and *château*. One type of *revenant* rattled his bones across that scene. "M. de Vitrolles," wrote Baron Eckstein in the article just quoted,[3] "a man of the world and of fashion; possessing the ear of Monsieur; without passion or violence; a Voltairean of the old school, but considering the clergy as the allies of the Bourbons and loving them as such." This

---

[1] *Rambler*, new series, i. pp. 50-1.
[2] *ibid.*, i. pp. 48-9.   [3] *ibid.*, i. p. 52.

gentleman with his decorous Church-supporting scepticism appeared in that age in every country where Catholicism in its regalian form had once held sway. There were as yet no Court chaplains to King Demos, but the old regime was lowered into its grave as the incense rose among the yellow tapers.

CHAPTER IV
TOCQUEVILLE

ANY STUDY OF ACTON'S EARLY LIFE is difficult because the layers of influence to which he was exposed were both simultaneous and successive. It may be said that he seems never to have turned away decisively from any of those men who influenced him except from certain Catholics in the years between 1864 and 1870. Thus Döllinger was always with him as a friend, although his direct effect was never so great after the end of Acton's tutelage.

In a sense the period of his intellectual tutelage and his legal minority ended together. Thus Lord Granville, who never seems to have wished to penetrate past an easy formalism, and Dr. Döllinger both ceased to have much actual contact with Acton's thought once he was master at Aldenham. He entered then upon a period in which he was the patron rather than the friend of those who came to him. These were the years of the conducting of Reviews and also of the first foundation of his great library at Aldenham. It was an unhappy era in which to have to play the young Maecenas, and only ended with the historian's submission to Mr. Gladstone's guiding star. These years, when Acton was approaching thirty, also cover the earlier of the two phases of his life in which his concern for current politics was acute. They further witnessed the development in Acton's thought of a political doctrine drawn from Burke and from those who looked to Burke as their master. It is these influences that we should now attempt to estimate.

The aftermath of the Crimean war was followed by the twelve years of struggle which ended in January 1871 with the proclamation of the King of Prussia as German Emperor in the *Salle des Glaces* at Versailles, while beyond the *Pickelhaube* of the German garrison lay a sullen and defeated France. On 19 April 1859 France and Piedmont declared war upon Austria. Three days earlier, as the southern spring came to the lemon groves above the Mediterranean, there died in a rented villa behind the Bois de la Croix des Gardes a French historian who more than any among his contemporaries foresaw the shape of things to come. In the days before the creation of the Riviera the eastern borderlands of Provence were very tranquil; the villa was only a few miles from Saint-Laurent-du-Var, the Piedmontese frontier. Down near the seashore in the Villa Eléonore-Louise lived old Lord Brougham, but Cannes was as yet far from the great world. The invalid historian read the Memoirs of Count Miot de Mélito, and quite till the end his thoughts were bent upon the literary exposition of his doctrine. Two sisters of charity nursed him as he still poured out replies to his correspondents. He had a consuming care for the arrangement and completion of his work, for he had a body of thought to communicate and a message for the theorists of politics, and not least for John Acton. On 16 April his life, so long endangered, flickered out, and his generation was left to assimilate the teachings of Alexis-Charles-Henri-Clérel de Tocqueville.

This teaching had a peculiar importance for Acton, who was well fitted to understand the basic conceptions and *milieu* of a writer whose world had very little in common with that of his admiring English friends Nassau Senior and John Stuart Mill. The influence exercised on the English historian was in some ways all the more powerful for being purely literary, since there seems to have been little personal contact between them. In fact, in the days of Tocqueville's last visit to Paris, Acton is found writing to Richard Simpson:[1] "Have you not made Veuillot's acquaintance? You pass by his door daily, 44 Rue de Bac, and Bonnetty is to be found hard by, 10 Rue de Babylon." Apart from his mother's fashionable friends, Acton was still in a measure tied to those to whom Döllinger had introduced him. He did not make effective contact with that circle where the former *Ministre des Affaires Étrangères* received his intimates in the Rue de Castellane.

Before discussing the influence of the author of *La Démocratie en Amérique* and *L'Ancien Régime et la Révolution* it is worth quoting some comments made by Acton in 1861 which show how seriously he was affected by his mentor. He was writing from Buckland, that great grey Georgian house lying in the Vale of the White Horse, and had found Tocqueville's "Life" in the Throckmortons' library. "To describe", he began in some notes upon this writer,[2] "what formed his mind and how it grew in power and how it developed in its views from American democracy to his last work, in which he stands in opposition to modern

---

[1] *Lord Acton and his Circle*, p. 22.
[2] *ibid.*, p. 223.

popular ideas far more than at first sight people suppose. Then to compare him to other Frenchmen—to show the very distinct limits and the very broad gaps of his genius and of his knowledge —how he occupies nearly the position of Burke to his own countrymen, minus the greatness and vastness of the other's mind, but plus much colder observation." With this indication of Acton's awareness and his concern we can return to a brief survey of the novel elements in Tocqueville's thought.

One phrase of his is most familiar: "Je n'ai pas de traditions, je n'ai pas de parti, je n'ai pas de cause, si ce n'est celle de la liberté et de la dignité humaine."[1] Two other expressions, both recorded by Nassau Senior, place this statement in its setting: "The great misfortune of France is the preference of *égalité* to liberty. I have long been convinced that the social soil of France cannot at present [1850] offer a solid and permanent foundation to any government."[2]

This last sentence well indicates that undercurrent of sadness in Tocqueville's outlook which went with an incapacity for working with colleagues in political affairs and a strange desolated sense of the extinction of his class. Through all his life, for all its great success, he has the quality of a *revenant*. An unremitting observation filters through his own remote exact astringent mind. In this connection Chassériau's crayon-drawing well conveys the delicate slight physique and the chiselled features, the long dark curling, almost d'Orsay hair, and that quiet manner which was at once contained and very easy. One can see that list of dinner guests which Senior sets out:[3] "Duc de Broglie, Monsieur de Viel Castel, the Baron de Billing".

Alexis de Tocqueville came, like most men acutely conscious of their rank, from the less prosperous section of his class, the Norman *noblesse de campagne* who would keep besides their *château* a small *hôtel* in some country town—in this case Valognes, the centre of society in northern Cotentin. His financial circumstances were easy and he was devoted to his granite *château* with its deep windows and the little careful park and the new billiardroom and the luxuriant creepers. In the coachhouse the family carriage stood with its armorial panels. Some dull days the sea

---

[1] *Correspondence and Conversations of Alexis de Tocqueville with Nassau William Senior*, ed. M. C. M. Simpson, i. pp. 90, 92.
[2] *ibid.*, i. p. 86.
[3] *ibid.*, i. p. 86.

mist would wreathe in across the heavy pastures, but usually the sun shone on his small constricted paradise.

Tocqueville's parents had been imprisoned during the Terror and his mother was a granddaughter of Chrétien de Lamoignon de Malesherbes, who had defended Louis XVI at his trial. At the Château de Tocqueville there was neither regret nor nostalgia but a sense of the loss of values. In Mr. Senior's journal there is a character of Napoleon drawn by his friend which bears this out. "Napoleon's taste", asserted Tocqueville,[1] "was defective in everything, in small things as well as in great ones; in books, in art, and in women, as well as in ambition and in glory." Here we have the pointed arid comment and the sense of a mould broken. With his attached friends he draws himself back into his own closed circle.

He had an approach to corruption which was both typical of the country *noblesse* and also French. In particular he detested the conception of the *pays légal*, the two hundred thousand voters who formed the electorate under the *bourgeois* monarchy. "With his [King Louis-Philippe's] two hundred thousand or rather four hundred thousand places, all the middle classes on whom his government rested, were his tools. He made the middle classes objects of hatred and contempt, and the people trampled them and him underfoot."[2] The next idea is expressed in a phrase particularly lucid and bitter:[3] "Bribery has enervated and degraded the middle classes, and filled them with a selfishness so blind as to induce them to separate their interests entirely from those of the lower classes whence they sprang."

He would then turn back to his own position. "When I talk to a *gentilhomme*," Tocqueville explained,[4] " though we have not two ideas in common, though all his opinions, wishes, and thoughts are opposed to mine, yet I feel at once that we belong to the same family. I may like a *bourgeois* better, but he is a stranger." Nassau Senior, whose reporting is so reliable, here makes a contribution. They had been discussing the statement of a very sensible Prussian, *bürger* himself, who maintained that it was unwise to send out any ambassador who was not noble. "You may be sure that when any of our *bürger* ministers meets one who is *von Adel*, he does not negotiate with him on equal terms; he is always wishing

---
[1] *Correspondence and Conversations of Alexis de Tocqueville*, i. pp. 113-14.
[2] *ibid.*, i. p. 78.   [3] *ibid.*, i. p. 37.   [4] *ibid.*, i. p. 69.

to sneak under the table."¹ So did Tocqueville think. He had been elected to the *Académie Française* in 1841 at thirty-six and had been Minister for Foreign Affairs for four months in 1849; but his mind would return to the powerlessness of his own class. "The people feel that as a political party the gentry are extinct." ² Guizot had said that in 1848 when the July monarchy fell the *Peuple* treated the aristocrats not as enemies, but as slaves, as a class to be kept in preserves, and consumed from time to time as the wants of the *Peuple* required. "Tocqueville said", we read in Senior's journal,³ "that the remark was very just, and that he had himself perceived the gradual transition in the minds of the people from dislike to indifference and ultimately to the sort of affection which one feels for one's milch cows."

At this point Tocqueville produces one of his ideas upon which Acton early seized, the notion of the Revolution of 1789 as a gradually developing event. He believed that after seventy years the Revolution still continued; it was an uncompleted process passing from stage to stage. "I have long seen that the Orleans family were mere actors, whose exit was approaching, and I fear that more actors have followed them." ⁴ The French aristocrats were very different from the other elements of the *noblesse* in Europe, for they alone were both physically and mentally dispossessed. Under a grey sky and from an immense distance Tocqueville viewed his times. His work was marked by a character essentially Latin, that swift and successive, that serial disillusionment.

Phenomena passed very slowly as in a kaleidoscope before that patient and unexpected observation. Tocqueville saw men in their categories. One morning he was speaking to Senior of the decrease of the influence of women. "Formerly every young artist, or poet, or preacher, or even politician, must come out chaperoned by some patroness." ⁵ This sentence with the word "preacher" so carefully placed by one who was most conscious of each *nuance* can serve as an introduction to an examination of Tocqueville's attitude to religion. He was in the first place a Catholic by that social inheritance which to him was inescapable. He attended Mass at Tocqueville as an obligation in the landlord-peasant relation, and he received the Sacraments in his last illness. At Sorrento he was accustomed to go to the country chapels; it

---

¹ *Correspondence and Conversations of Alexis de Tocqueville*, i. p. 69.
² *ibid.*, i. p. 51.   ³ *ibid.*, i. p. 50.   ⁴ *ibid.*, i. p. 89.   ⁵ *ibid.*, i. p. 51.

was a pleasure to him to witness the peasant faith. "The *curé* dined with us. He took scarcely any part in the conversation at dinner or in the drawing-room. This, Tocqueville said, was *convenable*."[1] One cannot help sensing that here was a world in which gravity of treatment sometimes took the place of faith.

The position was put to Senior very clearly. "The aristocracy tried to revive Christianity as a political engine. Accordingly no gentleman in the present century writes, or even speaks, irreligiously. None but the lowest classes now profess irreligion."[2] On another occasion we find the same metaphor:[3] "A much greater proportion of priests ... are constantly working on the minds of their flocks with the popular eloquence of a Catholic pulpit and the powerful engine of confession. The Pope", he observed,[4] "was most to be feared when he acted most silently."

It is an interesting position, for it has resemblances and contrasts with John Acton's. It has the same quality of the inescapable, but touched by a realism which is quite stripped of sentiment. Alexis de Tocqueville came from the matrix of a Catholic tradition which had created the great age of France. But his political and religious outlook both suggest an atmosphere of quenched hope. He was planted in Catholicism as in the midst of a moon landscape. It stretched away behind and all about him, but did much live in it?

In a letter to Henry Reeve, the first editor of the Greville Memoirs and a friend of Lady Granville, Tocqueville makes an illuminating comment. "That aristocracy", he explains in regard to the class from which he sprang,[5] "had ceased to exist, and one can be strongly attached only to the living." Few men were ever more conscious of the desolate character of their own world. This scepticism as to the vital elements in all old forces was reinforced in Tocqueville's case by a complete absence of regret and a clear lack of interest in history. In his view the *Ancien Régime* must have been extremely bad because it evoked such detestation. Tocqueville's conversations never deal with times earlier than those which his old friend Royer-Collard could remember. It is the characters of men of the generation of Danton and Lafayette and their successors which are alone passed in review. The whole

---

[1] *Correspondence and Conversations of Alexis de Tocqueville*, i. p. 116.
[2] *ibid.*, i. p. 106.   [3] *ibid.*, i. p. 185.   [4] *ibid.*, i. p. 179.
[5] Tocqueville, *Œuvres*, vi. p. 67.

bent of his mind was a-historical. He was influenced by the classic writers, and especially by Pascal. But they were regarded as timeless and as elements in the formation of the great tradition. He took for granted the *Grand Siècle* which had moulded his own class. Discussion of the Middle Ages does not appear.

His taste was not aesthetic but for a manner of life. His own *château* was a jumble of easy and unsorted styles. He was very far from Gothic feeling or Romanticism, whether French or German. He was utterly remote from the spirit which would lead his younger contemporary, Viollet-le-Duc, to embark upon his restorations. At Carcassonne the sharp grey towers of the restored *Cité* would have seemed trivial to one whose mind was concentrated on the shadow of the mass age. It is only partly true to say, as Acton did,[1] that Tocqueville was "no historian because he could not see things in their flow *im Werden*".

In certain aspects *L'Ancien Régime et la Révolution* follows Burke's thought in the *Reflections* closely. In a sense it may be said that Edmund Burke's position is Tocqueville's starting-point. The latter, in fact, foresaw the development of the powers which his great predecessor feared and analysed. "When", Burke wrote in the *Appeal*,[2] "the supreme authority of the people is in question, before we attempt to extend or to define it, we ought to fix in our minds, with some degree of distinctness, an idea of what it is we mean, when we say, the PEOPLE.

"In a state of *rude* Nature there is no such thing as a people. A number of men in themselves have no collective capacity. The idea of a people is the idea of a corporation. It is wholly artificial, and made, like all other legal fictions, by common agreement." Fragments from the succeeding pages stress this point. "When men, therefore, break up the original compact or agreement, which gives its corporate form and capacity to a state, they are no longer a people. . . . They are a number of vague, loose individuals, and nothing more. With them all is to begin again. They little know how many a weary step is to be taken before they can form themselves into a mass which has a true politic personality."

He then came to his view of the rights of a majority; this should be established because of its influence both on Tocqueville's and Acton's thought. "We hear much", wrote Burke,[3]

---

[1] *Lord Acton and his Circle*, p. 226.
[2] *Appeal from the New to the Old Whigs*, p. 169.
[3] *ibid.*, p. 170.

"about the omnipotence of a *majority* in such a dissolution of an ancient society as hath taken place in France. But amongst men so disbanded there can be no such thing as majority or minority, or power in any one person to bind another. The power of acting by a majority . . . must be grounded on two assumptions: first, that of an incorporation produced by unanimity: and secondly, an unanimous agreement that the act of a mere majority shall pass with them and with others as the act of the whole."

From these statements there follows one of the most familiar of all Burke's sayings: "Liberty, too, must be limited in order to be possessed."[1] With the contractual basis of the commonwealth upon which his suppositions rested it was natural for the Whig statesman to write:[2] "I flatter myself that I love a manly, moral, regulated liberty as much as any gentleman." There is one element in this picture that must be noted. "We have", he asserts in the *Appeal*,[3] "obligations to mankind at large, which are not in consequence of any special voluntary pact. They arise from the relation of man to man, and the relation of man to God, which relations are not matters of choice. . . . In some cases the subordinate relations are voluntary, in others they are necessary,—but the duties are all compulsive." A companion statement is set out on the preceding page of the same tractate.[4] "Much the strongest moral obligations are such as were never the results of our option. I allow, that, if no supreme Ruler exists, wise to form and potent to enforce, the moral law, there is no sanction to any contract, virtual or even actual, against the will of prevalent power." It is such sentences as these which lead Dr. J. P. Mayer to the conclusions which he has stated in his study of Tocqueville. "Both", he writes in speaking of Burke and Tocqueville,[5] "are profoundly religious, and are agreed that states lacking the secure foundation of a religious belief are doomed to destruction."

This judgment is one which might well be extended to include John Acton's name. The term "profoundly religious" sits ill upon the elder thinkers. It was rather, surely, that they were both in a stream of thought which in France had been interrupted by the *Encyclopédistes*. They belonged to the old tradition of Europe

---

[1] *Letter to the Sheriffs of Bristol.*
[2] *Reflections on the Revolution in France.*
[3] *Appeal from the New to the Old Whigs*, p. 166.
[4] *ibid.*, p. 165.
[5] *Prophet of the Mass Age, a Study of Alexis de Tocqueville*, p. 154.

in which the nature of man's obligations had been fixed for so long.

An element which is present in Burke's thought but absent from Tocqueville's is the note of regret. This corresponds to that "colder observation" which Acton discerned in the Frenchman when making a comparison of the two writers. Such a consequence is in part a result of the fact that Tocqueville throughout his life was never without his disillusion. Beneath a heavy sky he looked out on the waste of waters. A letter to M. Stoffels dated 28 April 1850 makes this point plain. "You wish", he wrote to his friend,[1] "for political prognostications; who can venture to make any? The future is as black as night; the most far-sighted admit that they cannot look forward. As for me, I see a tolerably clear outline of what seems to be the future destiny of this country. ... What I see clearly is, that for sixty years we have been deceiving ourselves by imagining that we saw the end of the Revolution. It was supposed to be finished on the 18th Brumaire, and again in 1814; I myself thought, in 1830, that it might be over when I saw that democracy, having in its march passed over and destroyed every other privilege, had stopped before the ancient and necessary privilege of property. I thought that, like the ocean, it had at last found its shore. I was wrong. It is now evident that the tide is rising, and that the sea is still enlarging its bed; that not only we have not seen the end of the stupendous revolution which began before our day, but that the infant just born will scarcely see it. Society is not in process of modification, but of transformation."

In this connection a conversation with Nassau Senior which took place in 1850 is worth recording. "He is", said Tocqueville[2] in speaking of the depression of spirits of the Duc de Broglie, "one of a numerous class who at each successive phase of our Revolution have believed that it was over, and that a settled state of things was to ensue.... The revolution of 1848 came, and these illusions were dissipated in an hour. The line along which they have been travelling since 1830 turns out to be only the segment of a circle."

The general conception of this movement is set out in. the preface to *L'Ancien Régime et la Révolution.* "Amidst the darkness of the future", Tocqueville writes, "three truths may be clearly

[1] *Memoir, Letters and Remains of Alexis de Tocqueville*, English edition, i. p. 423.
[2] Nassau Senior, *op. cit.*, i. p. 89.

discovered. The first is, that all the men of our time are impelled by an unknown force which they may hope to regulate and to check, but not to conquer—a force which sometimes gently moves them, sometimes hurries them along, to the destruction of aristocracy. The second is, that of all the communities in the world those which will always be least able permanently to escape from absolute government are precisely the communities in which aristocracy has ceased to exist and can never exist again. The third and last is, that despotism nowhere produces more pernicious effects than in these same communities." It is only a step to the conclusion. "Despotism . . . deprives its subjects of every common passion, of every natural want, of all necessity of combining together, of all occasions of acting together. It immures them in private life."

It was Tocqueville's great merit to detect that tendency towards absolutism inherent in a search for political equality. In this matter it was the plebiscitary dictatorship of Napoleon III which moved him. He had a special horror akin to Burke's as to what might be thrown up by a "mere majority". This led to his tempered dislike of universal suffrage.[1] The suddenly enfranchised elements might find their own needs mirrored in a dictator who proclaimed himself the enemy of property and the scourge of vested interests. A comment on Henri Martin "with his Asiatic democracy" is illuminating in regard to one angle of this subject. "He belongs", wrote Tocqueville of that publicist,[2] "to the class of theorists, unfortunately not a small one, whose political *beau idéal* is the absence of all control over the will of the people. Equality, not liberty or security, is their object. They are centralisers and absolutists." In general, this record of opinion conveys Tocqueville's standpoint in regard to Europe; but its consequences can only be drawn out when Napoleon III, who was the exemplar of so much that he distrusted, is seen through his eyes. This also has importance in the development of Acton's thought, for the Emperor of the French was the first political figure upon the Continent to loom across the threshold of his adult life.

Few moods slid away more rapidly than the revolutionary sentiments of 1848. They had few traces when John Acton left his boyhood. By the time he came of age the Second Republic had evaporated and Louis Napoleon had become Prince President and

---

[1] Nassau Senior, *op cit.*, i. p. 69.
[2] *ibid.*, i. p. 185.

then Emperor. He was to rule France from 1852 till 1870. During that period he incurred a dispassionate and remorseless opposition such as few princes reap. Tocqueville, to take one instance, came to regard him with an ice-cold distaste. A friend and one whom he regarded as a great authority upon this subject stated the case. "He is", said Lanjuinais of the Emperor,[1] "not a man of genius, or even a man of remarkable ability. . . . He is ignorant, uninventive and idle. . . . His great moral merits are kindness and sympathy. He is a faithful attached friend, and wishes to serve all who come near him. His greatest moral fault is his ignorance of the difference between right and wrong." And then Tocqueville himself took up the running. "He does not belong", he explained,[2] "to the highest class of hypocrites, who cheat by frankness and cordiality." With the admirable point that never left him the great sociologist passed judgment on those who opposed Louis Napoleon: "Our conspiracy was that of the lambs against the wolf." In a talk with Nassau Senior he spoke on another occasion for that world to which the travelled classes in both countries belonged. "We cannot bear", he began,[3] and his words here were surely Acton's, "that the fate of France should depend on the selfishness, or the vanity, or the fears, or the caprice of one man, a foreigner by race, and education, and of a set of military ruffians and of infamous civilians, fit only to have formed the staff and the privy council of Catiline. We cannot bear that the people which carried the torch of Liberty through Europe should now be employed in quenching all its lights. But these are not the feelings of the multitude."

There is here present a distrust of the judgment of the mass of men which is very striking. It was the plebiscite after Louis Napoleon's *coup d'état* which was responsible for the bitter quality of such a sentiment. That absolutism should be guaranteed by a popular vote on a wide suffrage seemed the death-knell of liberty. It was thus the plebiscitary dictatorship which instilled into Tocqueville that acute dislike which Acton in time would come to share. Both felt, and Tocqueville especially, that the peasants must support a continuing Revolution, while the huge new industrial populations, with which the old classes had so little contact, were unpredictable. Acton's own mind was normally not dramatic. The absolutism of the Second Empire was to him a bad principle

---

[1] Nassau Senior, *op. cit.* i. pp. 204-5.
[2] *ibid.*, ii. p. 12.   [3] *ibid.*, ii. p. 7.

in action. If Russia blanketed freedom, the new Imperial France imposed fresh fetters upon liberty.

In certain respects, and notably in regard to the actual new technique of State control, Tocqueville saw further than his pupil. He could imagine mass action and its strange consequences, and in a general way perceived the stair up which the national dictatorships would haul themselves. He felt acutely the insufficiency of that *bourgeois* monarchy which Acton valued on account of the measure of liberty which it supported. Guizot, who was not only the minister of Louis-Philippe but also the incarnation of his system, in particular had gained the young historian's admiration.

Broadly speaking there was, however, identity between Tocqueville and Acton in their approach to the Second Empire. A review which was published in 1863 in the *Home and Foreign* can mark the point at which the latter's outlook stabilised. The following sentences appear in a notice of *Le Fils de Giboyer* by Emile Augier:[1] "The things which he honours and believes are political views not moral laws. . . . His comedy is the savage protest of the men of 1789, translated into imperial materialists, against morality and religion. . . . The sum of the author's philosophy is that love of equality which is not only compatible with the love of distinctions, but a strong incentive to it, and the worship of the *fait accompli*."

The notice then continues with an examination of the popular absolutism then extant in France: "In the following words he [M. Augier] vindicates the imperialist theory of equality. 'Equality is not a level . . . the great word can have but one sense, to every one according to his works.'" Conceding to this authoritarian *régime* the term democracy, Acton probes further.[2] "What is it that this democracy hates, if it tolerates wealth, desires distinctions of honour, and worships power?" The answer that he arrives at is that the hatred is brought to bear on aristocracy. This is important, for it is around this conception of a natural aristocracy that the thoughts of Acton and his two teachers gather. The qualifying adjective is introduced to show that only the core of such an element would be hereditary. To Burke this was the corner-stone of the Whig policy; to Acton this was in its Whig sense the air that he and his had always breathed; to Tocqueville it was his

---

[1] *Home and Foreign Review*, 1863, p. 667.
[2] *ibid.*, p. 668.

own shell broken. Among these three men only Tocqueville was a sociologist, and he alone believed that his own world had gone out to a waste land.

To close this brief account we can give a judgment made by Acton[1] in reviewing the *Études critiques sur la Littérature contemporaine* by Edmond Schérer: "The author underrates the merit of Tocqueville, and exaggerates it at the same time, when he says that no political writer of this century can be compared to him, and that he deserves to have his bust placed beneath the statue of Montesquieu. Tocqueville was deeper than Montesquieu, and yet he had superiors even among his contemporaries." The reviewer then leads up through criticism to a panegyric: "The secure melancholy of his mind drives M. Schérer to seek an unreal explanation. Neither paganism nor Christianity ever produced a profound political historian whose mind was not turned to gloom by the contemplation of the affairs of men. It is almost a test to distinguish the great narrators from the great thinkers,—Herodotus, Livy, Froissart, Schiller, Macaulay, Thiers from Thucydides, Polybius, Tacitus, Machiavelli, Raleigh, Gibbon, Guizot, Niebuhr." This is an interesting glimpse of Acton's view of the high company.

[1] *Home and Foreign Review*, 1863, p. 719.

CHAPTER V
FERMENT

THE INFLUENCE OF EDMUND BURKE would penetrate and colour each aspect of John Acton's thought. In some sense it was, perhaps, those elements in the Burkian view which came to him direct that left most impression. Their impact was more immediate than those that filtered through Tocqueville's mind or Döllinger's.

In this connection a few propositions may be considered before examining that *Appeal from the New to the Old Whigs* which contains the teaching on the nature of liberty which was so crucial to Burke's thought. At any rate, during his early life the *Appeal* was John Acton's favourite among Burke's writings. Here are three sentences whose effect would in their different ways prove durable. "Abstract liberty, like other mere abstractions, is not to be found."[1] And again, "Individuals pass like shadows: but the commonwealth is fixed and stable."[2] Finally, with a note that has more in it of realism than disillusion, there comes this phrase: "The march of the human mind is slow."[3]

These lines of thought lead up to two expositions of doctrine that are familiar and memorable. Throughout his writings Burke displayed a temper in dealing with institutions which was both exact and serene. "But the liberty,[4] the only liberty I mean, is a liberty connected with order: and that not only exists with order and virtue, but cannot exist at all without them. It inheres in good and steady government, as in its substance and vital principle.... We are members", he went on in another of those speeches to the Electors of Bristol to which he would look back as his testament,[5] "for that great nation, which, however, is itself but part of a great empire, extended by our virtue and our fortune to the farthest limits of the East and of the West. All these widespread interests must be considered—must be compared—must be reconciled, if possible. We are members for a free country; and surely we all

---
[1] *Speech on Conciliation with America*, Everyman series, p. 91.
[2] *Speech on the Economical Reform*, 1780.
[3] *Speech on Conciliation with America*.
[4] *ibid.*, p. 97.   [5] *ibid.*, p. 98.

know that the machine of a free constitution is no simple thing, but as intricate and delicate as it is valuable. . . . A constitution made up of balanced powers must ever be a critical thing."

And then in the *Appeal* itself [1] there is expressed that view of the constitution which Acton was always to find so grateful. "Neither the few nor the many have the right to act merely by their will, in any manner connected with duty, trust, engagement, or obligation. The constitution of a country being once settled upon some compact, tacit or expressed, there is no power existing of force to alter it, without the breach of the covenant, or the consent of all the parties." "I am", Burke wrote,[2] "well aware that men love to hear of their power, but have an extreme disrelish to be told of their duty." In fact, it was just Mr. Gladstone's readiness to tell men of their duty which in the future had such great appeal for the historian.

It is here, perhaps, that a line of cleavage comes between the German and the French mentality. The conception of duty was indeed very central to nineteenth-century German life. The Prince Consort was himself in many ways an incarnation of this sense of poised and weighted obligation. In Bavaria in a less selfconscious fashion the same held good. With the greater lightness of the South there was still a sententious concept of what was owing from the German man. In time duty, conceived along rather different lines, would expel freedom. In Germany men's obligation would reveal itself in all the marching, riding, driving armies and in all the men who thought for them. Still, on the professorial side of Acton's Bavarian world it was civilian duty that appeared as freedom's guardian.

Compared to his deep understanding of the South German temperament, John Acton's approach to trends of French opinion appears as curiously superficial. He valued very highly the work of various French thinkers; but there is no doubt that he was irritated by certain tendencies which belonged rather to the sphere of mental habit. Thus he felt the absence of moral elevation, taking these words in their Gladstonian sense, and he was never to be at his ease with buoyant undefeated eloquence. This last factor may explain the lack of sympathy that Acton always felt for Dupanloup. It was the versatility and the quick fecund imagery of the great

---

[1] *Appeal from the New to the Old Whigs*, p. 162.
[2] *ibid.*, p. 153.

Bishop of Orleans that so repelled him. He believed in hewing and digging deep; he thought that rhetoric must expel learning.

To come to a very different field, it was of course inevitable that Acton should dislike *bondieusards*, but he was also untouched by all the history of chivalry. A matter-of-fact strain in his make-up debarred him from yielding to the appeal of that chivalric mediaevalism in which much French religious thought was dressed. There is no reason to suppose that he ever gave much heed to the Maid of Orleans. His whole approach was dry and penetrating. It is, perhaps, easiest to explain this by an example. At Rhodes there is a mediaeval inscription, one of those Frankish epitaphs familiarised in the romantic mood of the mid-nineteenth century:

> Ci-gît très-haut et très-puissant Seigneur
> Baudouin de Flandre, Comte de Courtenay,
> J'ai aimé, j'ai péché, j'ai souffert,
> Ayez pitié de moi, ô mon Dieu.

John Acton always turned against veiled sentiment.

Similarly he found himself opposed to all that mockery and disrespect which characterised one French mentality. In this connection there is an entry in Reeve's journal which throws light on an aspect of the religious policy of the Second Empire. "Persigny", this keen observer noted on 29 January 1856,[1] "said the Emperor of the French had not attended much to the religious disputes; that upon the whole the clergy had been useful to him, and were still so to a certain extent; but that when they became troublesome, the Emperor would kick them over like an ant-hill." This recalls a conversation which Greville had had with Acton's grandfather long ago. It had been at a dinner party in Rome with the La Ferronays in 1830. The principal guests had been the Dalbergs. "'Qui est cet homme?'", he records as the opening words of this exchange,[2] "I said to him [the Duke of Dalberg] when a ludicrous-looking Abbé, broader than he was long, came into the room. 'Que sais-je? quelque magot'." To Acton the comparison with a baboon was unappealing and the ant-hill metaphor but little better. The young historian's mind would always be severe and reverent.

[1] *Memoirs of the Life and Correspondence of Henry Reeve*, ed. John Knox Laughton, i. p. 352.
[2] *The Greville Memoirs*, ed. Roger Fulford, i. p. 473.

Thus he was never to lose his intense disapprobation of the free-thinkers. In this case it was intolerance with which he charged them. "The true sentiments of the free-thinkers of that age", he was to write in reference to Voltaire,[1] "may be found in a letter of the Economist Galiani written in 1771: 'Tous les grands hommes ont été intolérants, et il faut l'être.'" This sentence would sound upon his mind with a peculiar gravity. The necessity of intolerance was a secular dogma to which Acton was utterly opposed. The question of liberty was again the touchstone by which he would judge the aristocratic Parisian grouping *la vieille roche du faubourg Saint-Germain*. In regard to the Legitimists he was to state his convictions that their principles were generally adverse to intellectual labour. His scythe thus cut wide swathes through French opinion.

Acton's attitude towards French history has a great interest, for it would in time be widely endorsed by his English contemporaries and disciples. In the first place, it would seem to have been based on a great knowledge and appreciation of books but not on a great sympathy for men. It reflected a variant of the professor's teaching and was allied to a warm enthusiasm for the old French chronicles and for their presentation of established *fact*. In Munich he had learned to discriminate against historical treatises inspired by a concrete political intention. From this it followed that a scholar, disliking mythology and hating absolutism, must inevitably discount the body of writing tending to build up Napoleon's legend. To the myth of the Revolution he was no friendlier. Acton could never tolerate that historical truth should be brought to serve the ends of politics.

Some years later he was to write a notice on Huguenin's *Histoire du Royaume Mérovingien d'Austrasie* in which he sums up this point of view. "It [Austrasia]", he wrote of the Frankish kingdom centring on Metz,[2] "is a subject on which a Frenchman writes at a great disadvantage; for he dreams that he is dealing with his own country and people, whereas Austrasia was in fact Germany, and requires in its historian an accurate knowledge of German historical literature. Down to the time of Thierry, and, with the exception of Michelet and Pétigny, in most French histories even to the present day, the Franks are subjected to the same

---

[1] *Home and Foreign Review*, iii. p. 305.
[2] *ibid.*, iii. p. 284.

transformation as the Greeks and Turks undergo in the dramas of Racine." It will be clear, as we examine the great library that he was even now building up, that it was local history considered in its constitutional and legal aspect which gained John Acton's preference. It was probably his German training that made him impatient with that mass of centralised Court detail which meant so much to the society of the *Ancien Régime*. In this case a dislike for absolute government was linked in the historian's mind with a certain contempt for the artificial gradations of Versailles. A comment on the *Mémoires de Luynes*, composed in the reign of Louis XV, will make this clear. "There is", he was to write at the same time as the notice on Huguenin's history,[1] "a tone of dignity and morality about these Memoirs which forms a refreshing contrast to the society described in them; and they are less disfigured by pride, bitterness and hatred than those of Saint-Simon. But the discussion of the details of ceremonial is perpetual. In reading the book we are often reminded of the words of Paul-Louis Courier: 'L'étiquette rend les rois esclaves de la cour.'" This is the French century of which Acton wrote: "It is full of restraint but not in the moral order." [2]

From such considerations the historian would gladly turn to that world of ideas which seemed to him his own true country, to that consideration of doctrine and tendency which would always arouse his channelled and precise imaginings. A note on the Memoirs of the Abbé La Garde will show the lines of thought which roused his interest. "He was", wrote Acton of this commentator,[3] "the confidential secretary of the Archbishop of Paris in the best period of the reign of Louis XIV, at the height of the struggle with the Jansenists and with the Quietists, at the time of the Declaration of 1682 and of the revocation of the Edict of Nantes." Here was a field on which he could work out the waning and development of rival creeds, the Gallican influence and the pressure exerted on the Huguenots. This was history free from wars and campaigns, and equally remote from mundane politics. Nothing in the *Grand Siècle* could be far from the Court; but in this case Versailles was conceived as a battleground for forms of thought and not as the scene of the mere exercise of graded ceremonial rights and duties. Above all, the historian could now study

---
[1] *Home and Foreign Review*, iii. p. 239.
[2] *ibid.*, iii. p. 632.   [3] *ibid.*, iii. p. 303.

a panorama in that history of toleration which would for so long occupy his mind and labour.

Another judgment on an allied theme resumes so much of Acton's thought that it is worth weighing carefully : [1] "Ranke subjects Saint-Simon's Memoirs to that species of microscopic criticism, by comparison and analysis, in which he so greatly excels. Although his conclusion is extremely unfavourable to the credibility of the great historian, the religious opinions of the Duke, the strongest and most subtle influence by which his judgments are warped, are entirely omitted from the inquiry." Saint-Simon's religious outlook may be best described as that of an Erastian in a French setting; it was at once suspicious, desiccated, querulous, and patronising. The historian's sentence is quite remarkable; "warped" is the operative word.

It is possible that Acton never realised how very specialised were such concerns. The French traditions of an earlier time were seen across that gulf of the Revolution whose nature Acton hardly apprehended. He, who knew so much of Germany, did not perceive the tides that ran in France. His letters seem to show that in these years he found it difficult to grasp how very differently his own mind worked from that of Dupanloup. The same applies to Montalembert, who was editing the *Correspondant* while Acton was conducting his Catholic periodicals. Letters exchanged at this period sometimes indicate an identity of outlook which really was not there. "It must be remembered", Acton noted mildly,[2] "that the *Correspondant* themselves are not immaculate in their view or perfect in their knowledge, especially of Catholic England."

Possibly Acton's mind was too discursive for that French realism which was at once both logical and unhistoric. His thought worked up and down across the centuries. In a letter written in the summer of 1860 the young historian records a wandering soliloquy which very well conveys that swift unhampered thinking which cast a web around the generations. "Ideals in politics", he wrote,[3] "are never realized, but the pursuit of them determines history. *Such* was papal diplomacy in the Ages; the balance of power, all the attempts of universal empire which have broken down, but have carried things, ideas, institutions to places, like birds carrying

---

[1] *Home and Foreign Review*, iii. p. 543.
[2] *Lord Acton and his Circle*, p. 68.
[3] *ibid.*, p. 133.

seeds where they were wanted by God's design—Persians, Alexander, Romans, Napoleon. Also political principles as a panacea —LIBERTY, nationality, equality, unity of weight and measure, and language, Socialism. Other similar utopias,—Plato, Hesperides. Geographical ideals discovered all over the world—Cathay; Eldorado; Spaniards go to America expecting to get gold, else those countries would never have got a Catholic civilisation. Nations have had a star before them which they have followed in their migrations and which brought them to their allotted place, for all historically great nations *conquered* their homes. With the Teutonic race (and Aryan?) this was most the case. They had some mythological reason for going to Northern Europe, and then a similar impulse drove them South. Note Grey's line on the southward course of northern nations—Birds of passage:

> Where do they go, and what ideals do they seek?
> What the Jews have before them.

"All this is very crude and vain. It came into my head in the train coming up this evening." The self-accusation has much force if these sentences are examined one by one, but how well they do reveal that springing quick vitality? The French would accuse this thought of lack of realism. Surely Döllinger would have judged more kindly. It has a nobility struggling with its bonds. It was in England that John Acton could be best understood.

CHAPTER VI

THE ENGLISH HISTORIANS

AFTER THE SURVEY of the European political situation at the time when Acton came of age we can examine the general characteristics of the body of historical writing in English to which he was able to make his contribution. This was not a mould into which his thought was destined to run easily; rather he was among those who would help to break it.

In the first place, it is worth noting that few men using the English language could be so remote as was John Acton from the old school of insular antiquaries. Certainly he had no place in that succession. It was not that he was without interest in the local history, since information on that subject was to be found among the minor elements of his always expanding field of knowledge. On this matter we should pause a moment. There is a letter to Richard Simpson dating from the autumn of 1862 in which Acton gives his view [1] of the ingredients of a proposed article on Shropshire for the *Home and Foreign Review*. It sets out his approach with clarity. The books recommended are local histories of Ludlow, Bridgnorth and Shrewsbury, the *Reliquiae Baxterianae* for the countryside round Eaton Constantine, Dugdale's *Monasticon* for Wenlock and Buildwas, Blakeway's *Sheriffs*, biographies of the Clives and Hills, Smiles's *Engineers* for the life of the man who built the Ironbridge at Coalbrookdale. The writer, Acton goes on, should read about the ghosts at Acton Burnell and look up the history of the foxhounds to learn about Squire Forester. He should trace the journey of Charles II during his escape after Worcester from Whiteladies to the Severn ford at Madeley. It is an interesting catalogue and in an amateur fashion comprehensive, but there is no reason to suppose that Acton could have repeated it for other counties. His real concern would always lie in a very different quarter.

Nevertheless few historians have betrayed less appreciation of the value of detailed field work. Such minute application was quite foreign to his cosmopolitan far-ranging mind. As a man of the study he had no feeling for village history tracing the development

---

[1] *Lord Acton and his Circle*, p. 293.

and descent of local land, messuage by messuage. He was always very thorough and he lacked that brisk and evocative imagination by whose aid Lord Macaulay would design and colour in each famous scene. Small human concerns would not impede the ordered march of ideas in John Acton's processes. The freshness of his mind and the thought of Burke, his master, made much contemporary writing seem jejune. A brief survey of what went before will indicate not only Acton's mastery but also, at first, his loneliness. As an historical writer he was without English forebears; his inspiration was from the Continent, and in so far as it came from Germany it was not Prussian but Bavarian. He was back in England, but at this time remote from English Universities. Let us now study his strange company.

If there is one failing that can justly be attributed to the historical writers of this period it is a certain weakness for omniscience. In this weakness Lord Acton in his early life would fully share. Men had not yet escaped from the lure of the large canvas and from the interpretation of the massive theme. It is often stated that the *Encyclopédistes*, no less than the men of *Aufklärung*, were radically unfriendly to historical studies owing to their lack of interest in the past. The more conservative elements among the eighteenth-century reading public had, however, relished those great folios in which the history of a whole nation was set forth compendiously. The writers were intent upon the strategy of history.

It was a consequence of this presupposition that in the period before the Romantic revival the whole historical field tended to be envisaged as the subject of a very simple flow only impeded from time to time by cataclysms. Thus the world of England before the first Reform Bill appeared to stretch back across the centuries with little change. By a simplified process the past described in the current idiom seemed very near. This standpoint is frequently apparent in the writings of the older school of English literary antiquaries, a body of men who were so often to be found attached to Tory principles. Thus Edward Vernon Utterson, an equity draughtsman who was one of the six clerks in Chancery until that office was abolished, has a series of comments which are singularly illuminating. They draw attention sharply to the anachronism and lack of feeling for historic change which long persisted. The passages occur in Utterson's edition of Lord Berners's translation of Froissart's Chronicles which had been first printed in 1525.

"John Tiptoft was not the only peer whose literary acquirements and improved taste were ornamental to the era in which he flourished. John Lord Berners was not less ardent in the cause of reviving learning." Other assertions [1] are in this vein. "After Lord Berners had quitted Oxford, he went to the continent, in compliance with a custom at that time prevalent, and which has descended to our own times. The knowledge which Lord Berners acquired of men and manners in the course of his travels was afterwards highly beneficial to him." It is in consequence no surprise to read [2] that "the title of a valuable, if not the earliest English classic writer, may be conceded to his Lordship". It is true that these sentences were written in 1812, but Edward Utterson survived until 1856, into John Acton's early manhood. It was a curious approach to the Renaissance.

A similar impression is frequently conveyed by English historical writing before Macaulay. At the best it is a certain flat and arid elegance of phrase which carries us swiftly across the periods. The centuries slide past undifferentiated just as they do in the Byzantine section of Edward Gibbon's famous work. This character was partly due to a certain sameness of approach to the literary sources upon which such history was based. This was indeed the great period of the memoir and the chivalric chronicle considered as a part of the education of a gentleman. During the Napoleonic wars Thomas Johnes of Hafod had published translations of Froissart, Monstrelet and Joinville. To keep only to the French, there was Commines and there would soon be Saint-Simon. The gentleman of polite tastes would scan these works and consider in each age the secret springs of politics. The two elements reacted on each other. Politics was the *métier* of his class, and at the same time it was this concentrated political concern which enabled such vast tracts to be surveyed. It is noticeable that the chronicles were not linked up and were seldom compared with one another. It seems arguable that the study of Greek and Roman history solely by the aid of literary sources tended to make men believe that the illumination of the past was always fitful.

As a reaction from the artificiality of the chronicler or Court memoir-writer an interest developed in a continuous statistical

---

[1] Preface to the 1812 edition of Lord Berners's translation of Sir John Froissart's Chronicles, pp. 1, 5, 6.
[2] *ibid.*, p. 23.

record of modern fact. In the second quarter of the nineteenth century historical writing became discursive; it lost its point and measure. Long compilations crowded up the library shelves: the *Gentleman's Magazine*, the *Annual Register*, sometimes *L'Art de vérifier les dates*. Among these were soon to be found the twelve volumes of Sir Archibald Alison's *History of Europe during the French Revolution*, which were published between 1833 and 1842. Through volume after volume wound the long tired narrative. "The work", declared Alison in his preface,[1] "has assumed a dramatic air, unusual at least in modern histories; but it is the only method by which the spirit and feeling of the moment could be faithfully transmitted to posterity; and a modern author need not hesitate to follow an example which has been set by Thucydides, Sallust, Livy and Tacitus." These works of Alison's are a fit introduction to an history in which the old rhetoric gave form to a serried mass of information. It was the final example of historical writing conceived of as declamatory.

Another style of narrative also reached its last and typical expression at this time. William Roscoe's classic *Life of Lorenzo de Medici* had been brought out before the end of the eighteenth century, and attention had for long been fixed on Florentine, and especially Medicean, art and history. There is a lingering charm in the three volumes that James Dennistoun of Dennistoun now devoted to the Dukes of Urbino. The *Memoirs* appeared in 1852 and are perhaps the last example of the learned and discursive exposition prepared by a gentleman of leisure for the appraisal of his own compeers. A high conservatism inspired Dennistoun's labours. "When we contrast", he wrote of the state of Italy,[2] "the calm then around her institutions, the stillness of her everyday life, the careless ease of her nobles, the physical enjoyment of her middle classes, the simple well-being of the peasantry under their own vines and fig-trees,—we must sigh to see so much positive happiness perilled for contingent ameliorations which, if ever attained, may, like most political experiments, fail to realise the promised benefits." Thus the style rolled on, warm and complacent.

These comments will serve to indicate different types of historical writing against whose faults Acton was armoured from the start. He would always disclaim any intention of writing from a

---

[1] Alison's *History*, i. pp. xxxv-xxxvi.
[2] *Memoirs of the Dukes of Urbino*, edition of 1909, i. p. xxxvii.

purely party standpoint, although he was to fall into this practice in certain articles of his *Rambler* period. He would by instinct avoid the tendency to produce accounts which were exhaustive and burdensome and cumbrous. He would always sift his facts and train his searchlight. In one respect, however, Acton shared the outlook of his pedestrian English predecessors. To the last he believed in the great area of territory that he could cover. He was thus a survivor from the age of narrative.

A passage in Lord Acton's article on Wilhelm von Giesebrecht printed in the *English Historical Review* in 1890 is in this respect noteworthy: "He [von Giesebrecht] did not speak with authority of the things that came before Clovis or after Manfred."[1] Throughout his life Acton felt that it was possible to be an expert on many consecutive centuries. Yet, having made this statement, we must make one of those qualifications which this subject exacts continually. In the *Cambridge Modern History*, which he inspired, the relatively small area that each historian was expected to cover remained an axiom. He was thus the founder in England of cooperative study applied to political and general trends. It was one of Acton's charms that he possessed, at any rate on the technical question of presenting history, a very great swiftness and resilience. Upon this resilient and searching thought the influence of Lord Macaulay was brought to bear. This decade was that great man's heyday, for the fourth and last volume of the *History of England* had been published in 1855. That tree had put forth all its heavy fruit and Acton was to live henceforth beneath its shadow.

It is not easy to assess the impact that Macaulay made upon the young historian. Acton's comments on this subject for the most part date from his later life, but a letter to Lady Blennerhassett written in 1890[2] suggests that his first approach was marked by admiration: "Personne n'est plus persuadé que moi de la bonne cause de 1688: mais si je lisais Macaulay aujourd'hui pour la première fois il me ferait douter, parce qu'il est si sûr." He was to describe him[3] as one of the three greatest Liberals and again as one of the greatest of historians. "In description," he explained,[4] "not

---

[1] Acton's *Historical Essays and Studies*, p. 496.
[2] *Correspondence*, p. 297.
[3] *Letters of Lord Acton to Mary Gladstone*, p. 57.
[4] Letter to Mr. Gladstone, *Correspondence*, p. 261.

in narrative, I think he [Macaulay] is quite the first of all writers of history."

In the Whig world Macaulay was appreciated and unique. He had that secular confidence which his contemporaries of progressive views so fully shared. There was a public waiting for each clanging great antithesis. As Dr. Gooch justly remarks in regard to Macaulay's treatment of the historical essay,[1] "He found it of brick and left it of marble". Traces of his influence are discernible in Acton's early style. It is natural that after the years in Munich John Acton would turn to some English model for his presentation.

In the essay on James La Cloche, published by Acton in 1862 and reprinted by Figgis and Laurence after his death, we come upon a study in the pictorial style to which his talent, even when immature, was so unsuited. There is here a straining after what Sir George Otto Trevelyan calls the "telling sentence" which was foreign to Acton's native manner. The clashing of Macaulay's cymbals could but disturb the heavy straining effort that Acton put into his weighty half-expressed encumbered thought.

The Macaulayesque influence is even more perceptible in an essay on Henry Buckle's philosophy of history which dates from 1858. A quotation will illustrate this point. "Theodore of Mopsuestia, Julian of Eclanum, Calvin and Strauss, have not been without their usefulness. An able adversary, sincere in his error and skilful in maintaining it, is in the long run a boon to the cause of religion. The greatness of the error is the measure of the triumph of truth. The intellectual armour with which the doctrine of the Church is assailed becomes the trophy of her victory. All her battles are defensive, but they all terminate in conquest."

It is a mark of both Acton and Macaulay that they write from an immense security. The very phrases themselves fall into a singularly easy chessboard pattern. The element of tourney is persistent; thus virtue strikes down vice through helmet and through helm. Different as was their range of knowledge, both men belong to that high period of the supremacy of Western Man. It was a supremacy which was as patent as it was glorious, and still untarnished. Perhaps in the mid-twentieth century we are too much impressed by the absence of cataclysm in Acton's world.

This last factor may in some measure account for the independence of view, the contests and the hammer-blows which

[1] G. P. Gooch, *History and Historians in the Nineteenth Century*, p. 298.

diversified the whole field of Victorian scholarship. In Acton's case this sharpness of dispute was aided by the absence of social contact with his disputants. There was nothing to modify a severe judgment. This may be seen in his attitude to Froude, which had almost the character of a vendetta, and in his treatment of that gentle patient scholar S. R. Gardiner. The first two volumes of the latter's *History of England*, those dealing with the first part of the reign of James I, came from the press during the early period of Acton's reviewing. The comment is of interest since it reveals the young historian's first mature approach. "His faults", he writes of Mr. Gardiner,[1] "do not arise from any party spirit, or want of conscience, or want of knowledge, or study of inferior materials, but from his general conception of the province of the historian. In its general scope his history is not a narrative written to show the triumph of right, or what he conceives to be so, and viewing all events from the moral elevation of a strong antecedent bias; but neither is it a passionless exposition of the series of events in their mechanical and metaphysical relation of cause and effect."

These sentences may help to explain much in John Acton's career, including the slow recognition that he won in spite of his surpassing merit. He had come from a country where the Prussian and Bavarian scholars were almost at open war. He was thus early accustomed to strong controversy, and he regarded his own judgment as impregnable. All the same, it is a barrier to the growth of confidence to assert that your fellow-historian does not suffer from want of conscience, want of knowledge or from choosing to study inferior materials. It might well have been held that it was unnecessary for Sir John Acton to entertain the charges of which he proceeds to acquit his neighbour. It was long before he would understand the Universities and their ripe quietness. Döllinger had done much to shield his mind from knowledge of all the benefits that come from port and candlelight. "He belongs", Acton continued, proceeding with his analysis of Samuel Gardiner in another tone, "to Mr. Carlyle's school,—a school which seeks to unite the moral interest of the first kind of history with the veracity of the second, by making itself the partisan of the fact, by subjecting the right to the test of success, and by assuming that the conquering cause is the favourite of the gods." There are two

[1] *Home and Foreign Review*, iii. p. 296.

comments which rise to the mind in considering this whole long passage. The first and less important is that it is not accurate. It cannot now be maintained that Gardiner was a disciple of Thomas Carlyle. In all his wilderness of grey stone prose he never once sets up the image of the *fait accompli*. The most that can be said is that in his study of the Stuart reign he sees the Constitution in the light of a diluted optimism which is not imaginative. The more important element is Acton's moral indignation with its stern assurance. Gardiner is accused of subjecting "the right to the test of success". One feels that Acton did not know how very rude he was.

It is clear that he did nothing at this time to bridge the gulf which his Continental education had created. For decades he was to remain a stranger to that old suave English academic oligarchy which was not so much learned as receptive. In particular, he never came to care for the ripened form of Oxford sentiment. Acton's training made it certain that Dr. Newman's character was one that he would never understand.

CHAPTER VII
DR. NEWMAN

AFTER HIS RETURN from Munich one side of the historian's life was dominated by his long and unsatisfactory contact with John Henry Newman. There is reason to suppose that this alliance of a sort was doomed to failure from the start. So far as our present information extends it seems evident that the relationship of Sir John Acton and Dr. Newman was fundamentally unstable and that, during the sixteen fretting years of its continuance, it never achieved a clear mutual confidence of security. Newman, with his delicate and sensitive approaches, was already gathering to himself hesitantly and almost unconsciously the new disciples of his Catholic period. That affectionate bond, with its understood and careful intimacies, was one in which Acton could never be included. He kept his personal reverence for men very different from Dr. Newman, and was wholly uninterested in what Oxford had meant to the quiet and tentative and sweeping mind of the Oratorian. Munich had not prepared him to appreciate that fragile and sometimes tortured wit, the Oriel simplicity, so egalitarian and reticent, and the familiar spirit of that rain-swept charm. A cast of mind as positive as Acton's must have remained alike unaffected by Newman's self-raillery and his very English sentiment and the light burden of his miseries and his felicity.

The relations between them, carried on at first only by letter, had a comparatively auspicious opening. This was in 1854, when Newman was fifty-three and Acton twenty; the first year of the Irish journey and of the rectorship of the Dublin Catholic University. Three quotations, quite familiar, will give the measure of the older man's reactions in those months. They have no value in themselves as commentary but only as reflecting that room in Birmingham.

"Nor was this all," wrote Dr. Newman of one stage of his Irish journey,[1] "I had neither food nor sleep; I could not sleep upon the feather-bedded curtained four-posters, and I could not eat the coarse and bleeding mutton which was the ordinary dinner, and I created remark, of course, do what I would, by going with-

[1] Wilfrid Ward, *Life of Cardinal Newman*, letter dated February 1854, i. p. 338.

out it." And then comes the happy phrasing of his memorandum.[1] "Point 4. I shall come back from Rome with a prestige, as if I had a blunderbuss in my pocket." Finally he uttered that very simple cry at the loss of the Oratorian life which meant so much to him:[2] "Certainly it was very hard that I should be bound, for no end of my own, to leave my own dear *nidulo* in the Oratory, and plunge into strange quarters in order to wait at episcopal doors."

Such were Newman's true reactions as he forced himself to uncongenial employments. These were his inner thoughts as his delightful script slowly wound through his tedious official correspondence. Coming from the Oxford of an earlier and mellow day, Dr. Newman was incapable of taking seriously the mechanism of a University conceived in the decade of the Exhibition. The proposal that he first put before John Acton is clearly a routine suggestion which he presumably brought forward as a result of that meticulous sense of duty which oppressed him. "I now write", began Newman [3] in sentences which barely touch even the surface of his own concern, "to ask you [Sir John Acton] to let me put down your name in the University Books. This involves nothing at all except your goodwill to an Institution which the Church has sanctioned. ... I also wish to be allowed to enter on the books the names of Dr. Döllinger, Dr. Windschman (I know I do not spell his name rightly) and Dr. Phillipps; and should be much obliged to you if you would [4] obtain them for me. Mr. Hope Scott and Mr. Baddeley in London are going soon to send me a number of London names, such as Lord Arundel and Surrey etc. etc."

The whole angle of approach was ill conceived. For the Rector of the Catholic University was tired and sensitive and surely conscious of the meretricious quality of this unsatisfactory advertisement. It was equally natural that this letter on reaching Munich should arouse a keen delight in the flattered and young recipient. Acton was never light-minded about academic matters. The University books conveyed to him an impression at once more satisfactory and more clear than any *nidulo*.

---

[1] Memorandum dated 15 January 1854, *ibid.*, i. p. 329.
[2] *ibid.*, i. p. 325.
[3] Letter dated 5 June 1854, preserved in the Newman Correspondence, Acton Volume, f. i. in the Birmingham Oratory MSS.
[4] This letter is torn at the edge but the word in question appears to have been " would ".

In this instance he wrote back[1] conveying his own and Dr. Windischmann's satisfaction, and there began a desultory correspondence. In the summer of 1858 Dr. Döllinger came to Aldenham and was brought to the Oratory[2] by his host, and in the same year there commenced those negotiations concerning the *Dublin Review* and the *Rambler* which have been described at length in Cardinal Gasquet's book, *Lord Acton and his Circle*.

From this long story, very tedious to unravel, certain facts emerge with crystal clearness. Few men can have been less at home with the leaders of the Oxford Movement than was John Acton. The converts had now been established in their new Communion for several years, and he had been too young to witness the circumstances of their arrival. Already his attitude towards certain of the authorities of his own Church was shot with pity, an emotion almost incomprehensible to any neophyte. Very shy, but apparently never touchy, Acton held a standpoint grounded on a profound submerged assurance and fortified by a reasoned belief in the coming victory of Liberal principles. Each element in the Constitution worked loud and strong like the heavy grinding machinery, rocking in its bed, which was so visible an achievement of that new day. At his age and with his background Acton could have but little patience with the bending misty Toryism and the tentative and uncompleted Oxford prejudice. Again, he could never share the attitude of the converts towards the Church of England, neither the acerbity of the Ultramontanes nor those lucid views of Newman which were maintained with firmness and a tremulous affection. Still very young, Sir John Acton at twenty-four required only one thing from his co-religionists, that most depressing of instruments, a *platform*.

The idea of using the *Dublin Review* for such a purpose had been mooted, and he put this before Newman with no consideration for his reticent and hesitating mind. "My dear Father Newman," he wrote from Aldenham on 5 July 1858, "I have just been informed that a circular has appeared announcing that the *Dublin Review* is given up, and I am asked whether I would take it in hand myself. I do not entirely reject the idea because I think that it

---

[1] Letter dated Munich, 15 July 1854, Birmingham Oratory MSS.
[2] Three letters among the Birmingham Oratory MSS. deal with Döllinger's visit to the Oratory and a proposed visit by Newman to Aldenham which did not materialise.

would be a pity that it should cease to appear, or that it would pass into the hands of unsatisfactory persons."

Newman replied dissuading him from this course of action, and with great simplicity he wrote again in terms which could not but be uncongenial to one whose thought was always so precise and carefully qualified. Acton proceeded to set out three arguments. "I have often heard", he wrote,[1] "that the *Dublin Review* advanced money to the Cardinal, and that expenses of this kind outweighed the advantage derived from his very uncertain and unequal contributions. Again, the adulatory and undignified tone of the *Review* has alienated a good many subscribers. The literary wants of our Catholic public are unfortunately easily satisfied."

But Newman was not used to such heavy charges. His own attitude to the *Dublin Review* was very different: "a dreary publication which wakes up to growl or to lecture and then goes to sleep again".[2] It was not possible to reconcile these standpoints.

In December Acton approached the subject from another angle, stressing the good which would result from *Atlantis*, the projected quarterly in connection with Newman's University. "Indeed," he wrote,[3] "I should say that nothing can be more suitable than that the review which is to represent and lead Catholic opinion on every variety of subject should be conducted by the members of the Catholic University. It would be a great security against that levity and superficial popularity by which the English reviews have done so much harm to literature." And then again a few days later: "From your retirement, if I may use the term, during the last few years, at least as far as England is concerned, we are delivered over to the influence of very questionable masters."[4]

This was not the tone which might serve to reassure the Oratorian. In other quarters, too, Sir John Acton's concern for the presentation of Catholic thought could only receive a scant appreciation. "I never converse", he wrote at the beginning of this correspondence,[5] "with any even of the best and cleverest converts, Dalgairns, Morris, MacMullen, Oakeley, Allies, Marshall,

---

[1] Letter from Sir John Acton to Dr. Newman dated 5 July 1858, Birmingham Oratory MSS.
[2] Letter from Dr. Newman to Mr. Capes, quoted in Gasquet, *Lord Acton and his Circle*, p. xxiv.
[3] Letter from Sir John Acton to Dr. Newman dated 10 December 1858.
[4] Letter from same to same dated 20 December 1858, Birmingham Oratory MSS.
[5] Letter from Acton to Simpson dated Aldenham Park, 28 February 1858, printed in Gasquet, *Lord Acton and his Circle*, pp. 8-9.

Wilberforce, etc., without finding them stating what I hold to be most false. It is just the mistakes of these, our best men, that it will be best worth while to discuss." This is a comment well worth pondering.

Acton could hardly realise what it involved in a hierarchic body to have Fr. Dalgairns and Canons Oakeley and MacMullen, Mr. Allies and Mr. Marshall and even the gentle Henry Wilberforce aligned against him. It was a sad presage of the future that he should add: "I cannot look for sympathy with my ideas in any considerable body of men. Hope and Manning are the only ones that I feel likely on most occasions to agree with." If this was the situation, it becomes natural to enquire to whom Acton could look as his supporter. Very soon it becomes clear that this support was offered generously by Richard Simpson.

It is interesting to speculate as to how much of Acton's later attitude was to develop from his association with Richard Simpson. There is little doubt that he was for some years greatly fascinated by his ardent spirit, and that Simpson's intolerant and reckless integrity was a quality which never failed to rouse the future historian's admiration. It was also during the course of this association that Acton's detachment from the ecclesiastical world became charged with a novel and accumulating bitterness.

It was association with the *Rambler* which first drew the men together, and in 1858 Acton was already writing to Richard Simpson,[1] who was fourteen years his senior, "with the openness and confidence of an old friend". Simpson had been at Oriel. He had submitted to Rome when vicar of Mitcham and had held, since 1856, the assistant editorship of the *Rambler*. But the important factor in the situation was his twelve years of disillusioning experience of the outlook of his co-religionists. Simpson had come early to his maturity, and it was maturity which Acton so greatly valued. Full of enthusiasm and unbreakably sincere, he combined a strong pugnacity of temperament with an inability to take seriously either the office or the personality of Cardinal Wiseman. Gasquet has remarked on his very generous charity and the simplicity of his approach. The story of the apparitions of Notre Dame de La Salette claimed his enthusiasm.

It was, however, one of Simpson's central tenets that ecclesiastical authority was hindering the Catholic layman from his free

---

[1] Letter dated 16 February 1858, printed in *Lord Acton and his Circle*, p. 2.

expression. A letter written to his friend the Bishop of Southwark in April 1862 gives calm expression to his point of view. "I know," wrote Simpson,[1] "for I have experienced the thing, that the great prejudice against the Church among educated Englishmen is not a religious one against her dogmas, but an ethical and political one; they think that no Catholic can be truthful, honest or free, and that if he tries to be he is subjected to persecution." Surely a consciousness of this false opinion remained throughout life with Acton, whose mind was always open to the implications of such a standpoint. "They think that no Catholic can be truthful, honest or free."

This was a view which he could understand in contrast to the converts' Tory feelings or to their *fervorini* and devotions. His direct mind tended to the emphatic, and throughout there was a curious and youthful disillusionment. Again, he was naturally excluded from that common sympathy which at times could unite the converts so surprisingly. Two letters from W. G. Ward to Simpson, both written in 1859, bear on this point. "I never expected", so runs the first communication,[2] "to hear without lively pleasure of the *Rambler* being brought to an end, but certainly our eminent and Right Rev. Fathers have managed to do the thing in a way which effectually prevents any such feeling." This was a transient emotion raised by the heated feeling of that time; but Acton moved away from both their shores.

The *Dublin Review* project being now abandoned, he wrote from Aldenham in the New Year assuring Fr. Newman of his attachment. "May I write", he enquired,[3] "to one or two friends to ask them to join Lord Dunraven and myself in making a fund for the purpose of converting the *Atlantis* into a quarterly?" He was still patient, but his cordiality was waning. In an account given to Simpson at this time of a conversation which he held with Newman the note of respect is there no longer. "I had", wrote Acton,[4] "a three hours' talk with the venerable Newman, who came out at last with his real sentiments to an extent which startled me with respect both to things and persons, as Ward, Dalgairns etc.; natural inclination of men in power to tyrannize; ignorance

---

[1] Letter to Bishop Grant dated 23 April 1862, *ibid.*, pp. lvii-lviii.
[2] Letter dated February 1859, *ibid.*, p. xlvii.
[3] Letter from Acton to Newman dated at Aldenham Park 7 January 1859, Birmingham Oratory MSS.
[4] Letter from Acton to Simpson dated 1 January 1859, printed in Gasquet, *op cit.*, p. 47.

and presumption of would-be theologians. I did not think he would ever cast aside his diplomacy and buttonment so entirely, and was quite surprised at the intense interest he betrayed in the *Rambler*. He was quite miserable when I told him the news and moaned for a long time, rocking himself backwards and forwards over the fire, like an old woman with a toothache."

There were very few among the converts, or indeed among the general Catholic community in England, who shared this outlook on Dr. Newman. It was, perhaps, only Mr. W. G. Ward and Provost Manning who would savour the expression about Newman moaning and "rocking himself backwards and forwards over the fire". The point will serve to indicate Acton's isolation. It is clear that the years in Munich had not prepared him for the criticism to which his rash incursion into the control of Catholic periodicals exposed him. It is worth while to mention the chief dates in connection with these ventures, since it is unnecessary to recall their details in a study of the influence upon his thoughts.

The *Rambler* had begun as a weekly in 1848 under the proprietorship and editorship of Mr. Capes, a Balliol convert. Simpson, who had become assistant editor two years earlier, accepted the editorship in 1858. After difficulties with the ecclesiastical authorities it was undertaken by Dr. Newman in 1859. In September of that year he too resigned, after he had produced two numbers, and Acton came upon the scene as editor. He had been interested for eighteen months previously and was now co-proprietor with Capes and Simpson. The *Dublin Review* throughout this period was in close touch with the episcopate: the *Atlantis*, to which reference has been made, was a specialist venture of less importance.

In April 1862 it was determined to change the *Rambler*, which appeared bi-monthly, into a quarterly review. The *Home and Foreign Review*, as this was called, reflected the increasing seriousness of Acton's outlook. Here his thought moved towards maturity. In a later section of this study specimens of his writing in both these periodicals will be considered. After eight numbers Acton decided that the *Home and Foreign Review* should cease publication with the issue of April 1864. He had come to the end of his difficult course.

During these years Acton played a part in that English Catholic world which he only then entered and from which he subsequently almost withdrew. With his cosmopolitan upbringing and the Whig oligarchic clan so close about him, he seems always to have maintained that the Catholic community in England was *provincial*. He was never really familiarised with the life of the countryside, even in Shropshire. The English Catholicism of the soil meant nothing to him.

In consequence he could neither understand nor value the Bishop of Birmingham, who had held since 1848 the leadership of the Catholics in the Midlands and was the main support of all the moderate party. Dr. Ullathorne's strong and almost violent common sense; his rich undaunted idiom; his rooted Tory sympathies and bluff suspicions; his disgust at intellectual assertiveness; all these were alien to Acton's mind. That these two men could not pierce through to mutual understanding was a primary misfortune for John Acton.

There was nothing to counterbalance his uneasy correspondence with Dr. Newman. Without being sensitive, Acton was supremely unsuspecting, and he now learned that Father Faber, the superior of the Brompton Oratory, had denounced him,[1] apparently to the Cardinal, as an unsatisfactory influence in the world of letters. "I am too conscious", he wrote from Aldenham to Newman about this matter,[2] "of the questionable character of the reputation I have unfortunately acquired to allow my name to be publicly connected just now with anything in which I am deeply interested." In the summer, Newman, who was perhaps feeling the strain of these arduous letters, suggested with that delicacy which he had at his command that the correspondence should for the present cease. "To talk to you", he told Acton, "would be a recreation, but I am as sick of penmanship as a pastrycook of tarts."

Through the summer there was a desultory exchange of letters. About July, Acton, who had now taken over the *Rambler*,[3] was writing from Lord Granville's house, 16 Bruton Street, to ask for Newman's opinion [4] as to Döllinger's advice that "we should ask the co-operation [for the *Rambler*] not of Gratry but of Maret,

---

[1] In a letter from Acton to Fr. Darnall dated at Aldenham 3 February 1859 these words occur: "when Faber . . . had not yet denounced me as you wot", Birmingham Oratory MSS.
[2] Letter from Acton to Newman dated at Aldenham 25 January 1859, Birmingham Oratory MSS.
[3] This was announced to Newman in a letter dated from Aldenham "Feast of Corpus Christi" 1859, Birmingham Oratory MSS.
[4] Undated letter from Acton to Newman written at 16 Brutqn Street apparently in July or August 1859, Birmingham Oratory MSS.

among the French Divines, as he considers him much the most eminent". There were further letters about English contributors, and Acton crossed to Germany in August. It was in the next year, when Newman was beginning to dissociate himself from the *Review*, that the long dissatisfaction overflowed. The letter that follows represents a transient mood but is revealing.

"I beg of you," wrote Acton to Newman from the House of Commons,[1] "remembering the difficulties you encountered, to consider my position, in the midst of a hostile and illiterate episcopate, an ignorant clergy, a prejudiced and divided laity, with the cliques at Brompton, York Place, Ushaw, always on the watch, obliged to sit in judgment on the theology of men [Döllinger, de Buck and Gratry] you selected to be our patrons, deserted by the assistant whom you obtained for me, with no auxiliary or adviser but Simpson." There are few things that are more striking in this period than the literary temerity of the Victorians and their imprudence. When they committed to paper statements such as these, it is remarkable that they really managed their relations tolerably or that their enmities were ever healed.

He was calmer in his next letter,[2] writing of Lady Georgiana Fullerton's refusal to contribute and of Aubrey de Vere's offer of poetry. Perhaps the earlier onslaught is mainly valuable as an instance of Acton's immense vitality and of that slight tendency towards a persecution-complex from which in his isolation he somewhat suffered. The Newman correspondence was fading out, but there is from 1861 one further letter. It reflects a more peaceful outlook and will serve as a prelude to a consideration of Acton's thought in the early 'sixties. "I have studied politics", he wrote to Newman,[3] "very elaborately, and more as a science than people generally consider it, and I am therefore afraid of writing like a doctrinaire, or of appearing zealous to force a particular and very unpopular system down people's throats." It was clear that John Acton stood in pressing need of sympathy, and this he would receive from Mr. Gladstone.

[1] Letter from Acton to Newman dated 29 June 1860, Birmingham Oratory MSS.
[2] Letter from Acton to Newman dated August 1860, Birmingham Oratory MSS.
[3] Letter from Acton to Newman dated at 37 Half Moon Street 9 June 1861, Birmingham Oratory MSS.

CHAPTER VIII
THE " RAMBLER " PERIOD

THESE YEARS were also those of the historian's last consistent contact with the old Catholic families before he was absorbed in the Gladstonian world. Despite his editorial proclivities, Sir John Acton was first and foremost an eligible *parti* when such were rare in that closed grouping. It was in this capacity that he would go to Lady Petre's week-ends at Thorndon and would meet the other young Catholic landowners in his situation. John Arundell, who would in time succeed Wardour, was among these eligible bachelors. Here he met Frederick Weld, of a slightly older generation and already a colonial administrator. Both figure in John Acton's correspondence.

This was a world in which he was never easy and would with the passing years feel less and less at home. "I am almost afraid of John Arundell", he wrote on one occasion.[1] The old Catholics were changing since the Weedall period; now they would accept the converts of their own standing. The sons of the Rome-bound Tractarian peers were brought into this older Catholic grouping and married to the daughters of these ancient stocks. A Conservatism, very tenacious and unassertive, enfolded them; they were content and insulated. It was the heyday of that secure and static world which the fall in agricultural prices had not yet come to disturb.

In the great houses the higher clergy were found in some profusion. Thus in July 1861, when the London season was over, Acton met the Cardinal at Thorndon. It is interesting to note the historian's reaction to this encounter. Persistent opposition was always a surprise to him, and he complains [2] that Wiseman was "cold at first". Acton never knew how to play and gaff the well-placed prelate.

The setting was mainly Georgian, the Payne houses Thorndon and Wardour. The atmosphere was that of a closed preserve with the principals alike unaware either of their impending poverty or

---
[1] Letter to Richard Simpson dated from Aldenham 6 June 1858, printed in *Lord Acton and his Circle*, p. 22.
[2] Letter to the same dated from 37 Half Moon Street, 19 July 1861, *ibid.*, p. 191.

of their sometimes startling riches. Agricultural values in those decades before the great depression did well by the landlord of the Old Religion who spent his life on his own acres. There was all the business of a *coterie* as these cousins met with their great trailing families of Welds and Vaughans and Cliffords. This would prove intimately unappealing to a man of urgent intellectual capacity whose own diluted sense of kinship was clearly cosmopolitan. There the old phalanx stood, the red carpet laid for the Cardinal on the hall steps at Talacre, the parties gathering for the Twelfth, the silver cleaning and the cellars stirring, the young girls gossiping about their *prétendants*. The ladies stood ready in their crinolines, prepared to curtsey to His Eminence. The conversation feathered round the ghost at Ince, where Charles Blundell was still reported to drag his lame leg on the stone-flagged passage. It was a little society in which romanticism channelled religion, Mrs. Craven come again. The ladies would aver that the ghosts were souls in Purgatory demanding Masses. Upstairs the red lamp winked before the Spanish crucifix, and its light just defined the new work of devotion on the *prie-dieu*, the pages neatly marked with lace-fringed pictures. The air was laden with a warm, secluded piety. In the gun-room the servants worked away. It was not the place for John Dalberg Acton.

He neither shot the covers nor married the daughters; his reaction was not without robustness. "Tomorrow I eat orthodox fish with the Fullertons at two o'clock."[1] This couple formed a link between Acton's so different worlds, for Lady Georgiana would retain an understanding of how her brother Granville must affect this young Catholic, while she also had a perception of his intellectual interests. These latter were very far removed from the old philistine circle of their co-religionists. In particular, Lady Georgiana would comprehend the pleasure, though not the approach, of the historian in regard to patristic studies.

Döllinger's influence had led to the shaping of the mould into which the young man cast his learned and impressionable zest. Acton had gained by this time a very perfect assurance which never left him. He early formed a relish for the use of that store of bibliographical knowledge to which he would always add. The stream of Christian writing lay before him and his mind turned to the Fathers in their great folios and to the *Series Episcoporum*. It

---

[1] Letter to the same dated from 37 Half Moon Street, 10 July 1861, *ibid.*, p. 122.

was the continuing legal structure, ecclesiastical and civil, which had so soon come to dominate the historian's solid and retentive imagination.

Considering the great fields that he had taken for himself and the rapidity with which he formulated all his comments, Acton's slips were very rare. An instance of the type of trivial error which his correspondence with Mr. Simpson reveals is met with in his denial of the existence of the diocese of Tarrazona in Navarre. "I never heard", we find him writing in the winter of 1861,[1] "of a bishop of Tarrasona, surely *Tarraconensis*." He was only twenty-seven and the books which were to form that unique library were heaped up around him. His eyes would be raised from his crowded table to where beneath the December sunlight the rich lands stretched westwards towards Wales. Beyond the plate-glass there lay the policies of Aldenham. Tarrazona: *Tarraconensis*, this might be a seemly occupation for some old chaplain of antiquarian tastes; it was not the view of the Catholic squires that one of their number should be thus desk-bound.

In some respects there is no doubt that Acton's work gained from his really formidable isolation. The older generation of Döllinger's English friends had gone their way; to the contributors of the *Rambler* he was always the patron; he was not yet in the world of the Protestant historians. The Granville circle had not the interest to dispute his challenging judgments as they fell and rang. The phrases here given [2] will well serve to instance John Acton's early manner: "The followers of a writer so dazzling, but so little to be trusted and less to be imitated, as Count de Maistre. Montalembert is always rhetorical in his private letters as Macaulay is always antithetical even in private conversation. Robertson is clearly the best church historian in England now that Hardwick is dead. St. John Nepomucene, whose history I happen to know better than Anderdon, whose research has not extended beyond the Breviary." With energy he would snap down his own conclusion. A comment on the vaunted tiresome *History of Civilisation in England* just published by Mr. H. T. Buckle is a good specimen of his metalled style:[3] "I got through Buckle last night. Setting aside the theory, the learning of the book is

---

[1] Letter to the same dated from 37 Half Moon Street, 19 July 1861, *ibid.*, p. 164.
[2] *ibid.*, pp. 1, 68, 131, 108.
[3] *ibid.*, p. 13.

utterly superficial and obsolete. He has taken great pains to say things that have been said much better before in books he has not read." This is a rather fine example of the operation of Acton's mousetrap. The time of savage reviewing was not over and there was not much sympathy for the mouse.

The most amazing element in the whole range of Acton's knowledge was certainly his acquaintance, which was at once improbable and unrivalled, with printed sources. He was still able to take that broad and sweeping view which to a later generation seems so unattainable. He was strengthened in his adherence to his favoured methods by the great library which was growing all the time. His mind would go back to his rows of folios and all those dulled cloth bindings. The presence of this large mass of source-books accounts to some extent for the historian's insistence on texts of laws and bulls and ordinances. This last approach in particular was Germanic and tinged Acton's outlook on work on manuscripts.

In those early years of the opening of the State Paper Office and the publication of the Rolls series there was a natural emphasis on the official document. The scholar of that time would be a connoisseur of the printed register or the manuscript hand-list. The value of diplomatic correspondence was then seen to turn on the development and maintenance of treaties. There was perhaps an undue stress, especially in dealing with the sixteenth century, on the actual elaboration of the treaty system. This was the era of the study of political and legal and institutional history before the examination of the social structure. A letter written to Simpson from Carlsbad brings back the spirit of that epoch and that approach. "There is", explains Acton,[1] "a *published* report of about the date you mention. I do not remember it exactly nor the writer's name. Those reports are often extant in many more or less correct copies. The originals are all at Venice; copies were kept in families of ambassadors, others were made for men going on embassies. Thus they get multiplied. Ranke's peculiar knowledge and views of modern history are derived mostly from a set of those at Berlin. The cold-blooded acuteness of those Venetians singularly suits and attracts and often misleads him."

In this period manuscripts in private hands, with the exception of the almost official Roman collections such as those in the Palazzo

---

[1] Letter to the same dated from 37 Half Moon Street, 19 July 1861, *ibid.*, p. 109.

Barberini, hardly come within the scope of the student's interest. There was the great wealth of the national collections to be first ransacked. In this connection a suggestion made by Acton that one of Sir Richard Belling's letters might be found among the papers at Wardour Castle would seem to indicate that he had no personal acquaintance with the contents of that muniment room. The mention of this Catholic agent of the Restoration period brings us to Acton's solitary attempt to solve a problem of biography.

The contribution in question is an article of nearly forty pages entitled "Secret History of Charles II" and dealing with the life of that King's eldest natural son James La Cloche. Acton had been working on the matter for some time, and the results of his research were published in the *Home and Foreign Review* in July 1862. Properly speaking, this lies outside the *Rambler* period, but it is discussed here partly because it belongs to his term of interest in Catholic bypaths and partly because it is separated by a certain immaturity of tone from the bulk of his work in the *Home and Foreign*. There is much that is instructive in this study, and the marshalling of authorities is most impressive. The authors who deal at second-hand with the question of the religious faith of Charles II are first passed in review: Mackintosh, Hallam, Vaughan, Macaulay, Lingard, Dodd. This matter thus disposed of, Acton goes forward to his real *forte*, the examination of contemporary printed sources dealing from many different angles with the world of affairs. Here, with certain other matter, we find that body of writing upon politics to which the Victorian Age had grown accustomed, the serried rows of diplomats and placemen, Clarendon's *History of the Rebellion*, the *Mémoires de Mademoiselle*, Carte's *Collection*, Winwood's *Memoirs*, *La Vie de M. Olier* (to strike a note of ecclesiasticism), *Mémoires de Guy Joly*, *Mémoires de Cosnac*, *Mémoires de Turenne*, *Complément des Mémoires de Retz*.

Father Boero S.J. supplied transcripts of documents in the library at the Gesù, and there were despatches from the bundles labelled the Italian States and kept in the London State Paper Office. The article, however, leaves upon the reader the impression that Acton was not happy in attempting to reconstruct the details of a personal relation. It was public affairs and the great tides of thought to which his mind had found itself attuned. The swinging minatory phrases that he loved were inapplicable to that subtle world. He had no understanding of the Restoration *milieu* and did not like its bawdy wit nor the purposeful frivolity. In a letter to Simpson he exclaims that "Clarendon lies in his throat". This jars on those who feel for the high Cavalier dignity. Possibly the only man in all that period into whose mind Sir John Acton entered was Gottfried Wilhelm von Leibnitz; he was taken by his philosophic sweep, meticulous, courtierlike, Germanic.

However this may be, the historian did not return to this particular type of seventeenth-century problem, abandoning the personal side of dynastic history for wider issues. Acton was very far removed from the type of antiquarian which had flourished in the previous age. It was bibliography that fascinated him, and the study of the development of ideas to which he gave himself. Chronology and genealogy, which had so much exercised his predecessors, left Acton cold. In these matters he could be careless, referring [1] to Avellanedo's Empress as the wife of Rudolf II, who was in fact the only unmarried Hapsburg sovereign, and describing [2] Boniface IX as the successor to Pope Boniface VIII when he really meant Benedict XI.

Acton's attitude towards the Church was in these days undergoing change. He would always remain aware of the massive legal structure and of the documentation of pontificates and congregations; but the sunlight no longer fell upon that great façade. Nevertheless he would always give to the Church organisation what he believed to be its due. It lay across the background of that western history on which his attention was ever bent. At each stage he would meet with pontifical decrees and constitutions. "Cardinal Toleto", he noted,[3] "generally Toletus; but I suppose you have authority." "An invaluable book", we find Acton pointing out,[4] "Guerra, *Constitutiones Pontificiae*, 4 vols., folio, 1772, with an index rich enough to make your mouth water. It gives under distinct heads ... often the very words of the essential portions, together with references."

Meanwhile the historian set out in terms stronger than he would subsequently have used the errors of the naturalism that he saw around him. "Certain Germans of the last century remind me of him [Boz] as to religion. They saw 'no divine part of

---

[1] Letter to the same dated from 37 Half Moon Street, 19 July 1861, *ibid.*, p. 185.
[2] *ibid.*, p. 238.   [3] *ibid.*, p. 164.   [4] *ibid.*, pp. 243-4.

Pope Gregory XVI, Tsar Nicholas I and Cardinal Acton.

Christianity', but divinified humanity, or humanized religion, and taught that man was perfectible, but childhood perfect. So they used to die full of benevolence and admiration of the sun and moon, and for their children and their dog and for their home. They hated intolerance, exclusiveness, positive religion, and with a comprehensive charity embraced all mankind and condemned alike differences of faith and distinctions of rank, as insurrection against the broad common humanity." It is an interesting expression of Acton's views, and all the more so since it introduces the only discussion which the historian permits himself of Dickens and Thackeray.

"Their religion", he continued in this long stiff-jointed letter to Richard Simpson,[1] "was a sort of natural religion adorned with poetry and enthusiasm—quite above Christianity. Herder was a man of this stamp. Surely Dickens is very like them. He loves his neighbour for his neighbour's sake, and knows nothing of sin when it is not crime." Here was something of Acton's moral fire, but the analysis which follows belongs manifestly to his early period. "Our recent novel literature", he declared,[2] "seems to me to be our great glory in literature since Bulwer's reformation. They are nearly all respectable except Currer Bell and Kingsley—but at least the masters, Neo-Bulwer, Thackeray, Dickens, Reade, Trollope." It was now six years since Charlotte Brontë, who had used the pseudonym Currer Bell, had died. Charles Kingsley had published *Westward Ho!* in 1855: it is not difficult to see how that book and *Jane Eyre* would rile John Acton. He was always hostile to any emotional heightening of a situation. Bulwer Lytton's appeal is more difficult to fathom.

The letter dealing with his views on Thackeray was written rather more than two years later, in January 1864, just after the novelist had died. "I am sorry to say", Acton explained to Simpson,[3] "I have neither his books nor any good ideas about him. His views of history are surely very superficial, and he is not in the first rank of literary critics, but he can go to the bottom of small minds in a way which is wonderful because he was not a first-rate judge of character among his acquaintances. Thackeray was extremely sensitive in the great world. I certainly did not think him *distingué*. The marvel is how he knew the ladies of the great

---

[1] Letter dated 8 December 1861, *ibid.*, pp. 241-2.
[2] *ibid.*, p. 241.   [3] *ibid.*, pp. 310-11.

world so well, for that is his strongest department. *Esmond*, again and again I assure you, is a masterpiece for that sort of knowledge. Also, in the *Virginians*. . . . Dickens is far below Thackeray in his characters." A final note in the same letter will bring back a theme of these passing years: "In the *Newcomes*, to the matchmaking mammas I could add a touch or two."

CHAPTER IX

THE HOUSE OF COMMONS

THE DESCRIPTION of Acton's links with the English Catholic world has a bearing upon the relations which took long to forge and then were quickly severed with the members of the House of Commons, whose number he joined in 1859. There seem to have been two opinions as to the purpose of the parliamentary career which was now opening. In Lord Granville's set, which was so easy and yet profoundly political, a seat in the House was the obvious first move for any young man entering on public life. In John Acton's case a special difficulty was caused by his Catholicism, but in that fortunate and experienced society on which the light of reason fell like barred sunlight, difficulties existed to be overcome. The Whig managers scrutinised the roll of Irish seats which were not unduly expensive to contest and could in those years be disposed at will. A first proposal in regard to Clare having miscarried, Sir John Acton was elected in 1859 for the borough of Carlow. It was a project that had been considered for some eighteen months, for a testimonial letter from Cardinal Wiseman designed to be used with bishops and clergy in Ireland was dated 27 November 1857. As far as Granville and his friends were concerned, it was a very simple routine matter. It is not surprising that this was not the light in which his stepson viewed the subject.

A letter on this question is illuminating. It was sent as a reply to a note offering Acton a hope of entering "the noblest assembly in the world". The young historian made it clear that, while there was no political party with which he could act so well as the Whigs, he could not always undertake to vote with Lord Palmerston's Government or with any other. "There is", he wrote,[1] "a sort of fastidiousness produced by long study which public life possibly tends to dissipate, but although the profession of anything like independence of party appears ridiculous, I am of opinion that to a Catholic a certain sort of independence is indispensable. Reasons of religion must separate me occasionally from the Whigs, and political convictions from the Irish party." In this letter,

---

[1] *Lord Acton's Correspondence*, i. p. 28.

which has more than one revealing passage, Acton goes on to say that "my opinions and character are not such as to ensure the support of the Irish Catholics". This was certainly a just observation.

In many ways Acton would have been more at home in the unreformed House of Commons. It was in part a legacy from his German years that, on the social side, club life appealed to him: breakfast clubs, dining clubs, the Athenaeum, which he joined early. In this connection one of the few friendships which he gained through being a member of Parliament was that with Sir Mountstuart Grant Duff, which had the quality of unimpeded and unhurried exchange of view. Acton had by this time come to enjoy a modicum of discussion, an element of thought, both in good company. This was the world of Burke rather than that of Cobden. Besides, the historian was no speaker, nothing of a committee man, and wholly unfamiliar with industrial and commercial questions.

Acton's writings give the impression that he conceived his role as that of a political philosopher. What Burke had done he perhaps too might do. He knew, besides, so much about the detail of Continental politics; in these last years he had studied so closely. This last quality was, however, not destined to help him. The atmosphere of the House of Commons was as yet unsympathetic to the expert. It was still the opinion that the gentlemen of England were sufficiently informed in regard to the interest of their country. They did not need any foreign-bred young member to instruct them.

In general the temper of the House, both among the Whigs and Tories, was profoundly conservative, a Conservatism in which Acton shared. The knowledge possessed by most members of the conditions of life and way of thought of the urban proletariate was as sketchy as his own. It was the manufacturer and the farmer whose needs were understood, and as far as the labouring classes were concerned it was only the agricultural world which could come clear to them. Patriarchal benevolence in its Victorian guise, the landlord-tenant relation, was well developed. The concept of the "deserving poor" had been acquired; the parson and the squire now ruled the English village. The Erasto-Christian feudalism which this involved was accepted by the Victorian squirearchy as the normal pattern of life in the best of countries, but for Acton there was something laboured in such acceptance. A letter which the historian wrote to his mother from Munich in regard to the school which she had established at Morville on the Aldenham estate will serve to emphasise this point.

It should be explained that the letter in question was written after a summer visit to the Arcos and was dated only 26 October. The year is not given, but it seems probable that Acton was then twenty-two. "Comme je pense toujours", he explained,[1] "plus au devoir qu'au droit, il m'a paru que ce qui décide de la question c'est le fait que ceux auxquels l'école est destinée sont presque sans exception protestants." Always putting duty first, he recognised that the school would be almost entirely filled by Protestant children. The lesson that he drew was that it would be just to appoint a Protestant schoolmaster. "Il est donc plus juste qu'ils aient un maître protestant. Les Catholiques n'y perderont rien, si la personne choisie est modérée et libérale dans ses opinions, et si elle ne se mêle pas de sujets dans lesquels la controverse peut entrer." Acton had been staying with his cousins on their Austrian property at St. Martin. The peasantry of Europe lay stretched out before his mind; the German world and the Slav borderlands; the prayers taught by a Bohemian nurse, the carols and the snow upon the shield above a wayside cross. The roots of human relationship struck very deep, and there was also the memory of Revolution. The fidelity of the house servant was directed rather to the great family than to any nation. Such appreciations were the shared background of the European landowning class throughout the eighteenth and nineteenth centuries. At home at Morville the children sat in their neat rows in smocks and pinafores. It was essential that the teacher should be "modérée et libérale". What did this signify in the English shires?

Still, if Acton and his English contemporaries were at cross-purposes in regard to the rural picture, they shared an incomprehension of the great industrial masses. It is worth examining this aspect of the scene in politics, for it is related to the fear which the spectre of absolutism inspired in the historian. It will be recalled that according to his doctrine this absolute power could be exercised from above or from below. He feared a despot or a despotic mob which would itself in turn create a despot.

The old Whig world looked out over the troubled waters. This

[1] *Lord Acton's Correspondence*, p. 22.

was a scrutiny not devoid of hope but unenlightened by any practical experience. The new voters, which the impending Reform Bill, passed actually in 1867, would bring to the poll, could only make their choice among the existing political parties. There was no secure way to tell which side would benefit. Chartism was over, and the struggle for Education not begun. Beyond the mass of voters there still lay the wide sections of the unenfranchised, and when Acton entered Parliament only one adult male in six was a voter.

It is well to stress the ignorance of this new factor throughout the prosperous Victorian world. The urban population lay far beyond the sight of Acton's circle. Bridgnorth was a pleasant little country town which shared in the agricultural prosperity of the decade before 1862; there was nothing to assist him there. In London Sir John Acton's journeys took him to the sections of the capital which lay between Bryanston Square and Portman Square and the Houses of Parliament. Consultations with his solicitor or man of business might lead him to Bedford Row or to the City. There were no rookeries near 16 Bruton Street, that sober house from which he would emerge on his quiet occasions. The air of St. James's brooded on his London life.

On train journeys, of course, the traveller would view the stretches of mean houses as the swaying first-class carriages of those days ground into Wolverhampton or passed slowly over the arches above the lines of chimneys at Bethnal Green. Apart from such glimpses, caught as the draught penetrated past the rug to the footwarmer while the gloved hand lay on the window-strap, the sight of industrial poverty must have come but seldom. Leaving travel aside, it was, perhaps, only as the brougham breasted the slope above Snow Hill on that journey from the railway station to the Oratory which the historian took so rarely that his eyes would fall upon the crowding roof-lines of the vast new city slums.

In Charles Greville's diary there is an entry made in the year before John Acton entered Parliament. It shows how the old high Whigs would speculate about the subjects that they did not know. "Among the events of last week", he noted on 22 June 1858,[1] "one of the most interesting was the Queen's visit to Birmingham, where she was received by the whole of that enormous population with an enthusiasm which is said to have exceeded all

---

[1] *The Greville Memoirs*, ed. Roger Fulford, vii. p. 374.

that was ever displayed in her former receptions at Manchester or elsewhere. It is impossible not to regard such manifestations as both significant and important. They evince a disposition in those masses of the population in which, if anywhere, the seeds of Radicalism are supposed to lurk, most favourable to the Conservative cause. . . . This great fact lends some force to the notion entertained by many political thinkers, that there is more danger in conferring political power on the middle classes than in extending it far beneath them." Thus the old gentlemen would consider how best they might preserve a natural aristocracy.

Nevertheless this particular speculation possessed no great appeal for the historian. The form in which it was set out was clearly insular. It was a result of the nature of his upbringing that Acton was entirely free from any feeling against the middle classes; that was peculiar to England, a sentiment among the old Whigs and the old high Tories. In Germany and Austria, for instance, and indeed across all Europe, the middle classes were the buttress of the constitutional position. In each country they formed that bureaucratic *cadre* by which the Government was carried on. It was a very different thing to trust the mass of unskilled labour or the artisans.

In this connection there was unanimity in the House of Commons about the question of democracy. A speech by Disraeli, made in the year that Acton took his seat, will bear this out. The occasion of the utterance was the abortive Reform Bill which the Tories had sponsored. "If you establish a democracy," affirmed Disraeli,[1] "you must in due season reap the fruits of a democracy. You will in due season have great impatience of the public burdens combined in due season with great increase of the public expenditure. You will in due season reap the fruits of such united influence. You will in due season have wars entered into from passion, and not from reason; and you will in due season submit to peace ignominiously sought and ignominiously obtained, which will diminish your authority and perhaps endanger your independence. You will, in due season, with a democracy find that your property is less valuable and that your freedom is less complete." Six years later he would revert to the same theme.

"You have", declared Disraeli,[2] "an ancient, powerful, richly-

[1] *Life of Disraeli*, by W. F. Monypenny and G. E. Buckle, i. p. 1608.
[2] *ibid.*, ii. p. 144.

endowed Church, and perfect religious liberty. You have unbroken order and complete freedom. You have landed estates as large as the Romans, combined with commercial enterprise such as Carthage and Venice united never equalled.... You have created the greatest Empire of modern time. You have amassed a capital of fabulous amount. You have devised and sustained a system of credit still more marvellous." From this it was a simple step to show that any interference would spell the nation's ruin. It would not be Old England—"the England of power and tradition, of credit and capital, that now exists." The point of view was set out once again in a final sentence. The Tory leader hoped that the House would "sanction no step that has a tendency to democracy, but that it will maintain the ordered state of free England in which we live". Lord Shaftesbury wrote a letter on the delivery of this second speech which in its turn is most revealing. "The sentiments and the language", he told Disraeli,[1] "were worthy of each other, and a masterly protest against any truckling to democracy. I believe that, in proportion as a man is a deep, sincere, and consistent lover of *social*, civil and religious liberty, he will be a deep, sincere and consistent hater of pure democracy as averse to all three."

Here after all were those great phrases which bound the thinking part of the electorate: "a love of social, civil and religious liberty". They would create complacency, and men from both parties could ring this coin. A cliff divided the unenfranchised mass from those to whom these warming fine ideals sounded gratefully. The abstract right of increased numbers to vote had been conceded in 1832 by the first Reform Act. The feeling that then ran high was by the Crimean war years quite exhausted. The unreformed House of Commons had been based upon an electorate of half a million. This figure had been increased to rather more than a million when the second Reform Act added another nine hundred thousand. The unskilled urban worker, and in particular the casual labourer and the young lodger, were in these years beyond the pale of all discussion. The crucial fact was this, that even for the skilled artisan the right to vote was of much less consequence than the right to combine. The active thought of such men was bound up with the development of unions on a craft basis; the first Trade Union Congress met in 1868. This was a world to which John Acton did not penetrate.

[1] *Life of Disraeli*, ii. p. 145.

THE HOUSE OF COMMONS 137

Within the House itself there was a certain homogeneity of wealth and background. All members already formed a part of (or wished to be accepted into) the aristocratic *milieu*, with its hangers-on, or the solid Victorian middle class. Thus Richard Cobden, who among Acton's leading colleagues had known most of real poverty in his own life, would sign his writings by the pseudonym of a "Manchester manufacturer". Wealth or inheritance had stepped each man into his place. Few members, and they perhaps among the Tories, would have disagreed with the necessity for the moral education of the poor. "We are bound", Acton was to write in discussing an erring minister,[1] "to make the rude workman understand and share our indignation against the grandee." At the same time yet another factor would tend to bind the House together. The Radicals Bright and Cobden were among the most travelled members. Sitting in their top-hats in the Continental railway coaches or in the old *diligences* they would make their own sharp observations. They were thus linked with Tocqueville through Nassau Senior and John Stuart Mill.

It was, perhaps, insularity that most antagonised the young member for Carlow. This was the reason why he was not at ease with his own leader, Palmerston, then entering on his final long administration. "A gay old Tory of the older school," so the *Press* described this Whig premier,[2] "disguising himself as a Liberal and hoaxing the Reform Club." This appealing description was not likely to endear him to the historian. The jaunty manner, the intense masculinity of the aged buck, the large sophisticated ignorance were all abhorrent to John Acton. There in the House of Commons the prime minister would sit in his place with his white hat pulled down over his eyes pretending to be awake before he left to go to his dinner, the turtle soup, the cod, the oyster sauce. Twenty years later, writing in the *English Historical Review*,[3] Acton would call him a "master of expediency and compromise". These were hard words; but Palmerston's attitude to the ballot may serve to explain them. He regarded the franchise, so his biographer explains, "as a trust reposed in the electors for the public good". For this reason he opposed the ballot. "Poking in a piece of paper," he once declared,[4] "looking round to see that

[1] *Letters of Lord Acton to Mary Gladstone*, p. 96.
[2] Quoted in *Life of Disraeli*, i. p. 1415.
[3] *English Historical Review*, 1888, p. 476.
[4] *Life of Lord Palmerston*, by R. Ashley, i. p. 362.

no one could read it, is a course which is unconstitutional and unworthy of the character of straightforward and honest Englishmen." Though they belonged in name to the same party, Lord Palmerston was almost everything that Mr. Burke was not; but after all, John Acton had been warned. When only fourteen he had written to his mother describing the political views of the Professor. One phrase remained upon the memory: "Il déteste Lord Palmerston."[1]

*　　*　　*

To Acton's mind the association of politics and the turf was wholly uncongenial. For this reason he felt little more respect for the Tory leader, the fourteenth Earl of Derby, than he did for his own chief. There is a note made in the previous year by a Tory henchman invited to Knowsley. "As a leader of a party he [Derby] is more hopeless than ever—devoted to whist, billiards, racing, betting." It was not in the historian to develop a Newmarket side. Acton was to prove in middle life an adept courtier on the German model. He was already an easy conversationalist, with a rather heavy sense of social *nuances*. If we seek for an explanation of his failure to accommodate himself to either House of Parliament, the reason would seem to be that he was too professorial for that assembly.

This comes out in his whole approach to politics. He was at once a Burkian Conservative and anti-Tory. The *odium theologicum*, which in time would burn so brightly, was in these years concentrated on a deep doctrinal opposition to the Tory cause. In this connection a notice in the *Home and Foreign Review* dealing with Thomas McKnight's *Life of Bolingbroke* throws light on Acton's attitude. This is the review which contains the well-known statement that the greatest Tory chieftains were "all reckoned by their party either converts or apostates". It is perhaps one of the least mature of the pronouncements for which Acton would be responsible; but it gives the standpoint which he adopted and the angle from which he would judge Mr. Disraeli.

"The author of the Peace of Utrecht", we read in a consideration of Bolingbroke's career,[2] "is memorable in history for the greater achievement of having elevated Toryism for a moment to the dignity of a political theory. No other man ever attempted

[1] *Lord Acton's Correspondence*, p. 9.
[2] *Home and Foreign Review*, 1863, p. 635.

this. . . . For it was in the nature and definition of Toryism that it lived on class interests or on religious opinions, and borrowed the elements of its vitality from a different order of ideas. . . . The cry that the Church was in danger or the landlord threatened did duty instead of a political idea, and acted far more powerfully than anything based on reasoning could have acted on uneducated minds. Therefore the most illustrious chiefs of the party either were not reared in its arms or deserted it in the maturity of their powers; and they are all reckoned by their party either converts or apostates." So much for the general line, and now for the personal attack on Bolingbroke; it is clear that he is regarded as *the* theorist and a precursor. "In later life," we are told of this statesman,[1] "when he was a confirmed infidel, too bitter if not too sincere for hypocrisy, he argued that an established Church was an essential institution of good policy. He accommodated his really liberal ideas to the party with which he acted, by extravagant errors in political economy such as his hatred for capitalists and for the Bank of England." Alongside this severe judgment can be placed Disraeli's view of what Bolingbroke had achieved for the Tories: "He restored the moral existence of the party."[2]

There were many counts on which John Acton was opposed to Disraeli, who in these years stood revealed as the mentor and future leader of the Conservatives. In the first place, there was his paraded attachment to the doctrines of Bolingbroke and the younger Pitt. The review just quoted gives Acton's measure of the latter figure:[3] "Mr. Pitt who led the Tories without dreaming of inspiring their minds with an idea." And then there was that high flamboyant fantasy which was so repugnant to the historian's solid processes. An example will make this clear. In the year following Acton's entry into Parliament, Disraeli wrote to his friend Mrs. Brydges Willyams. "Once I said, in *Coningsby*," he exclaimed,[4] "there is nothing like Race: it comprises all truths. The world will now comprehend that awful truth." It is to Lord Acton's honour that this was a conception which he appreciated exactly and against which he always fought.

[1] *Home and Foreign Review*, 1863, p. 636.
[2] Buckle and Monypenny, *op cit.*, i. p. 671.
[3] *Home and Foreign Review*, 1863, p. 635.
[4] Quoted in Buckle and Monypenny, *op cit.*, ii. p. 55.

CHAPTER X
VICTORIANA

THIS SURVEY has given a brief impression of certain trends in politics. Clearly it can only serve to emphasise the links and contrasts between the political forum narrowly considered and the general social order in which this was enshrined. It is striking with what ease men would pass over from the last brittle romanticism of a world made safe by Metternich to the very solid appurtenances of life in the mid-century.

In this connection Acton was ever on his guard against all rhetoric and was surely characteristic of his generation in disregarding aesthetic values. Sir Mountstuart Grant Duff particularly noted that he had no care for his books' bindings. Again, in Acton's case his mind moved so much in the circle of ideas that he seems to have manifested no reactions when confronted by the solid material aspects of that world into which his life now swung.

In the volume of correspondence with Mrs. Drew there is reproduced a photograph of a group at Tegernsee taken in the autumn of 1879. Lord Acton in black coat and dull white trousers is seen leaning back on an iron garden chair with his round black hat reposing on his crossed knees. His left foot rests on a little woven mat which lies on the flat raked expanse of gravel. The virginia creeper hangs over the *persiennes*. Opposite him across the gravelled space is Mr. Gladstone's visage, composed and leonine, while in the background sits the old professor. These points are here recalled, for John Acton had now entered that age of burgeoning material ease which was to characterise the middle and latter portions of the reign of Queen Victoria. It was a period of facilities which he accepted, comforts which were in the background of his swift mental activity, and a social ritual which he observed. It is easier to picture Acton in his manhood if we recall the actual facilities and comforts which built up the physical surroundings of that clear-cut personality.

A few details may be mentioned merely to establish the position. Galoshes had been introduced some years; the Inverness cape was now in fashion; phosphorus matches he had known since boyhood. These were the days of carriage exercise in the afternoon and the rite of the dinner party. It was a period of shooting in the Highlands and summer holidays in Brittany and Normandy. Henry Reeve, who was one of Lady Granville's circle, followed both these pastimes. It is worth noting that these observances and recreations had in the main the *patina* of a new fashion. Railway travel was satisfactory for daylight journeys; at night a gentleman did not attempt it. Reeve on his summer visits to the deer forest which his friends had leased was accustomed to take a stateroom in the steamship sailing from London to Aberdeen. On the railroad the well-packed luncheon hamper, the grouse, the flask of brandy against the cold, sustained the traveller. The fog closed in past the massive archway before that station which was still known as Euston Square. The travelling valet with the folded rug borne on his left arm stood waiting beside the door of the first-class railway coach with its grey and swiftly soiled upholstery.

In the country lamps were universal, lit by paraffin and burning in a globe of white ground glass. The incandescent gas was still confined to the town houses. There had now come into fashion striped wallpapers, royal-blue curtains, gilt pelmets, inner curtains of Nottingham lace, Brussels carpets with their thick sharp pattern and Berlin woolwork enriched with beads.[1] We are approaching the naming of magenta; this was the period of shades and dyes. On the tables stood silver tureens, epergnes and bread baskets. Beside the hostess would be placed the tea equipage. In the dining-room wine-coolers rose beneath the sideboard under the family portraits in heavy oils. The bell-pulls were of woolwork in subdued colours. Knick-knacks were dusted lightly with a feather brush.

Far off down the long stone corridors the bells would jangle by the servants' hall. The silver shone; it was the time of massive trophies. As one passed through the green baize door towards the servants' quarters, and moved beyond the smell of metal polish, the air was heavy-laden with beer and porter. The sum of these impressions always lingered with every window tightly closed against the night air and the draught. In the reception-rooms the great fires roared, and in the bedrooms firelight played about the whitewashed ceilings and the new beds without curtains, and lay on the large china jugs and basins and the shining soap-dishes and sponge-trays.

[1] Cf. *Early Victorian England*.

Amid this wilderness of production two other trends may be observed. The years which brought the great development of Victorian furnishing, the heavy desks of rich moulded mahogany, and the invention of machine-made blotting-paper, saw the grave rise of the Pre-Raphaelites. In 1858 William Morris had published *The Defence of Guinevere* and Millais had exhibited "Sir Isumbras at the Ford". It was seven years since society had been made familiar with the bright unnatural sheen of Ophelia's tresses as they lay outspread upon the water. On the other side, time could not quell Disraeli's curveting romanticism. There is a letter from this period written to Lady Londonderry[1] in which he describes Mentmore, a house lately completed by the Rothschilds. "The hall ... glowing with colour, lit by gorgeous Venetian lamps of golden filigree that once were at the head of Bucentaurs. Such chairs—Titian alone could paint them, such clocks of lapiz lazuli, such cabinets of all forms and colours, such marble busts of turbaned Moors." Still, this was not the dominant impression of the post-Crimean period; that was of plaids and tartans brought to favour by Balmoral, Birmingham ware and mass-produced effects, the mists about Sir Edwin Landseer's cattle, the English Sunday, domesticity.

The Sabbatarian customs had just established themselves in the world of fashion when Acton came to manhood. There was already a tendency positively to go in search of sermons which is surprising. "I am just come", noted Greville in regard to C. H. Spurgeon,[2] "from hearing the celebrated Mr. Spurgeon preach in the Music Hall of the Surrey Gardens. It was quite full; he told us from the pulpit that 9000 people were present." The next quotation is little less improbable. "Went", wrote Henry Reeve,[3] "to hear Dr. Guthrie preach at a Scotch Presbyterian chapel near the Edgware Road. ... Guthrie's preaching was a finished performance, but I could hardly trace an idea. He passed from one topic to another, as if he were exhibiting dissolving views of the perdition of man."

This zeal for Scottish or dissenting preachers was incomprehensible to any foreigner, nor could John Acton understand it. Certainly it seemed to manifest the gulf that was now opening between the way of life pursued in England and on the Continent.

---

[1] Letter dated 29 April 1857, printed in Buckle and Monypenny, *op cit.*, i. p. 1477.
[2] *The Greville Memoirs*, vii. p. 265.
[3] Entry in journal dated 10 February 1856, printed in *Life and Correspondence of Henry Reeve*, ed. John Knox Laughton, i. p. 357.

The perfunctory attendance at the formal service of the Established Church which characterised the Georgian period was easily understood by Catholic *émigrés* whose *berlines* had crunched the paving-stones of little Lutheran capitals. Across Europe society would appreciate Lord Chesterfield's nice approach to social obligation. The situation now was very different, nor was the Court in this instance responsible. The Queen herself was content with an ordered Protestant approach, Lutheran in inspiration and Erastian in temper. She held herself towards her clergy with a condescension companioned by that unselfconscious dignity which was at times agreeable. It was among the well-to-do section of her people that the Evangelical tide was flowing, and the Sabbatarian impulses. It was in these years that Trollope placed the promotion of Dr. Proudie to the see of Barchester.

The position is well expressed in a note made by Henry Reeve in his journal on 21 February 1856 in which he sets down the memories of Lord Clarendon's mother and beside them his own reflections. "Mrs. Villiers", he records,[1] "said a little time before she died that no change had taken place in her time more remarkable than the change in the observance of the Sabbath. Queen Charlotte used to have drawing-rooms after church, and women went in full dress to the Chapel Royal. Everybody had dinners and some people played cards." This note was probably inspired by the incident that Greville relates on the same day:[2] "Last night the Evangelical and Sabbatarian interest had a great victory in the H. of C. routing those who endeavoured to effect the opening of the National Gallery and British Museum on Sunday.... It will be very well if we escape some of the more stringent measures against Sunday occupations and amusements with which Exeter Hall and the prevailing spirit threaten us." In May he noted further [3] that the "puritanical and Sabbatarian party" had prevented the playing of military bands in Kensington Gardens on a Sunday. There seems to be some ground for Reeve's comment: [4] "Now we are Judaised, and the whole idea of the Sabbath is brought back from Christian holiday to the Mosaic observances." This is an interesting sentence and especially that phrase "now we are Judaised".

[1] *Life and Correspondence of Henry Reeve,* i. p. 358.
[2] *The Greville Memoirs,* vii. p. 203.
[3] *ibid.,* vii. p. 228.
[4] Reeve, *op cit.,* i. p. 358.

Naturally, in a society which was in such a high degree political, the religious question was in the first place examined in its bearing upon policy. Thus Greville in his first entry dealing with the Mutiny labours this note. "G. Anson", he explains,[1] "writes to me from India that there is a strange feeling of discontent pervading the Indian Army from religious causes, and a suspicion that we are going to employ our irresistible power in forcing Christianity upon them." Two comments made in January 1858 [2] amplify the same idea: "Shaftesbury is stirring up all the fanaticism of the country.... The real meaning of the Exeter Hall clamour is that we should commence as soon as we can a crusade against the religions of the natives of India."

Parallel in many ways to Greville's standpoint is the old-fashioned Conservative position reflected in the first Earl of Lytton's biography of his father, which, though it was not written until 1883, will serve to plot a permanent trend in nineteenth-century English thought upon the true sphere of religion. "By taste and temperament," we are told,[3] "by training and family tradition, and by the force of political as well as religious instinct, he [Edward Bulwer-Lytton] was attached to the Established Church. He regarded it as a great bulwark against religious tyranny on the one hand, and religious anarchy on the other. He valued it also as a vehicle for the salutary association of religious teaching with intellectual refinement and learning. He appreciated the generally tolerant spirit of its divines." This is surely a fair analysis of a widely held belief. It came within Acton's purview in a way that Puritan literalism could never do; above all it put stress upon that ethical content for which he always craved, a bulwark against tyranny.

The final passages of the same statement are much in character. "Attaching, as he [Bulwer-Lytton] did at all times, great political importance to the maintenance of kindly relations between rich and poor, he believed that such relations are better promoted by the influence of our educated rural clergy than by the order of men who exercise the function of dissenting ministers in the lower ranks of Nonconformity."

With this we come once more to the curiously tight and class-

---

[1] *The Greville Memoirs*, vii. p. 285.
[2] *ibid.*, vii. pp. 329-30.
[3] *The Life, Letters and Literary Remains of Edward Bulwer Lord Lytton*, by the Earl of Lytton, ii. p. 15.

Marie Countess Granville.

bound concepts of the solitary oligarchy which had still retained its power. "Breakfasted", noted Henry Reeve, then editor of the *Edinburgh Review*,[1] "at Lord Stanhope's, with Macaulay, Gladstone and his wife, and Lord Stanley. A breakfast party of that size and that quality is certainly as perfect an occasion of table talk as ever existed, but it is exhausting from the brilliancy of the performance." Two further phrases from this time bite into the memory. "Show me", exclaimed Bulwer-Lytton,[2] "a class of gentlemen, an Aristocracy in short, and I will form a conjecture as to the duration of any free constitution; without that, between Crown, soldiers, traders and mobs, I am all at sea." The next sentence comes from the same figure, who was then secretary for the Colonies. "Democracy", he declared in 1859,[3] "is like the grave; it perpetually cries 'give, give', and, like the grave, it never returns what it has once taken."

At that time Monsieur Guizot, the veteran statesman of the reign of Louis-Philippe, was living in retirement at Val Richer in Normandy within very easy reach of English summer visitors. "We had no support", he wrote,[4] "but the middle classes; they alone were really with us in wishing to restore the younger branch of the Bourbons and free institutions." After a description of the French position in 1848 which need not detain us here, he closed the letter with a pregnant utterance: "I should not have had the least objection to extending the suffrage, if it had been likely to strengthen our cause; but it promised us nothing but danger or embarrassment." Throughout these quotations, and especially in this last, there sounds a single note, expediency. Against expediency John Acton's life was to be one long protest.

There is, however, another angle from which the period of the historian's entry into the House of Commons can be approached. A letter to Lord Canning written from Aldenham by Lord Granville in September 1859 gives a clear view of the impression that the young man created on his carefree and unselfconscious stepfather. "I came down here", he began,[5] "immediately after writing my last letter to you, and have consequently nothing to tell you.

---

[1] Reeve, *op cit.*, i. p. 350.
[2] Quoted in *Life of Edward Bulwer First Lord Lytton*, by the second Earl of Lytton, ii. p. 309 note.
[3] *ibid.*, ii. p. 314.
[4] Letter dated 4 November 1858, printed in Reeve, *op. cit.*, ii. p. 377.
[5] Letter dated 4 September 1859, printed in Fitzmaurice's *Life of the Second Earl Granville*, i. p. 358.

Johnny Acton, who is extremely agreeable, left us two or three days ago to go to Germany, with the intention of coming back to study in the middle of October. His library is becoming immense. He has remodelled the old library. He has entirely filled the hall; he has furnished his own room with books, and he has bagged a bedroom for the same purpose. I can hardly open a book without finding notes or marks of his.

"His new position as M.P. has done him much good. It has taken away from him the suspicion that people undervalued him, and he appears to appreciate some of the fine ladies being coquettish with him. Lowe (the fat keeper) gave me a day's shooting on his own preserves. I know no one more agreeable. I asked him whether Acton did not manage to kill the deer. 'Well, my lord, I don't think he ever takes aim' : adding with much feeling, 'I am sorry to say'."

This letter with all its implications seems to mark the end of the youthful phase. Acton's political life was just begun, and perhaps the closing act of his apprenticeship was that by which he was almost bear-led into the seat for Carlow. Henceforward, in company with Mr. Gladstone, he would give his life its own direction.

These last two chapters have concentrated on an effort to build up a certain picture of Church and State in England, those two great elements around which Acton's mind revolved and lingered. If many political phrases have been recorded, this is because he was so avid of every thought on politics. This was the air he breathed when he returned from Munich with his swift processes and that crowded mind and all his student seriousness. It is for this reason that for our purposes the other aspects of the time have less significance. Thus there has perhaps been insufficient emphasis upon the element of sport in this English life because John Acton took so little part in it. All the same, it is hardly possible to exaggerate the general social preoccupation with the series of race meetings, especially in Lord Granville's set. Old Greville in these years was always on the move, staying at Wynnstay for the Chester Races, going to Doncaster, going to Goodwood.

The Queen herself was not a factor in Lord Acton's life until much later; but in English social history these years were crucial. In 1861, when the Prince Consort died so suddenly, the widowed Queen would enter into a hierarchy of mourning. Custom was fixed and the Queen's mind would turn back to these happy years, to the Prince's view and the Prince's counsel. Material prosperity lay over all this period. John Acton's cares were not concerned with place or money. He would soon make that marriage which his world considered so appropriate. His bride was now eighteen and he had watched her growing, for she was his second cousin, Countess Maria-Anna-Ludomilla-Euphrosyne Arco-Valley. As well as his great gifts he had the virtues; it was this combination that endeared him to Mr. Gladstone.

A letter written on the occasion of Heine's death in 1856 may be inserted here, since it stands in contrast with all that way of life that Acton knew. Karl Marx is explaining to Friedrich Engels how Heine's wife Mathilde was waiting for her *maquereau* as her husband's coffin lay in their poor apartment. By way of example he quoted the poet's verses which tell how the man was hanged at six and buried at seven; "but at eight she drank red wine and laughed". This was the underworld of insecurity so many miles from Aldenham.

    Sie aber schon um achte
    Trank roten Wein und lachte.

PART III: THE FIRST ACHIEVEMENTS

CHAPTER I
ACTON AS A REVIEWER

THROUGH THOSE FIRST FIVE YEARS in which he sat in the House of Commons, and past his first contacts with Mr. Gladstone, there was always one shadow in Acton's background, the long uneasy history of the monthly and the quarterly which he successively conducted. It was his chief misfortune that the *Home and Foreign Review* was a religious organ. After all, John Acton was only twenty-eight when he undertook that weighty periodical which emerged as a quarterly on the cessation of the *Rambler*. It cannot have appeared to Provost Manning that there was a sufficient reason for this young man to set up as a leader of opinion. The history of the *Rambler* was rehearsed and not considered satisfactory.

The position was not made easier since there was present in John Acton's mind a sharp defensive outlook when confronted by the Hierarchy, and especially by their leader Cardinal Wiseman. It may be hazarded that in this early period of his life he made too much attempt to penetrate to where the opposition lay concealed, so bland and kindly. It does not seem to have occurred to him that there was anything strange in the place he occupied or the authority that he brought to bear. Since childhood he had been accustomed to his own massed knowledge, to his youth and to his loneliness. Without selfconsciousness he knew the buttress of his strong opinions. It was perhaps a pity that he should have tried to probe the elements opposed to him; he was so very early on his guard. This last quality stands out most strongly in a letter to Simpson written in May 1858:[1] "All this would lead us to the cave of Aeolus, and explain whence the winds come that blow at Brompton and York Place, in Maynooth and in Birmingham." Acton made only too much attempt through all these years to unravel each thread of opposition.

Nevertheless in this matter also the year 1862 is something of a watershed. With the emergence of the new quarterly a definite

[1] *Lord Acton and his Circle*, p. 16.

cleavage is apparent. In the fresh setting John Acton could give full play to his erudition. The earlier periodical had been taken over from others; its rather ragged form and the way in which the articles slipped over in instalments from one number to the next were legacies from another time. The books selected for review appear to have been chosen quite haphazard. Throughout there was an absence of that leisured scholarly concern which marked the *Home and Foreign*.

In some ways Acton was in a stronger position than he would ever be again until he came at last to the Cambridge chair. The Herrnsheim properties had come to him with his mother's death in 1860. He was in no sense dependent on Lord Granville; he had that full freedom which wealth and leisure bring. At the same time he had found his place in the House of Commons. It is true that he did not speak there, but he put in some work upon committees and the very fact of being an M.P. would give him standing. Viewed from the personal angle, there was now less tendency to have recourse to Döllinger and on the other hand he had worked free from that patron-client relation which coloured all his early years with Richard Simpson.

This being so, it may be asked why he did not launch out into that world of scholarship and general politics which might have given us the *English Historical Review* (linked to a survey of foreign policy) a quarter of a century before its time. The answer seems to be that Acton was not yet in touch with those who alone were qualified to aid in such an enterprise. Familiarity with the Universities lay in the future, and it is doubtful if the history of that day was ripe for this experiment.

Acton was antagonistic to certain historians, and notably to Froude and S. R. Gardiner. The professorships were held by men who would not be congenial. Three names of young historians spring to mind, but their world and Acton's was still far apart. They were linked with one another but not with him; the two first had been unsuccessful candidates for the Chichele professorship at Oxford. Edward Augustus Freeman was a man of means, a candidate for Parliament, living near Wells at Someleaze. The Reverend William Stubbs was vicar of Navestock, a Trinity living deep in Essex, and was also librarian at Lambeth. The Reverend John Richard Green was rector of Holy Trinity, Hoxton. James Bryce, who was to be a friend and warm admirer, was a young Fellow of Oriel sharing rooms in London with Kenelm Digby and eating dinners at Lincoln's Inn. Acton was not yet made free of the academic circle. There was, and would be for many years, an air of political ease about his life, the Athenaeum, Grillion's, The Club, The Breakfast Club.

There is a phrase in one of his letters [1] at this time in which he speaks of asking old George Finlay to act as a reviewer; the younger men he did not know. It is ironic that Sir John Acton should have been prevented from entering upon his true country by the presence of two obstacles. The weight and presentation of his German learning was at this date a barrier, as was his politico-social position, which was smooth and impregnable. How could he persuade men that he was not an amateur?

This is the position in the light of which the *Home and Foreign Review* can be examined. We have now reached the stage of Acton's positive achievements and of his matured thought. His contributions to the new quarterly fall into two distinct sections: the reviews of books and the articles on contemporary foreign politics. In the articles, which were a continuation of those printed in the *Rambler*, Acton considered the developments of current policy in the light of the great principles that he held to be immutable. He harnessed his doctrine to these surveys just as his erudition came to bear on each book notice. It is perhaps simplest to begin with the examination of the reviews, which bring together a body of learning altogether incomparable. After studying his work we can examine that great library which was his workshop.

In the quarterly some sixty or seventy pages were devoted in each number to notices of books. This was an entirely fresh departure, and it is seldom appreciated how much work Acton himself put into the new venture, for in fact it very well reflects his mind and thought. Thus in the *Home and Foreign Review* for January 1863 the historian himself contributed thirty-one reviews, most of them over a page in length. The remaining thirty-two books noticed were divided among nine reviewers. It is worth examining the notices in this number rather closely, for they indicate more clearly than the set pieces Acton's immense and catholic range of knowledge.

In considering his work at this time the clearest picture is presented if we begin with a discussion of Acton's attitude to those

---

[1] Cf. letter dated 20 January 1863, printed in *Lord Acton and his Circle*, p. 397.

current books which caused him to define his own approach to history. It was a textbook for use in schools in which Professor Wilhelm Putz dealt with the Middle Ages that gave the first occasion for comment. "Nothing", wrote Acton,[1] "causes more error and unfairness in men's view of history than the interest which is inspired by individual characters. The most absolute devotion to certain ideas and opinions is less dangerous, for they may be perfectly true, while no character is perfectly good." And then his mind would move to the teaching of history. "An indiscriminate admiration and jealousy of criticism marks the feeling of a sect and a party towards its leaders. Now this is a disposition strengthened in early life by the manner in which history is generally learnt. The interest of biography awakens a thirst for knowledge long before history can be understood; and we have our minds crowded with objects of hero-worship before we can understand the intricacies of character, and before we can appreciate the sanctity of a cause." Here we have the standpoint of the historian's maturity as he moved towards Gladstonian Liberalism. "In this way", the review continues,[2] "the imagination may be aroused and the memory stored; but the judgment is warped instead of being formed, and the historical faculty and habit, which is the most valuable fruit of historical study, and may survive even historical knowledge, is spoiled. . . . Something is wanted to counteract this effect and to educate minds to take an interest in impersonal history, in events so great as to conceal the actors, and in a process more regular and instructive than the vicissitudes of fortune and adventure."

It may be suggested that various factors had gone to form this judgment. There was the general approach to history which Döllinger favoured and the subjects about which his mind was exercised. There was again a certain sharp difficulty about Cardinal Wiseman's leadership. Praise which outstrips sincerity even by a little is liable to curdle, and in Acton's mind, very critical and not yet poised, the notion of the Cardinal had turned sour. He had a young man's resentment at being patronised. He would not go a step with those who gave to Cardinal Wiseman what he considered to be adulation; "no character is perfectly good". At the same time there is another element which seems to have entered into Acton's plea that history should be impersonal. He could not rival those great scenes that Lord Macaulay painted with their built-up

[1] *Home and Foreign Review*, ii. p. 219.   [2] *ibid.*, ii. p. 219.

Titian colours; he had nothing of the scenario contriver and it was difficult for him to value work so much at variance with his grey semi-tones. The deep contrasts that John Acton framed were in the world of thought and not in the sensibilities.

Macaulay in any case was much in his mind, for among the books upon his desk for notice in this number there was a volume on that historian's public life by Frederick Arnold. It was now three years since his sudden death, and we feel as the review proceeds that Acton was clearing his thought upon the subject of his predecessor. "Lord Macaulay", we are told,[1] "was by the character of his mind averse to the niceties of political speculation. His own views on all public questions were free from the exaggerations of absolute Liberalism; but he was unable to discern the speculative origins of these errors, or to ascertain the necessary application of first principles. Hence he is not always just in describing the doctrines of different parties, nor always consistent in his own relations towards them. For the party to which he belonged has a double pedigree, and traces its descent on the one hand through Fox, Sidney and Milton to the Roundheads, and on the other through Burke, Somers and Selden to the old English lawyers. Between these two families there was more matter for civil war than between Cromwell and King Charles." We are away on one of those surveys which through his mature life would always fascinate John Dalberg Acton.

"The divergence' he went on with that gathering assurance which was so much in character,[2] "between any two systems that result in arbitrary power cannot be so great as that between either of them and a system which subjects the sovereign in law; and there were more principles held in common by Falkland and Selden, when one was Secretary of State and the other the colleague of Pym, than by Fox and Burke when they were in office together."

"According to one theory," he explains,[3] "the King as well as the people was subject to the law, and both were bound to prevent or to avenge the breach of the constitution by the other. The men of the other school maintained the contrary principle of the right of every people to choose, and therefore to change, its own rulers. Not only a revolutionary but also an unpopular act on the part of the King might forfeit his crown. The legitimacy of resistance

---
[1] *Home and Foreign Review*, ii. p. 258.
[2] *ibid.*, ii. p. 258.   [3] *ibid.*, ii. p. 259.

was to be tested not by the laws of the land, but by the consent of the people; and the cause which justified rebellion was not the arbitrary violation of unquestioned rights, but opposition to an arbitrary caprice."

Acton here sets out his views, with that opposition to dynastic Legitimism which was so deep-seated, and then places his subject with great neatness. "Macaulay began life, we are told, as a Tory and was converted by distinguished friends. The Whiggism that prevailed at that time in the society to which he was soon introduced, was the Whiggism of Holland House,—the Foxite school of Lord Grey and Lord Russell. This is the school which he always acknowledged as his own. He would 'defend with unabated spirit the noble principles of Milton and Locke'. Again and again the utilitarian notion of government recurs in his writings, and the writer seems as sincere a believer in the sovereignty of the people as Sidney, or Paine, or Lord Russell. 'The Whig theory of government', he says 'is that kings exist for the people, and not the people for kings.' It is evident that he never mastered the real point at issue between the Whigs and all other parties; for in all these passages he overlooks the fundamental distinction between sovereignty and authority, and between rights in the sense of power and rights which imply duties. He was not acquainted with the political writings of Plato and Aristotle, in which he would have found more of the Whig doctrine than in the men he delights to quote. But he was guided throughout, and preserved from many errors to which his superficial treatment of principles would have exposed him, by an unswerving admiration for the writings of Burke."

Upon Acton's desk there also lay a *Manual of English Literature, Historical and Critical* just published by Thomas Arnold, the younger son of the Headmaster of Rugby and at this time a Catholic. We can see Acton's mind running on his former subject as he turned the pages. "Political truth", we read,[1] "is identified with Whiggism, and the other schools exhaust the various forms of error: the Cavalier Tories represented by Filmer; the philosophical Tories by Hobbes; the Puritan Whigs by Milton and Sidney; the philosophical Republicans by Harrington. This exclusion", continues Acton, "of Milton and Sidney from the ranks of the true Whigs shows that Mr. Arnold is fully conscious of the

[1] *Home and Foreign Review*, ii. p. 254.

difference between the highly constructive, positive and definite theory of Whiggism and the generalisations of an ordinary Liberalism. Speaking of Johnson he identifies Conservatism and Whiggism. 'His influence upon England was eminently conservative. . . . After his death Burke carried on the sort of conservative propaganda which he had initiated.' He is not quite true to himself when he places Locke in the line of the Whig tradition." Here we meet again that high doctrinal emphasis that Acton loved.

"Now the essence of Whiggism", he explains, "is the acknowledgment of the supremacy of the divine Will, or as we should say, if the term has not been degraded, of divine right over the will of man, whether represented by the sovereign or by the people, in the institutions of the past, or in speculative theories. It is the absolute exclusion from politics of the arbitrary element which asserts itself in Toryism by denying the claims of principle, and in Radicalism by rejecting the authority of fact. In this way Selden shared in the Great Rebellion, Somers justified the Revolution, and Burke defended the constitutional idea in the American and the revolutionary wars. But Locke derives civil society from a voluntary contract and thus introduces a principle as arbitrary in its nature, and as dangerous to right in its consequences, as the maxim that kings are above the law."

Acton's mind was now running upon systems and he turned to a volume which MM. Schauer and Chuquet had just edited containing the letters exchanged during 1792-97 between Kirchberger and Louis Claude de Saint-Martin. The latter had played a part in influencing Döllinger's thought,[1] for Baader had brought the young professor to a study of Saint-Martin's writings. The note which we now quote is interesting partly on account of the exhaustive examination of Saint-Martin's reading and also possibly as indicating a sympathy with those whom the orthodox Catholic world did not appreciate. "Frederick Schlegel," Acton explains,[2] "who described Saint-Martin as the greatest master of a spiritual philosophy in his time, anxiously vindicates him from the charges of a silent and passive opposition to the Church to which he belonged. . . . Kirchberger was a Swiss Protestant, who had studied deeply some of the mystics of the seventeenth century,—German writers whom Saint-Martin could not understand, and especially

---

[1] "Döllinger's Historical Work," pp. 376-7.
[2] *Home and Foreign Review*, ii. p. 241.

Madame Guyon whom he had not read. He [Saint-Martin] declared that up to the age of fifty he had known nothing of the writings of Jacob Böhme, and that when he became acquainted with him through the English translation of Law, he discovered his own system in a much more perfect form of development."

These extracts in particular throw light on Acton's determination always to *place*. Whether it was in the descent of ideas or in the wider field of literary or political inheritance, he would always bring his ranging information into a clearly marked schematic frame. It seems reasonable to claim that this was a new conception in English history.

Acton was always especially keen to trace the unexpected intellectual filiation. An example of this interest is provided in a generally unfavourable notice of a biography of Freiherr von Wessenberg. "Baron Wessenberg", so runs this extract dealing with the Josephist administrator of Constance,[1] "was educated for the priesthood at a time when the reforms of the Emperor Joseph, the writings of Febronius and the later Jansenists, and the influence of Rationalism and Illuminism, had conspired to reduce the religious spirit of the clergy to the lowest point of fervour. He studied under the celebrated Sailer." It is the next note [2] that contains the special point. "The man", we read, "to whom Wessenberg owed his promotion and with whom during many years he was most intimately connected was the Primate Dalberg. . . . Dalberg had grown up in the same school as his younger contemporary, and he had imbibed more deeply than any Catholic ecclesiastic the tone and ideas of the rising literature of Germany, which had its centre in his own neighbourhood at Weimar." Acton was particularly drawn to study lines of influence that intersect the national and religious boundaries. Thus he would map out the effect of Goethe's work, the Goethe of *Hermann und Dorothea*.

And then Acton's notice returned once more to those who were almost his own contemporaries. Here we find again that standard by which he would always judge political ideas. The Burkian concepts were not forgotten, and to them was fitted that new emphasis which nineteenth-century experience had brought the later writer. The leaven of his views on sovereignty was always working in John Acton's mind.

[1] *Home and Foreign Review*, ii. p. 248.
[2] *ibid.*, ii. p. 250.

In a series of studies Alfred von Reumont, who was for so long Prussian minister to the then grand ducal Court of Tuscany, devoted a volume to Cesare Balbo. Two sentences from this notice are worth quoting:[1] "In his hatred of revolution he [Balbo] seems to have invested legitimacy with some of the virtues of legality." And again: "The germ of his later opinions was laid by Chateaubriand's *Génie du Christianisme*—a work the success of which is a decisive measure of the intellectual condition of the period in which it was admired." This pleasant tartness of expression was characteristic of John Acton's mind.

Beyond these salient points the historian possessed two other qualities as a reviewer which these notices bring out. He liked to let the wide sweep of his thought play on the sources as they were calendared in the great collections or appeared in the archaeological transactions which were so marked a feature of mid-nineteenth-century writing on this subject. Thus in this number of the *Home and Foreign* he greeted the Calendar of Letters, Despatches and State Papers relating to the negotiations between England and Spain in the reign of Henry VII. Dr. Bergenroth, the editor, was placed in his setting:[2] "a scholar who has shown a very eminent capacity for the study of English history which already owes so much to his countrymen Lappenberg, Ranke, Phillips and Pauli". Then came the note on sources: "The archives of Simancas . . . are in good order and prodigiously rich."

To this same subject Acton would return as he surveyed the report made by Anton Gindely to the Imperial Academy at Vienna. "Dr. Gindely", we read,[3] "was at Simancas at the same time as Mr. Froude and Dr. Bergenroth, who is making researches on behalf of the English Government. For a hundred and fifty years, from the death of Isabella to the Peace of Utrecht, the archives of Simancas are the richest in Europe. . . . The most interesting documents they contain are the correspondence from Rome, and the report of the deliberations of the Council (of Castile). We can believe our author when he says that the publication of these reports will topple over the current views of history like a house of cards. But we have reason to expect that they will not present the government of Philip III and Philip IV in a more favourable light."

Here we find again that liking for a wide canvas and the striking

---

[1] *Home and Foreign Review*, ii. p. 272.
[2] *ibid.*, ii. p. 227.   [3] *ibid.*, ii. p. 235.

and far-reaching implication. In an earlier review dealing with Van Male's *Commentaries of Charles V*[1] Acton had made the observation which now follows: "The Emperor, though he writes with his crown on his head and his sceptre in his hand, is ever ready to acknowledge his own faults and mistakes; but not ready to be saddled with those of his counsellors and allies, on whom he always contrives to fasten their own burdens." Now, in welcoming a study written by Professor Wilhelm Roscher, "the most learned political economist on the Continent", and issued in the Transactions of the Saxon Academy, he drew attention [2] to a judgment on the general course of German history: "The war of the Peasants, whose rising and defeat in 1525 I [Roscher] consider the great turning-point which occasioned all the misery of the following centuries."

Acton would thus place in juxtaposition a view of Charles V and of the great Peasants' Rising in his reign. One is tempted to believe that at this time the historian's mind was deeply occupied with the main lines of German history. To the *Mémoires de Luynes* Acton was cold,[3] and to the French translation of Dom Ruinart's travels, published by the Archaeological Society of Lorraine, even colder.[4] One phrase in his review of Gindely [5] seems to forecast the future: "If we are not misinformed, a complete elucidation of the intrigues and mysterious end of Wallenstein will be the most interesting fruit of his labours." When he abandoned impersonal history it was to the weakness of political man that Acton turned.

A final thread running through these notices is that unstrained bibliographical erudition which we have come to expect from the historian. In this respect Acton's criticism of vol. xl. of the *Nouvelle Biographie Générale* is very damaging. "For instance," he writes,[6] "out of fifteen Lives of Pius V only three are named, and they are not the three best." And again: "Ritschl's edition of Plautus, and Sillig's edition of Pliny are not spoken of; in the article on Pliny a book is referred to which the writer cannot have seen, and he knows nothing of the important fragment of the *Natural History* discovered a few years ago by Mone." Acton was nothing if not categorical. His tone towards Hugo Laemmer's work is lofty: [7] "His only real defect as an editor of unpublished

---

[1] *Home and Foreign Review*, ii. p. 540.
[2] *ibid.*, ii. p. 234.   [3] Cf. *ibid.*, ii. p. 239.   [4] Cf. *ibid.*, ii. p. 238.
[5] *ibid.*, ii. p. 235.   [6] *ibid.*, ii. p. 275.   [7] *ibid.*, ii. p. 232.

manuscripts is an immaterial one. He does not always know what has been printed among the papers he finds. Thus he gives an account of Bellarmine's discourse to Clement VIII on the office of the Pope, without being aware that it is to be found in at least three printed and not uncommon books." In general, Acton is already somewhat severe towards contemporary ecclesiastics. In reviewing Dom Gams's first volume of *Die Kirchengeschichte von Spanien* he makes this comment:[1] "The fourth book is much more rich. The passions of the martyrs who suffered under Diocletian and Maximin carry us into the principal churches of Spain. The author . . . sums up all that others have said before him on these remarkable martyrdoms,—all the commentaries of the Bollandists, of Ruinart's *Acta Sincera*, Tillemont's *Mémoires Ecclésiastiques*." It is in this notice [2] that Acton cites the German Benedictine against the English Cardinal who always riled him: "Father Gams proves that all the so-called African words which the Cardinal [Wiseman] found in the pre-hieronymic version were in use in Rome and in the Roman provinces of Europe." It is surely remarkable that all this learning and these vivid judgments are found in Acton's book reviews in a single number of one quarterly.

The *English Historical Review* was only founded in 1886, but more than twenty years earlier Sir John Acton was ready and equipped to play his part in working up a technical quarterly. One final quotation [3] from these notices has an especial interest in view of the writer's lifelong ambition: "Raleigh's History of the World, though quite valueless in execution, is perhaps in design the greatest conceived by an historian." Acton sat in his library at Aldenham. There lay spread out before him the many stones with which he would plan and never build his great History of Liberty.

[1] *Home and Foreign Review*, ii. p. 210.
[2] *ibid.*, ii. p. 209.   [3] *ibid.*, ii. p. 254.

CHAPTER II

THE LIBRARY AT ALDENHAM

BEFORE CONSIDERING THE GREAT LIBRARY which Acton was now steadily building up it is worth examining the method of his work and the form in which he desired to present it. Above all, he loved to penetrate sequence of thought. Parallel to such an exploration he would track down the successive formulation of policy; it was almost a recreation to open one Chinese box after another. One example of the latter process will show how he would use his serried folios. It is to be found in his celebrated study of German schools of history. "Much", Acton wrote,[1] "has come lately to light touching the partition of Poland. Who proposed it? It was Catherine or Prince Henry in 1771, Bibikoff at Christmas 1770, Joseph II in July, Wolkonsky in March. It was Count Lynar in 1769, or a mightier person wearing his mask. Or it was Kaunitz in 1768, if not Choiseul in the same year. Panin started the idea in 1766, Czernitcheff or the electress of Saxony in 1763, Lord Stair in 1742, the King of Poland himself in 1732, or the crown prince of Prussia one year earlier."

It is in such sequences that the reader feels a lightness of touch which is seldom revealed in Acton's published letters or his more elaborate works. In the instance that we have quoted he seems to give himself up to the joy of the chase. This same quality is said to have appeared in that general social intercourse which, in his middle years especially, he so much valued. It may be suggested that it was the necessity for giving judgment which expelled his humour. As long as he was on the social level or merely following out a chain without regard to its content he could be light-hearted.

In regard to the method of Acton's work Mountstuart Grant Duff has preserved a note. "His usual rate of book-consumption", he explains, "was a German octavo *per diem*, and he had one of those faultless memories on which everything imprinted itself at once and remained for ever." Grant Duff, however, goes on to draw attention to the complete system of cross-references and notes that the historian built up although he did not seem to need

[1] "German Schools of History," *Essays on Modern History*, p. 366.

this apparatus. Macaulay had the prodigious memory of the nineteenth century, but in his case it was so to speak pure memory and took in every kind of list and fact; Acton's was a memory of erudition. Both men would seem to have strengthened this faculty by a continual exercise. Thus Acton never would allow the instrument to grow rusty; as his letters show, he kept it for ever at a stretch. Moving through the masses of his books, he probed and probed. He had a feeling for encyclopaedias.

No study is yet available of his great library, which now rests at Cambridge. It is simplest to pursue quite briefly a few lines of enquiry. A first impression gives rise to the belief that the books which were at Aldenham when John Acton was a boy were never brought into his historical library as we know it. Certainly they were sharply contrasted. Thus it would seem that the library which the historian's father found when he returned from Naples to his Shropshire seat was more extensive than might have been expected. A few items will indicate the scope. There was the Livy, in an Amsterdam edition of 1661, inscribed "W. Acton". Then Sir Whitmore had added a copy of the first part of Jeremy Taylor's *Antiquitatis Christianae*; a rather fine edition of a *Dictionnaire Royal, François-Anglois*, had been purchased for the young girl who would marry Sir Whitmore's heir. It is inscribed "This is the book of the Lady Anne Gray". The whole effect produced is of a true country-house library.

Against such a sober background stood the volumes brought from Italy. There was a *Specola Astronomica* bought when John Acton's father was fifteen. It is marked "Richard Acton, Londres, 21 April 1816". In the year after the historian was born some recent purchases, thirty-one volumes in all, were sent to be rebound. They included Botta's *History of Italy*, Lingard's *History of England* and the first part of the *Dictionnaire analytique d'Economie politique*. Lives of the saints were kept in Aldenham chapel, and Elizabeth Acton on her marriage had left behind the edition of La Fontaine's *Fables Choisies* which she had been given as a child. A list of books possessed by the Chevalier Acton at Naples includes the *Mémoires de Mirabeau*, Madame Campan's *Correspondance* and an Italian edition of Benvenuto Cellini. So much for the Acton background.

By contrast the books from Herrnsheim seem to have been incorporated into the historian's general store. At Cambridge there are neat little volumes, *Œuvres de Montesquieu, Œuvres de Machiavel.* Each carries a small plate "Bibliothèque de S. E. Mr. le Duc de Dalberg". It is worth noting that they seem all to be in French. Lady Granville's contributions included four volumes of S. Alfonso Liguori and a rather elaborate copy, "M. D. Granville, Aldenham 8 Sept. 1848", of the proceedings of the Court of Peers when taking evidence relating to the assassination of the Duchesse de Praslin.

With this beginning, and urged by Dr. Döllinger's example, John Acton set about his great collection. This has been described as a library from which an history of liberty might be constructed. It is, perhaps, more accurate to consider it as primarily devoted to the elucidation of law and custom, a purpose supported by a mass of biography and correspondence and by the existing encyclopaedias in all European languages.

The library is incomparably rich in regard to French local history, a richness reflected in the appreciation which Acton always showed for the work of the eighteenth-century French historians and chroniclers. It is equally extensive in matters both ecclesiastical and secular, a remote province such as Quercy being much better covered than most English counties. There are various reasons which may account for this tendency towards a French preponderance in the collection of an historian whose main interests, as well as his sympathies, lay elsewhere. In the first place, it is clear from the actual volumes that Acton employed three or four booksellers in Paris. They must have searched and brought many volumes to the notice of so persistent and valuable a customer. Another factor was that great interest which Acton inherited from Döllinger in the religious controversies of the seventeenth and eighteenth centuries whose literature was, in great measure, French. The *Bibliotheca Dollingeriana,* a printed catalogue issued in 1893, contains the titles of nearly twenty thousand volumes in the professor's collection. A very considerable number of these books were acquired by Dr. Döllinger in later life, but in each case the date of publication is provided. Under the combined heading "Molinismus, Jansenismus und Gallikanismus" there are listed some four hundred and fifty titles. This interest is well reflected in Lord Acton's library and constitutes another reason why this book-buying was so largely concentrated on Paris.

After the very remarkable French section, which includes

L

printed works of every school of thought and on most subjects, one of the pleasantest portions of the library is the collection of Italian and Spanish Church histories, ecclesiastical constitutions and synodal laws. The printing and the general production of the Italian volumes of the *settecento* is particularly lavish and attractive. Both these sections are close to the spine of Acton's interest, which was at one time so concentrated on the legislative framework of religion. Parallel with those sections is a series of small works dealing with the reigns of Pius VI and Pius VII or with that of Clement XIV. The latter turn upon the controversy relating to the suppression of the Jesuits. It is worth noting that Acton was at pains to collect every type of book and pamphlet relating to the history of the Society of Jesus.

Few private libraries have contained such a rare series of local Church histories, the synodal constitutions of the dioceses of Calahorra and Cuenca, the catalogue of the Bishops of Cordova, Martin de Ximena's *Annals of the Church of Jaen*. We must underline Acton's tendency to purchase the complete works of standard authors; the forty-two volumes of Antoine Arnauld provide a case in point. The books bought were not necessarily expensive. Seven volumes of Beaumarchais cost £1. Inevitably many books had come from the secularised religious houses of South Germany and Austria. The Benedictine monastery of St. Stephen at Würzburg provided several volumes, a work on Richelieu came from the Munich convent of the Augustinian Hermits, Greiderer's *Germania Franciscana* had belonged to the Franciscans at Bözen. In this connection a copy of *Florus Anglo-Bavaricus* can be traced to Benediktbeuren. The suppressed houses of the Society of Jesus provided their own quota. Laureto de Franchis on the controversy between Bishops and Regulars had made its way from the episcopal seminary at Culm. Some books, including Armellini's *Bibliotheca Cassinensis*, had belonged to the Electoral, later Royal Library at Munich. In general these are duplicates.

Books from French monastic sources were much more rare. There is a fine copy of Jean Besly's *Histoire des Comtes de Poictou* from the Benedictine abbey of Moyen Moutier in the diocese of St. Dié. The Carmelites of Turin had owned one volume, while the magnificent edition of the Consistorial Orations of Innocent XI from the Marucelli Library is, perhaps, the most distinctive of the few Italian works whose *provenance* can be traced. The ecclesiastical antiquities of the town of Brunswick come from the library of "Stadt Stralsund". In regard to the classical section of Lord Acton's library it should be remembered that it incorporates the books of Ernst Lasaulx purchased in 1862.

The standard English political histories and memoirs were all included. Acton was not contented with one copy where the subject interested him. There are no less than six variants of Platina's *De Vitis Pontificum*. The historian's copy of Wiseman's *Recollections of the Last Four Popes* in the edition of 1859 remains uncut. Inevitably the library has some of the limitations of the period in which it was assembled. Ranke's *History of Servia* has a prominent place in the section devoted to Eastern Europe. There were on the whole not many books of travel. The three volumes of Lord Valentia's journeys stand out in this respect.

The majority of the books were purchased between John Acton's coming of age in 1855 and his construction of the library some ten years later. This building was described by Henry Tedder, who was librarian at Aldenham in 1873, as a fine cruciform apartment lit by lantern lights and large french windows. An iron gallery, also shelved with books, ran round the walls. The restrained gilding and the moulded iron beadwork recalled the British Museum reading-room.

After this quick impression of the library, a note can be inserted of one aspect of the use that its possessor made of it. At the University Library at Cambridge there are preserved a large number of boxes each containing a card index of a special subject. They vary greatly in size and contents. One labelled "Burke" contains a series of notes of that statesman's sayings, without, however, giving any impression of Acton's view of these propositions. The box entitled "French character" contains only two cards. One of these carries this sentence: "When Burke says that a man has a right to the fruits of his labour, he gets behind the north wind, and accepts the Revolution." The box described as "Monacensia" gives a considerable number of brief details of Baader and the Munich school. The very interesting series entitled "Döllinger's table talk" belongs for the most part to a later period.

There is, however, another approach which throws light not so much on Acton's commentary as on the essentially solitary character of his great knowledge. Viewed from one angle, the notices which date from this period form a most valuable illustration of Acton's attitude towards his library and its use. A careful study will suggest those periods of western history in which he was most at ease as also those in which his erudition ground forward somewhat heavily. Across the period one can observe a very gradual shift away from ecclesiastical history, a change of emphasis which goes with the development of that flair for the distant paternity of ideas. It is this last point which one feels that Acton found at once so attractive and so rewarding.

Beyond the monumental character of Acton's erudition there was an adventurous element in his study. The quality of adventure in his nature was in fact poured out into research. Here he was, perhaps, the stronger because he had no companions. Nothing was less static than his history and his mind. This is possibly the reason for his impatience with Macaulay's high polemic. With all its merits the *History of England* was what Acton never cared for, a narrative without surprises. This note of adventure was Acton's own; it did not come from cautious Döllinger, still less from the Whig world. It was a quality which needed for its fruitful exercise a range of erudition such as Tocqueville did not possess. Fearless of criticism, and unafraid of seeming paradox, following where each track led him, Acton went forward quite alone over the wide tracts of his great knowledge.

There was always present an experience of the world which is most refreshing. Naturally this operates most easily where the subject-matter belongs to his own or to the preceding century. It is an approach devoid of all pretence, and has a realism that is singularly encouraging. Two passages in the *Home and Foreign Review* will bear this out. "Few modern periods of history", wrote Acton in a notice dealing with the eighteenth century in Austria,[1] "have been so little studied as the reign of Maria Theresa. The absence of great intellects or eminent characters in the Austrian state at that time has generally deterred historians. . . . Maria Theresa introduced a new system of government . . . which is a remarkable instance of the absolutism of the eighteenth century, aggravated rather than tempered by the sovereign's regard for morality, and, as in most cases where absolutism is not intensified by centralisation, neither oppressive nor unpopular in the more remote dependencies." The generalisation in the last clause lies spread out on the table neat and fair. Surely this is an epoch in modern history?

[1] *Home and Foreign Review*, 1863, p. 703.

CHAPTER III
THE EMERGENCE OF THE HISTORIAN

AT THE VERY BEGINNING of his association with the *Rambler* Acton laid down certain principles which governed his thought in these years before he reached maturity. "I have thought and read a good deal upon political subjects," he wrote to Simpson in February 1858,[1] "and have read a great lot of the famous writers, to try to find out a clear view which I could rely on in public life. I will endeavour to turn these studies to account and to pursue them farther in the service of our common undertaking.

"Now the first point about it is that I am very far from agreeing with any of the more famous Catholic writers, or with any of the political parties in England. But I think that there is a philosophy of politics to be derived from Catholicism on the one hand and from the principles of our constitution on the other—a system as remote from the absolutism of one set of Catholics as from the doctrinaire constitutionalism of another. I conceive it possible to appeal at once to the example and interest of the Church and to the true notion of the English constitution. I am not on this account an admirer either of all Catholic governments or of all constitutional governments, but I think that the true notion of a Christian State, and the true latent notion of the constitution coincide and complete each other. In this way it is possible to obtain a singular repose and confidence in judging political events and men both at home and abroad."

This is a clear and valuable expression of Acton's then standpoint. Already there is discernible the sweep of his measured thought and the neat dove-tailed synthesis. He was only twenty-four, and from the clumsy phrases there emerges a profound vitality of mind.

The concrete application of his principles is seen in his comment on the Roman Government which, after the unification of Italy in 1859, was buttressed upon an occupation by the troops of Napoleon III. "*Dolus*," he wrote on 20 August 1859,[2] "I know, *latet in*

---
[1] Letter to Richard Simpson dated 16 February 1858, printed in *Lord Acton and his Circle*, pp. 3-4.
[2] Letter to Richard Simpson, *ibid.*, pp. 79-80.

generalibus. The Roman system since the French occupation and reforms is no longer what it used and ought to be. This is their great difficulty, the discrepancy between their natural and their traditional policy and that which was imposed upon them after the Revolution. One cannot briefly explain the details of this. The absence of conscription is a remnant of the old system. Forced military service is, I should say, entirely incompatible with what I call the Catholic notion of the State. Yet that is the great source of trouble and contempt to the Roman Government of the present day, that they have no soldiers of their own. But if we go into detail, we shall find many things which date from the Napoleonic period, and apparently contradict my theory. All the plans of improvement are on the modern system and can only make the discrepancy greater. England for instance would have a constitution after our model. Well, it is impossible for the Pope to recognise the right of his Chamber to refuse supplies." In some respects this letter is a good example of the way in which the historian's mind now turned as he bent his attention to the theory of the constitution.

In some notes sent to Simpson in July 1860 Acton returns to this same subject. They were intended as a commentary on despatches written between 1854 and 1857 by the second Lord Lyons, who had at that time served as secretary to the Legation in Tuscany. "Lyons", began Acton,[1] "repeatedly recognises the good will of the Roman Government to make reforms, and also the determination of the people, of the discontented part of it, not to accept them. The opposition is not to definite grievances but to the Government altogether, not because it is bad but because it is clerical, and therefore not suited to the spirit of the times. Therefore the disaffection in the Papal States is, like that in Tuscany against the Grand Duke, not like the Sicilian movement, a protest against real, distinct wrongs. The Grand Duke attacked because he was an Austrian, the Pope because he is a priest.

"The readiness to concede very much on the one side, the resolution to be satisfied with nothing on the other, is the most striking result of these papers. Nothing can be conceived more criminal than the unwillingness to see reforms made which Lyons perceives among the malcontents, lest they should consolidate the Government.

[1] *Lord Acton and his Circle*, pp. 141-3.

"Secularisation will satisfy nobody, yet it is the great remedy dwelt upon by Lyons, because it is only a means, not an end. It is the means by which the opposition hope to get power to alter all things according to their own particular designs.

"These are eminently hostile to the Catholic system and not less to English ideas of liberty. See what Lyons enumerates as the peculiarities of the Code Napoleon. In fact, Italian liberalism for the most part is not far removed from the system which finds its most natural expression and development in French Imperialism. Conscription, for instance, he himself says, is advocated by the liberal party, as it has been imposed on the Italians by Garibaldi, though it was one of their great liberties under Naples. Now conscription is not tolerated by a people that understands and loves freedom. . . .

"Lyons sets up a memorial to the infamy of Italian liberals, which they do not all of them deserve. But the first aspirations of the moderate and conservative among them, like the Marchese Carlo Bevilacqua [1] of Bologna, whom Lyons often mentions with praise, are baffled by their unscrupulous allies, who strive to make things worse under the present system in order that they may become better only by the supremacy of their own system. Revolution is the great enemy of reform: it makes a wise and just reform impossible."

It is all very clearly laid out, that fear of the Revolution and the reverence for the Burkian principles. Two years earlier Acton had proposed to write an essay on Edmund Burke as a teacher for Catholics. "In the writings of his last years," he had declared, speaking of the period between 1792 and 1797, "whatever was Protestant or partial or revolutionary of 1688 in his political views disappeared, and what remained was a purely Catholic view of political principles and of history."

The ideas of Burke in his later phase, clamped to this somewhat forced interpretation, were accepted by the young Acton's judgment, which was calm and so inexorable. These notes can conclude the account of Acton's standpoint. He had a profound dislike for those forces which he termed the Revolution. The Garibaldian approach was the negation of his view of the Constitution. Yet above all he had a horror of expediency and compromise and easy shifts.

[1] In the Gasquet edition of these letters this name is printed Berilacqua, a mistake surely impossible to Acton, who knew so intimately the Palazzo Marescalchi at Bologna.

It is interesting to watch with what ease Acton could deal with general principles as opposed to the impatience which he displayed when confronted by the manipulations inseparable from the world of politics. "The Pope", Acton is found writing to Simpson in October 1861,[1] "was at the head of a great *immunitas*, like many other prelates. The similarity of the two things, Papal and episcopal independence, appears best under Charlemagne."

"Observe," he continues, "with reference to the analogy with all other freedom, that bishops etc. belong to particular nations, but the papacy (as representing unity and government of universal Church) is not national. So it is natural that its freedom should be secured in a different way. . . . The *right* of liberty is a *claim* not always admitted. The Church's right is denied by the pagan State, which denies distinction between religious and civil authority, and by the modern absolute State. The temporal sovereignty is the only plan we can devise to secure liberty for the Pope, but it is a means subsidiary; in fact it is a negative idea, the not being governed, not the right of governing, though governing is the only way to avoid being governed. It is stated as a basis, an acknowledgment of independence, not as a means of defence or a source of political power. The extent therefore is not essential."

A long letter written in the December of this same year sets out still more clearly the basis and the application of his ideas. "The revolution", Acton explains to Richard Simpson,[2] "teaches that a government may be subverted by its subjects, irrespective of its merits; while that theory lasts, the Pope can never be safe against his own subjects except by force. Even good government is no security in a revolutionary age—see the cases of Louis-Philippe, of Tuscany in '59. While the revolutionary principle has power, therefore, the papal sovereignty must depend on the aid of its neighbours against its subjects. But the revolutionary theory has also an international application and teaches that a State may be absorbed by its neighbours even if it has not attacked them, when a wish of the kind is presumed on the part of the people, or expressed by insurrection, or ascertained afterwards by vote, or even for rectification of physical boundaries, or for the sake of ethnological connection. Therefore (which is *a priori* necessarily obvious, as it cannot contradict itself), the same revolutionary

[1] Letter dated 9 October 1861, printed in *Lord Acton and his Circle*, pp. 212-13.
[2] Letter dated 20 December 1861, *ibid.*, pp. 248-51.

doctrine which puts governments at the mercy of the people prevents neighbours protecting it against the people. Therefore in an age where the duty of allegiance and even good government are no security, treaties, and international guarantees, and public law, can be no security."

And then Acton moved forward to an *excursus* on papal history. "In the Middle Ages", he continued, "the Popes preserved their liberty by their authority, by the faith of nations, not by their own political sovereignty; by the moderating influence they exercised over States, which was the keystone of the European system. Simultaneously almost with the final destruction of that system by the cessation of unity of faith and the nationalization of the Churches (Concordat of Francis I in 1516, Luther, 1517), the Popes obtained a material basis for the freedom which was losing its spiritual guarantee—through the formation of the sovereign dominion in central Italy by the Borgias, Julius II and the Medici. On this theory they straightway built up a new system to take the place of the old, and this was the system of the balance of power. The political support of the mediaeval system was the empire; this had now fallen, and as much of it as remained was an alarm to the Pope as an Italian sovereign. The army of Charles V took Rome, and the reluctance of the Holy See to assist the empire in the Thirty Years war was due to Italian politics.

The Popes undertook to maintain their spiritual freedom through their territorial independence by the opposite plan to that of the *republica Christiana* under pope and emperor, by *preventing* predominance of any one power, not by courting it. So they created the system of balance of power as the security of their temporal power, as of old the imperial supremacy had been the implement and safeguard of their spiritual predominance."

The connexion", continued Acton after giving some examples, "between the Temporal power and the balance is so clear that when Napoleon raised up a new universal empire, Pacca imagined that Temporal power would become superfluous. Now as balance of power is made up of alliances, it depends on the security of the alliance, that is, on the sanctity of treaties. The revolution, just now in the shape of Caesarism, naturally upset both. *Result :* in an age of revolution the temporal power has no security against rebellious subjects or ambitious neighbours. The spiritual liberty of the Church has no safety in a revolutionary State. No solution, therefore, is to be looked for till the revolution has exhausted itself." The remedy which Acton then suggested involved the seeking by the Pope of provisional safety in some State which was neither despotic nor revolutionary.

It was in the following month, while still at Aldenham, that Acton's thought upon the government of the Papal States took final shape. "In all secular States", he wrote to Simpson on 5 January 1862,[1] "the existence of great classes, nobles, clergy, etc., limit the Royal or State power. In Rome the great class of the clergy is the mere creature and instrument of the sovereign. In Protestant countries and those Catholic countries where Church property was seized [Austria, etc.] the monarch had to call into existence a new class for administration of Church property. This was the origin of the modern bureaucracy, that is of a class irresistible as against the people, merely an implement as against the Crown. This was the step by which loss of Church power or freedom led to absolutism. But in Rome the clergy is the bureaucracy.

"All liberty consists *in radice* in the preservation of an inner sphere exempt from State power. That reverence for conscience is the germ of all civil freedom, and the way in which Christianity served it. That is, liberty has grown out of the distinction (separation is a bad word) of Church and State." Here quite early in Acton's development one reaches phrases which were to embody his lifelong doctrine. "All liberty consists *in radice* in the preservation of an inner sphere exempt from State power."

It is the wellsprings of his thought which are so valuable, and the theories which issue from them in their clear integrity. Even in the 'sixties they attain to that high individualism which in time would mark his gathered writing. But at this early stage we also find such positive and garish statements as: "This was the origin of modern bureaucracy." In later years his wide experience in part concealed the incapacity to hesitate.

It may be noted that at twenty-seven he had very naturally not yet come to that meticulous and detailed accuracy which was to illumine his great range of knowledge. There is a boyish quality in the zest with which he puts in order the rather vague general information which surrounded the core of Richard Simpson's history. "But stick to this," he wrote to his friend in that winter

[1] *Lord Acton and his Circle*, pp. 253-4.

of 1861-2 at Aldenham which proved so fruitful,[1] "that in that society out of which modern European States have grown, the corporation was the first thing, the sovereign State the second. But the State gradually gained ground, and took into its hands what was common to all. The Church accomplished the first by borrowing from the Jews the notion of an anointed king, thus elevating by a divine sanction a power which the then society could not develop out of itself.

"Afterwards came Roman law (about the time of Frederic I), in which the State is the first thing; law comes downwards from the sovereign, does not grow upward from the people, as in the Teutonic State. This difference is not, however, in the original principle of the two legislations but in this that the Roman law which began to be studied was that of a finished State, of a mature, yea an old people, of an empire that had developed the most extremest absolutism on the ruins of the *Populus*."

This was the period of Acton's earlier attitude towards the Hapsburg Monarchy, which, like his views upon the Papal States, was characteristic of his years of transition. He could refer to his "Austracism" and he had not yet reached the full Gladstonian sympathies. This appears plainly in an undated letter written to Simpson, apparently in 1862.[2] "Now", declares Acton, "the only real political *noblesse* on the Continent is the Austrian. So the tendency of France and Piedmont, whose system is averse to real aristocracy, denying primogeniture and having no hereditary senators. Palmerston's strong and open feeling against Austria, and her great perplexities in the last three years, have strengthened this feeling far beyond what it was when they were in office. Lord Malmesbury still speaks the old language, not really Austrian. But his far abler under-secretary, Seymour Fitzgerald, shows this clearly enough. Now inasmuch as aristocracy is the framework of liberty, sincere friends of liberty must have the same sympathy with Austria. Accordingly the Conservative reaction in foreign affairs manifests itself most oddly, though quite logically, in Roebuck's speeches.

"Whereas moreover this is a class tendency, it is shared partly by the old Whigs—'the old gentlemen who go to bed at 11 o'clock', as Bernal Osborne defines that political connexion. These are the old stagers and fogies at Brookes', old Ellice, Sir F. Baring, Charles Greville and a coterie of Whigs."

[1] *Lord Acton and his Circle*, pp. 232-3. [2] *ibid.*, pp. 263-4.

In this letter, quoted at length, there were present two contrasted elements, the current political judgments of no great interest and the world view of an historian of ideas. In a continuation of his argument Acton set out the following statement in which he is describing his prime minister. "Then", he wrote, "there is the position of Palmerston, who is tolerated because he is cheerful and wounds no pride, and because he is old and excites no envy." There is a touch of Macaulay in this antithesis, and it is one evidence among many that, had his standards been less austere, the young Acton would have proved a facile writer.

But, beyond these *causeries* and the domestic turmoil of the *Rambler* and the *Home and Foreign*, one can trace the emergence of that broad and generalised discussion which issued in those letters from the quiet of Aldenham. There he sat, determined and unharried, building up with competence some great construction. "Then there is this great difference", he began in an account of the English and the Spanish Colonial systems,[1] "the English colonies in general were founded by the emigrants, for themselves, not by or for the State. They were in opposition to the home country, and were, more or less, originally sectarian—that is, exclusive in their religion, not members of a great, spreading religious organisation. In these two respects the Spaniards were entirely different. They went forth as emissaries of the State, labouring for it, helped and guided by it, and controlled, at the same time, by a Church which had very similar duties towards the natives as towards them. Thus they were under a double control which was wanting in North America.

"The English colonists could only ignore the natives because their political principles were liberal; there was no overwhelming State power over them. Where class rules over class, a strong supreme power is (1) *necessary*, because one must be watched and the other protected, as the duties of the State and its interests oblige it to preserve both alike; and (2) *possible*, because the dominion of one class over the other gives to the dominant class a compensation that makes it tolerant of oppression from above, whilst it partly deadens to the lower class the force of the State, partly represents it as a protection from the social domination (as in Russia). Thus absolute monarchy delights in *castes*, in the modulation of citizenship fixed and determined by blood (Creole, Octoroon

[1] *Lord Acton and his Circle*, pp. 278-9.

etc.), in *slavery*, which even when there is no monarchy tends to make the State absolute, and absolutism a blessing."

This was written in 1862. Such suppleness of expression as he attained to in his middle period had now been reached. There was a mathematical character in his work. The lines of his thought sprang from his mind, soaring and rigid.

CHAPTER IV

THE INFLUENCE OF MR. GLADSTONE

ALL THESE MATTERS were the preparation for that intimate friendship with Mr. Gladstone that Acton would now receive. It was not only a close friendship but also a willing and permanent submission to the singularly massive influence that radiated from Gladstone's hearth. This was a relationship prepared for in part by isolation but much more by a native and increasing affinity of mind. The initial obstacle to such a friendship was Acton's emphasis during the *Rambler* period on his position as a leader of more or less official Catholic thought. The whole range of character and outlook displayed at this time in the Catholic body and ranging as it did from Provost Manning to Dr. Newman was in the last analysis painful to Mr. Gladstone. At the same time, as long as she lived, Lady Granville had retained her son socially in the Whig grouping, which was in spirit so remote from Gladstone's circle.

Just as the Whig contacts were decreasing, so also was Acton's intercourse with his co-religionists. He no longer desired to give "political education" to his fellow-Catholics. The visits to York Place ceased in those years when Provost Manning came to dominate the ailing Cardinal. From the giving up of the *Rambler* these contacts languished. This was a tide in his affairs, and all the time he was moving towards a world in which neither the old Catholics nor the converts counted. At the same time Acton had little in common with young Englishmen of fashion and was as yet remote from the Universities. He was ready for some great impression.

There is extant a letter written by Mr. Gladstone, then Chancellor of the Exchequer and at the height of his powers, to acknowledge the receipt of an article on "The Political Causes of the American Revolution" by the young member for Carlow. It was dated from 11 Downing Street on 8 May 1861. "I have read", begins the statesman,[1] "your valuable and remarkable paper. Its principles of politics I embrace: its research and wealth of knowledge I admire: and its whole atmosphere, if I may so speak, is that which I desire to breathe. It is a truly English paper." And, as the friendship thus begun unfolded, Gladstone

[1] Letter printed in *Correspondence*, ed. J. N. Figgis and R. V. Laurence, p. 158.

came to admire the mind of the younger man increasingly. On his side Acton reached out towards a more concrete application of his Liberal principles. Apart from Lord Granville, all his political contacts in this country were made through Mr. Gladstone and his friends and centred on that statesman's progress. At Hawarden he had found his star.

Gradually his "Austracism" peeled away and he came to regard the Italian Government with peace and a measure of content. He became more *rangé* and his thought moved securely along party lines. Nor was Acton unaffected by the cold distaste with which his new mentor regarded the phenomenon of English Roman Catholics. For the first time he could see Oscott and Faber and York Place as these were viewed by Mr. Gladstone.

To the new friendship John Acton brought that fund of ordered information illumined by principle which was so grateful to the mind of the Chancellor of the Exchequer. It followed that it was in the strictly political circles rather than among the Oxford converts or the old Catholic squires that the young historian's thought would find response. *There* lay the understanding of his piled knowledge and of his carefully cast appreciations. Some passages from the leading articles in the *Rambler*, even as far back as 1859 and 1860, will make this clear.

"Baron Hübner", wrote Acton in his survey of events,[1] "was replaced as Minister of Police by Baron Thierry. Hübner was popular; and his retirement was caused by a difference with Baron Bruck, the Minister of Finance.... It was hitherto unusual for a difference of opinion among themselves to cause the retirement of any of the ministers, or even to become known to the public. Men of the most opposite opinions administered separate departments without discussion or communication with each other. The Ministry did not form a unity; and under Metternich and Buol there was no Council of Ministers. Each reported separately to the Emperor; each had their own organ, and could exercise a control, so far as his own office was concerned, over the official organ of the Government, the *Wiener Zeitung*. Schwarzenberg was president of the first Council of Ministers, of which he had the entire command. It was a natural result of the situation, in which the Empire had to be reconstructed by united councils; and the position of the young Emperor, who owed his throne to some of

[1] *Rambler*, new series, ii. pp. 262-3.

the new Ministers, made it easy for them to form themselves into a powerful and united body."

Yet from this detail Acton would launch out on that examination of the theory in which he rightly felt himself so much at home. "In the concession of the [Austrian] Concordat itself", he continued in this same article, "a principle was acknowledged and adopted by the Government which was susceptible of the widest application in every department of the State, and by which the Government was necessarily bound in respect of all other corporations.

"This is the principle of self-government; the notion that the power of the State is limited to certain definite functions; that all that lies beyond its immediate sphere is subject to different local authorities; and that in its own sphere the business of government is, for the most part, to issue orders, not to execute them;—in a word, that government, but not administration, is an attribute of sovereignty. The Concordat bestowed no privileges on the Catholic Church, but gave her freedom by acknowledging the limits to the authority of the State. For the Church in Austria was deprived of her freedom for the same reason that all other liberties were assailed,—in order to establish the absolute powers of the Emperor. The establishment of the Josephine absolutism weighed on civil and religious liberty alike." "Now the principle of self-government", he concludes,[1] "does not divide the power of the State, but limits its extent."

Before leaving the consideration of the Hapsburg realms, the situation in Hungary led Acton to put forth his theories in another field. It was still seven years before the *Ausgleich* and the formation of the Dual Monarchy, and the Constitution had been suspended since the time of Kossuth's Rising. "With ridiculous hypocrisy", began Acton,[2] "the nobles desiring to recover their ancient supremacy, and to reduce the peasants once more to the level of serfs, appeal to the principle of national independence. In every way the restoration of the Hungarian Constitution would be a retrograde step in civilisation; and this character is most visibly shown in the appeal to the theory of nationalities. It is one principal result of the progress of mankind that physical causes are gradually overcome by moral motives; that history is influenced more and more by mind, and is less dependent, as time goes on, on matter.

---

[1] *Rambler*, new series, ii. p. 265. [2] *ibid.*, ii. p. 269.

The effect of this law on States is that their formation is determined by political reasons, not by natural influences. The lowest influence is that of the earth, of geographical causes, as in the case of Egypt. The influence of blood is higher; but, where that alone prevails, a State can hardly be a political body, but it can exist only by a political cause. A State exhibits political maturity when it represents a political unity, the predominance of some political purpose or system over national and physical barriers."

A very similar point of view finds its expression in Acton's attitude towards the Liberation of the Serfs in Russia which the Tsar Alexander II was pressing forward. "All nations", he wrote in the *Rambler*,[1] "have passed through the stage of slavery on their way to civilisation, and the process now going on in Russia has occurred, under many varieties of circumstances, everywhere else. For liberty is a plant of slow growth and late maturity, and belongs only to nations that have reached their prime and have not approached decay. An institution, so universal and apparently inevitable, cannot be treated as simply an evil or a wrong. Helplessness or childishness is contemptible only in a grown-up man, and slavery is criminal only when it is artificial.

"The notion of personal rights and freedom", he continues, "develops itself even with the progress of civilisation. In the lower stages the individual is very little considered; he acts only in a collective capacity; the State deals with groups and corporations. For, as the State performs very few of the services required for the existence of society, society is then obliged to provide its own organs for the purpose, in its orders, communities, corporations and other natural associations. The supreme power is designed to do little more than to preserve the nation from external danger, consequently the sovereign is usually only the most powerful member of the community; as the most suited to perform that function; otherwise he has little authority, and does not interfere in internal concerns.

"It is hard to say whether the local communities are part of the State, or whether the State is an alliance of separate communities. But as it has little power, and little to perform, the corporations which supply its place naturally possess great authority over individuals. This is the character of mediaeval society."

From this *excursus* the historian brought his thought back to

[1] *Rambler*, new series, iii. pp. 281-3.

a consideration of the Russian situation. "The only probable result of the undertaking as it now stands", concluded Acton in regard to the Tsar's measure, "will be an enormous increase of the aggressive power of Russia, without any security at home against tyranny or any restraint upon ambition."

Ranging over the European problem he came to Naples, and his attitude to this question was of an especial interest at the time when he was moving into close association with that Gladstonian world which had been always so much concerned at the Two Sicilies. "The oppressive character of the [Neapolitan] system", declared Acton, "was felt chiefly by the educated classes—the nobility and the Church. The former were the principal enemies of the Government; the latter its principal victims. There is no more perfect test of the character of a Government than its position towards the Church. A Protestant State may exclude her, or persecute her on religious grounds; but the modifications of her relation to a Catholic State depend entirely upon political considerations.

"Politically it is no reproach to a Catholic country that it refuses to give perfect equality to a Protestant minority, or to a Protestant country that it denies equal rights to a minority of Catholics. Civil disabilities on religious grounds are not only consistent with the true notion of government, but essential to it, provided they are founded on a great inequality of numbers. In Spain, for instance, and in Sweden certain restrictions have been founded on reasons both of religious feeling and of political expediency. . . .

"In a country wholly Catholic or wholly Protestant religious intolerance is not necessarily incompatible with civil liberty. Where different religions subsist together in one State, religious intolerance implies political tyranny. But when in a purely Catholic country the Church is deprived of her independence, it is the surest and strongest sign that can be given of a false theory of government. For the only system which is absolutely contrary to the freedom of the Church, and necessarily at war with her, is the system of arbitrary power. The freedom of the Church in Catholic States can only be asserted in conjunction with other liberties, and is obnoxious only to a policy which endangers in like manner every species of political independence."

"Besides," concluded Acton, "the sufferings endured from

heretics and infidels have not the corrupting influence which is exercised by the jealous protection of Catholic sovereigns. This poisonous effect of Catholic despotism has nowhere been more fatal to religion than at Naples." The whole statement of this point of view is interesting. The effect produced upon the minds of Cardinal Antonelli and Mr. Gladstone by a careful perusal of these statements would necessarily be most divergent. This manifesto on the realm of the Two Sicilies is in a sense a presage of the future.

More characteristic of the permanent element in his outlook to which the historian had now come was a study of Nationality contributed to the *Home and Foreign Review* in July 1862. "Liberty", begins this statement,[1] "provokes diversity, and diversity preserves liberty by supplying the means of organisation. All those portions of law which govern the relations of men with each other, and regulate social life, are the varying results of national custom, and the creation of private society. In these things, therefore, the several nations will differ from each other; for they themselves have produced them, and they do not owe them to the State which rules them all. This diversity in the same State is a firm barrier against the intrusion of the Government, beyond the political sphere which is common to all, into the social department which escapes legislation and is ruled by spontaneous laws. This sort of interference is characteristic of an absolute Government, and is sure to provoke a reaction, and finally a remedy. That intolerance of social freedom which is natural to absolutism, is sure to find a corrective in the national diversities, which no other force could so effectively provide.

"The co-existence of several nations under the same State is a test, as well as the best security, of its freedom. It is also one of the chief instruments of civilisation; and, as such, it is in the natural and providential order, and indicates a state of greater advancement than the national unity which is the ideal of modern Liberalism." Each detail of this standpoint has its interest, the survival of certain prejudices of the author's youth, and those smooth antitheses of reaction and remedy.

"The greatest adversary of the rights of nationality", the article continues,[2] "is the modern theory of the nationality. By making

[1] *Home and Foreign Review*, i. p. 17.
[2] *ibid.*, i. pp. 17-23.

the State and the nation commensurate with each other in theory, it reduces practically to a subject condition all other nationalities that may be within the boundary. It cannot admit them to an equality with the ruling nation which constitutes the State because the State would then cease to be national, which would be a contradiction of the principle of its existence. According, therefore, to the degree of humanity and civilisation in that dominant body which claims all the rights of the community, the inferior races are eliminated, or reduced to servitude, or outlawed, or put in a condition of independence.

If we take the establishment of liberty for the realisation of moral duties to be the end of civil society, we must conclude that those States are substantially the most perfect which, like the British and Austrian empires, include various distinct nationalities without oppressing them."

Two other statements in this article are in their way illuminating. "The theory of nationality therefore", writes the historian,[1] "is a retrograde step in history. It is the most advanced form of the Revolution, and must retain its power to the end of the revolutionary period, of which it announces the approach." And again: "Although the theory of nationality is more absurd and more criminal than the theory of socialism, it has an important mission in the world, and marks the final conflict, and therefore the end, of two forces which are the worst enemies of civil freedom;—the absolute monarchy and the revolution." Here is that theory of the Revolution which was to mark Acton's writing throughout his middle period.

[1] *Home and Foreign Review*, ii. p. 25.

CHAPTER V
CRYSTALLISATION

IF A POINT IN ACTON'S DEVELOPMENT must be chosen at which the reader will first meet those accents and that matured outlook which the historian would retain, there is much to be said for fixing the year 1862. This date has already been stressed as a turning-point. Men could at last detect the political content of coming decades. The American Civil war was under way and the Italian situation had achieved a very uneasy equilibrium with Florence as the capital of the new kingdom and French troops in garrison at Rome. Bismarck became head of the Prussian Government in September of this year. The materials on which Acton would form a judgment in contemporary affairs had for the most part already come to hand. This was the setting in which all his life would pass, and the scene would only be gravely modified in a single particular, by the disappearance of Napoleon III and the emergence of the Third Republic. To a man with Acton's knowledge of the field of German politics the appointment of Otto von Bismarck-Schönhausen would seem a clear portent.

Sir John Acton was now approaching thirty, and we can mark out the system of his somewhat rigid preferences. By this time that dislike of the French scene, which was purely personal to him, was balanced by a political distaste for Prussia which was apparently hereditary, the whole dominated by a feeling for Germanic values which was to prove the most persistent of the historian's sympathies.

Acton's marriage would link him yet more closely to Bavaria, but already the general outlines of the late nineteenth-century polity were taking shape; that particular type of mercantile utilitarian privilege with a military flavour and an heraldic setting which was to mark the German, Austrian and Russian Courts as they sat somewhat uneasily to their bureaucratic administrations. The sovereigns of that era were long-lived and so, often, were their great ministers. Queen Victoria and the Emperor William I and Francis Joseph were all exceptional in their length of life, as were their ministers of the *Risorgimento* period, Gladstone, Bismarck and Beust. Even in Russia the changes lay far ahead. It would be almost twenty years before the Tsar Alexander would meet his death beside the Catherine Canal, and Prince Gortchakoff was to survive him. Allowing always for the rise of Prussia, this was politically a static time.

In Acton's youth the political scene upon the Continent had altered swiftly; but he would soon reach to a period of quietude and of exhaustion after effort in which a delusive stability would allow the mind to concentrate on general problems. His matured thought was in fact given to the physically contented generations of that high *bourgeois* life in the opulent western world which drew its financial life-blood from the easy streams of capital.

It is well here to insist on the singularly unchanging character of Acton's outlook. To a mind bent upon the principles which govern politics there was but little to rouse interest in the men who were the instruments of nineteenth-century policy. This has its bearing on a point which his editors, Mr. Figgis and Mr. Laurence, notice. "Acton's political conscience", they write,[1] "was also very broad on the side technically called moral. No one had higher ideals of purity. Yet he had little desire to pry into the private morality of kings or politicians. It was by the presence or absence of *political* principles that he judged them." It was only the public, and within that division only the political, acts which the historian felt called upon to subject to examination. It is a consequence that the men in public life whom he reviews are presented to us as two-dimensional like figures cast upon a screen. This method produced two results: the judgments as such hardly "date" and the principles are thrown into relief. A survey of the comments on Lord Acton's general standpoint made in 1907 by the editors of his collected writings will bear on the first point.

The introduction which Mr. Figgis and Mr. Laurence contributed to their edition of *The History of Freedom and other Essays* has admirably withstood the test of time. While the value of certain aspects of Acton's thought has become more apparent in the last forty years, their statement very well conveys the historian's inexorable pulsating energy. "His scholarship", so runs a memorable phrase,[2] "was to him as practical as his politics, and his politics as ethical as his faith." Again, they note [3] the absence of *chiaroscuro*

---

[1] *Essays on Liberty*, introduction, p. xxxii.
[2] *ibid.*, p. xviii.
[3] *ibid.*, p. xvi.

in his imagination or of half-tones in his vein of thought. "There was no haze in his mind. He judges, but does not paint pictures."

Another judgment bears on this point:[1] "He felt the danger that lurks in the charm of literary beauty and style, for he had both as a writer and a reader a strong taste for rhetoric, and he knew how young minds are apt to be enchained rather by the persuasive spell of the manner than by the living thought beneath it. He was interested in knowledge—that it might diminish prejudice and break down barriers. To a world in which the very bases of civilisation seemed to be dissolving he preached the need of directing ideals."

Their comment on the Acton-Gladstone relationship needs citing here:[2] "What Acton most admired was what many condemned. It was because he was not like Lord Palmerston, because Bismarck disliked him, because he gave back the Transvaal to the Boers, and tried to restore Ireland to its people, because his love of liberty never weaned him from loyalty to the Crown, and his politics were part of his religion, that Acton used of Gladstone language rarely used, and still more rarely applicable, to any statesman." In a very true sense, "it was not his [the Prime Minister's] successes so much as his failures that attracted Acton".

It followed that the historian moved in the wake of Gladstone's social programme:[3] "While he felt the dangers of Rousseau's doctrine of equality, declaring that in the end it would be destructive alike of liberty and religion, he was yet strongly imbued with the need of reconciling some of the socialist's ideals with the regard due to the principles which he respected. He was anxious to promote the study of Roscher and the historical economists, and he seems to have thought that by their means some solution of the great economic evils of the modern world might be found, which should avoid injustice either to the capitalist or the wage-earner."

Yet with this there went the views that Acton absorbed from his own environment:[4] "Provided that freedom was left to men to do their duty, he was not greatly careful of mere rights. He had no belief in the natural equality of men, and no dislike of the subordination of classes on the score of birth." A close examination of this description will indicate that conservative approach to the more radical aspects of social progress which was a characteristic

---

[1] *Essays on Liberty*, introduction, p. xxii.
[2] *ibid.*, p. xxiii.
[3] *ibid.*, p. xxix.
[4] *ibid.*, p. xxxi.

of the old high English Whigs. The sense of duty and guardianship was very strong, and it was a mark of the inner Whig circle that its members regarded themselves as natural trustees. A broadening oligarchy, strengthened by fresh recruitment, had all the attributes which Acton sought. "He was not greatly careful of mere rights."

At the same time there was already present in the historian's outlook that intense distaste for the wielder of power which was to leave so deep a mark on the output of his maturity. The scepticism with which he approached the political world owed little to any English influence. Here the aristocratic Continental *milieu*, with which Acton had so many ties, brought him a *realism* which was very far removed from the insular wisdom which marked Macaulay and the naïve enthusiasms of Carlyle. And it was just during these years that the latter writer was completing his lyrical and gusty *Frederick the Great*, the first volume being published in 1858. No views of Frederick II of Prussia were likely to be more diametrically opposed than those held by Acton and Carlyle.

There is reason to suppose that the historian had already come to those judgments on his senior that he was to formulate much later in a letter to Mrs. Drew. "Excepting Froude," he wrote in 1881,[1] "I think him the most detestable of historians. The doctrine of heroes, the doctrine that will is above the law, comes next in atrocity to the doctrine that the flag covers the goods, that the cause justifies its agents, which is what Froude lives for. Carlyle's robust mental independence is not the same as originality. The Germans love him because he is an echo of their own classic age. He lived on the thought of Germany when it was not at its best, between Herder and Richter, before the age of discipline and science."

Acton in time would carry very far his dislike of the "doctrine of heroes". From the outset this view affected his whole approach to those who had inherited or would attain to power. There is, however, no doubt that it was deepened by the inflexible character with which his ideas were marked after he had sustained the influence of Mr. Gladstone. The actual expression of this view is found comparatively late. In the postscript of a letter to Mandell Creighton written in 1887 we find that experienced and serene pessimism to which Lord Acton was led by his inflexibility. "No public char-

[1] *Letters of Lord Acton to Mary Gladstone*, p. 70.

acter", he wrote on this occasion,[1] "has ever stood the revelation of private utterances and correspondence. . . . Be prepared to find that the best gives way under closer scrutiny."

This was the fruit of his accumulated knowledge of the political rulers of his age. We meet traces of this standpoint very early, and it was characteristic of that tranquil generation that decade by decade Acton could lay down those undeviating steel tracks of his system along which his thought went forward so remorselessly. "The inflexible authority of the moral code", he explained to Creighton,[2] "is to me the secret of the authority, the dignity, the utility of History. Progress in ethics means a constant turning of white into black, and burning what one has adored. . . ." One feels that the historian savoured such phrases. "Historic responsibility has to make up for the want of legal responsibility. Power tends to corrupt, and absolute power corrupts absolutely. Great men are almost always bad men, even when they exercise influence and not authority, still more when you superadd the tendency or the certainty of corruption by authority."

These sentences, among the most familiar from all his writings, indicate the final form in which Lord Acton wore his prophet's mantle. It was a standpoint which was to be deeply grateful to all who came beneath the spell of Mr. Gladstone's processes. From one angle the point of view to which he reached can be considered as a rather unexpected consequence of Acton's early fixed determination to know and judge the history of his day. At the same time it is worth noting that a certain scepticism, which was never far from his austere conclusions, assisted the historian in his approaches to the contemporary scene. "Both parties", he was to declare in speaking of the causes of the Franco-Prussian conflict, "laboured to bring about war—the one after the conclusion of alliances, the other before."

Nevertheless it is not Acton's judgment but his analysis which seems to have imperishable value. He was singularly fitted to enter into the minds of constitutional theorists of the eighteenth and early nineteenth centuries. He perceived, with a thought which was both dry and very clear, the consequences of each different theory. He was, as we have noted, an opponent of those dogmas of racialism which were to grow to such proportions. As a

[1] *Essays on Modern History*, p. 506.
[2] *ibid.*, p. 505.

member of a class which was both privileged and cosmopolitan he scented them very early with all their consequences. Working so much in solitude and for long hours, he had an uncanny power of tracking down and isolating the component elements of current thought on politics. He never showed more prescience than in his constant opposition to the overriding State.

It was, indeed, one of Acton's great services that he gave such minute scrutiny to the State, its operations and the restrictions which it imposed. By his whole training he was uniquely fitted both to examine and demolish its extreme pretensions. It was here that there came into play that keen unfaltering integrity. All his coldness and that strict criticism, which was never diluted by expediency, was brought to bear upon the Moloch-State which man had created to the detriment of his own ordered liberty. It is here that we see the value of his cool distaste for the operation of men in power.

It was natural, given his period, that it should be the great bureaucrats, and not the myriads of little *fonctionnaires*, that awoke in him the sense of peril. It was a merit that he conceived the generous life without reference to class boundaries. His imagination, which so seldom reposed on the concrete example, enabled him to form a concept of that abstract liberty which all men need. He had a wide, if rather bookish, sense of freedom. There was in his whole idea of liberty a largeness and a wide untrammelled franchise. He would set no limit to man's choice except that he believed that all might come in time to live within an ethic of proved value. So far as one can enter into Lord Acton's mind it would appear that he conceived of a world whose members would be guided by conscience, free of every realm of knowledge, prizing tolerance and ideals of liberty. It can only be said that this was a lullaby, *la plus douce cantilène*, of a civilisation which was very old, generous as wine, experienced, culturally rich. Sharp as is the divergence, the mind is led back from that milk-heavy nineteenth century to the Rome of the Antonines. In each case a range of thought poured out in generous measure while the bases of society waited to be transformed.

At the end of their introduction Mr. Figgis and Mr. Laurence print a document found among Lord Acton's papers. They state that it records in an imaginative form four ideals that he set before him. "I could see indeed, at the same time," so runs this exercise in describing an imaginary figure Adrian,[1] "that his conduct was remarkably methodical, and was guided at every step by an inexhaustible provision of maxims. He had meditated on every contingency in life, and was prepared with rules and precepts, which he never disobeyed. But I doubted whether all this was not artificial,—a contrivance to satisfy the pride of intellect and establish a cold superiority. In time I discovered that it was the perfection of a developed character. He had disciplined his soul with such wisdom and energy as to make it the obedient and spontaneous instrument of God's will, and he moved in an orbit of thoughts beyond our reach." It is necessary in thinking back to Acton's earlier years to disengage the mind from the *Gaston Latour* evocations with which this style oppresses us. He was very far, in fact, from Walter Pater. "He could not", so the character concludes, "easily enter into their [other men's] motives when they were mixed, and finding them generally mixed, he avoided contention by holding much aloof. Being quite sincere, he was quite impartial, and pleaded with equal zeal for what seemed true, whether it was on one side or on the other. He would have felt dishonest if he had unduly favoured people of his own country, his own religion, or his own party, or if he had entertained the shadow of a prejudice against those who were against them, and when he was asked why he did not try to clear himself from misrepresentations, he said that he was silent both from humility and pride. At last I understood what we had disliked in him was his virtue itself."

This links up with sentences written long before to Richard Simpson:[2] "You want things to be brought to bear, to have an effect. I think our studies ought to be all but purposeless. They want to be pursued with chastity like mathematics. This, at least, is my profession of faith."

Acton's devotion to historical studies was singularly wholehearted. His channelled strength of purpose could co-exist with an easy if rather measured social life. His family grouped around him, and beyond them stretched the very catholic gathering of his friends. Yet in spite of these many ties he had a certain loneliness of spirit, an isolation which would grow sharper in his middle life. It is clear that it was in solitude that he came to his stern judg-

---

[1] *Essays on Liberty*, introduction, p. xxxix.
[2] *Lord Acton and his Circle*, p. 57.

ments; these were not tempered by submission to another mind. Acton was generous and rather wonderfully freed from self-interest. Already his great erudition was available to those who came to draw at that deep well. Viewing the whole number of the historians, it may well be maintained that he gave the perfect example of a selfless scholarship. His thought on politics possessed a deep essential wisdom. His mind would range continuously across the wide landscapes of history. It has been indicated that his judgments were affected by reactions which were almost instinctive. He lacked the gift of equanimity.

The abiding memory that Acton leaves with us is that of an analysis which is singularly penetrating and a power of correlation in regard to lines of thought that is surely quite unequalled. Above these stood the ark of Acton's covenant, a dominant integrity, high, dedicated, cutting as a sword, inviolable and pure.

INDEX

Abel, Karl, 64
Aberdeen, 141
Abingdon, Montagu seventh Earl of, 36
Acton, John Emerich Edward Dalberg first Lord, *passim*
  Marie (Arco-Valley), Lady, his wife, 20-8, 46-51, 147
  Sir Ferdinand Richard Edward, his father, 21-2, 27-8
  Marie (de Dalberg) later Countess Granville, his mother, 20, 26-9
  Sir John Francis, his grandfather, 11-19
  Marianne (Acton), Lady, his grandmother, 18, 28
  Charles Edward Januarius, Cardinal, his uncle, 19, 28-9, 34, 37, 73
  Elizabeth, his aunt, *see* Throckmorton, Lady
  Sir Richard, fifth Baronet, 14-15
  Sir Whitmore, fourth Baronet, 17, 160
Acton Burnell, 38, 106
Ailesbury, Charles first Marquess of, 81
Albemarle, William seventh Earl of, 36
Albert Prince Consort, 76, 100, 146-7
Alcester, 43
Aldenham, *passim*
Alderbury, 14
Alexander II, Tsar of Russia, 79-82
Alison, Sir Archibald, 109
Alopeus, Alexandrine d', 24, 36
Alton Towers, 40
Anderdon, William Henry, 125
Angers, 30
Anson, George, 144
Antonelli, Giacomo, Cardinal, 143
Antonius or Antonio, Nicholas, 74
Arco-Valley, Count Johann Maximilian von, 28, 133
  Anna (Marescalchi), Countess, his wife, 28
  Marie, his daughter, *see* Acton, Lady
Armellini, Mariano, 162
Arnold, Frederick, 152
Arnold, Thomas, 153
Arundell of Wardour, Mary Lady, 33, 43
  John Francis twelfth Lord, 123

Aschaffenburg, 8
Ashburnham, Bertram fifth Earl of, 36
Astley Abbots, 14
Augier, Emile, 97
Augustinus or Augustin, Antonio, 75
Auldjo, John, 21
Austerlitz, 19

Baader, Frank Xavier von, 65
Baddeley, Edward, 115
Baden, 27
Baggs, Charles Michael, 34
Baines, Peter Augustine, 34
Balbo, Cesare, 156
Ballerini, Pietro, 74
Balzac, Honoré de, 26
Baring, Sir Francis, 171
Baronius, Caesar, Cardinal, 73
Beauharnais, Maximilien de, 82
Beaumarchais, Pierre-Augustin Caron de, 162
Bellarmine, Robert, Cardinal, 158
Belling, Sir Richard, 179
Benediktbeuren, 162
Bennettis or Beneti, Cyprianus de, 74
Béranger, Pierre-Jean de, 65
Berardi, Carlo Sebastiano, 74
Berlin, 3, 126
Berners, John Lord, 108
Berry, Duchesse de, 23
Besly, Jean, 162
Beuron, 61
Bevilacqua, Carlo, 167
Bianchi, Giovanni Antonio, 74
Bibikoff, Alexander Ilitch, 159
Birmingham, 3, 142
  Oratory, 115
  Snow Hill, 134
Bismarck-Schönhausen, Prince Otto von, 70, 78
Blakeway, John Brickdale, 106
Blenheim, 3
Blennerhassett, Charlotte Lady, 110
Blondel, Pierre-Jacques, 74
Blundell, Charles, 124
Böhme, Jacob, 155
Boisserée, Sulpiz, 63

Bolingbroke, Henry Viscount, 138-9
Bologna, 167
Bonald, Louis de, 83
Bordeaux, Duc de, 24
Borgia, Girolamo, 74
Bossuet, Jacques-Bénigne, 58, 68
Boulton, Mr., 15
Bozen, 103
Bramston, James Yorke, 33
Brantôme, Pierre de Bourdeilles de, 69
Bridgnorth, 106
Bright, John, 49, 137
Bristol, 101
Broglie, Albert Duc de, 80
Brontë, Charlotte, 129
Brougham, Henry Lord, 87
Brunswick, 162
Buccleuch, William sixth Duke of, 80
Buckland House, 43
Buckle, Henry, 111, 125
Buildwas, 106
Burghersh, Lord, *see* Westmorland, twelfth Earl of
Burke, Edmund, 5-6, 49, 75, 92-5, 97, 99-100, 107, 132
Burnaby, Andrew, 13
Burnand, Sir Francis, 36
Burton Constable, 41-2
Bute, John third Marquess of, 36
Byng, Frederick Gerald, 80
Byng, George Henry, 80
Byron, George Gordon sixth Lord, 23, 67

Calahorra, 162
Cambridge, 52
   Magdalene College, 27-72
   Trinity College, 6
   University Library, 160
Campan, Madame, 160
Canning, Charles John Earl of, 8, 145
Capes, John More, 120
Carcassonne, 92
Carlisle, Georgina Countess of, 51
Carlow, 131, 137
Carlsbad, 126
Carlton House, 44
Carlyle, Thomas, 112-13
Carrington, 39
Carte, Thomas, 127
Caserta, 16, 24
Castel Gandolfo, 34
Castellamare, 22

Catherine II, Tsarina of Russia, 82-3
Cellini, Benvenuto, 160
Charles V, Emperor, 157, 169
Charles X, King of France, 65
Chassériau, Theodore, 88
Chateaubriand, François René de, 83-4
Chatsworth, 80
Chester Races, 146
Chesterfield, Philip Dormer, fourth Earl of, 143
Chevreuse, Duchesse de, 79
Chideock, 9
Choiseul, Étienne-François Duc de, 159
Clarendon, Edward first Earl of, 127, 128
Clifford, Hugh seventh Lord, 70
Coalbrookdale, 106
Cobden, Richard, 49, 132, 137
Coburg, 29
Cologne, 55 ; Cathedral, 63
Condillac, Étienne Bonnot de, 84
Confucius, 60
Constance, 155
Constantinople, 18
Cordova, 162
Costessey, 39
Coughton Court, 44-5
Courier, Paul-Louis, 103
Cousin, Victor, 79
Cox, Edward, 70
Craven, Mrs. Augustus, 20-3, 124
Creighton, Mandell, 184-5
Cromwell, Oliver, 152
Croy-Dülmen, Cardinal Gustave de, 26
Cuenca, 162
Culm, 162

Dachenhausen, Baroness von, 28
Dalberg, Emerich Duc de, 20, 26-7, 76, 101
   Marie (de Brignole-Sala), Duchesse de, his wife, 28
   Marie, his daughter, *see* Acton
   Primate Karl Theodor, his brother, 20
Dalgairns, John Dobree, 117-18
Dalkeith, Lord, *see* Buccleuch, sixth Duke of
Danton, Georges-Jacques, 91
Darnall, Nicholas, 121
Darrel, Mrs., 12
Dartmouth, George second Earl of, 16
   William third Earl of, 16
Deloraine, 64
Dennistoun, James, 109

INDEX

Devonshire, William sixth Duke of, 80
   Georgiana (Spencer) Duchess of, his mother, 47
Dickens, Charles, 129
Digby, Kenelm, 150
Dittisham, 71
Dodd, Charles, 127
Döllinger, Ignaz von, 8-9, 67-75, and *passim*
Doncaster, 21, 146
Dryden, John, 67
Dublin, 114-15
Dugdale, Sir William, 10
Dunraven, Edwin third Earl of, 119
Dupanloup, Felix-Antoine, 100, 104
Durham coalfield, 39

Eaton Constantine, 106
Eboli, Duchess of, 21
Eckstein, Baron, 83
Edinburgh, 72
Eglinton Tournament, 48
Eichhorn, Gottfried, 68
Elgin, Thomas seventh Earl of, 18
Ellesmere, George second Earl of, 73
Ellice, Edward, 171
Engels, Friedrich, 147
Enville Hall, 14
Eshe, 39
Eton, 21
Eugene, Prince, 56
Exmoor, 44

Faber, Frederick William, 121
Falkland, Lucius second Viscount, 154
Fantuzzi, Giovanni, 74
Febronius, Justinus, 58
Fénelon, François de, 68
Ferdinand I, King of the Two Sicilies, 15-18
Ferdinand II, 23
Finlay, George, 76, 150
Fitzgerald, Sir William Seymour, 171
Florence, 42
Floridia, Duchess of, 21
Fox, Charles James, 51, 153
Fox, Hon. Henry, 23-4
Foxcote, 41
Francis I, King of France, 69
Frankfort Diet, 68
Frascati, 23
Frederick II, King of Prussia, 184
Frederick William IV, 63

Freeman, Edward Augustus, 149
Freiburg-im-Breisgau, 63
Froude, James Anthony, 149
Fullerton, Lady Georgiana, 48-9
Granville, 48

Galiani, Ferdinando, 102
Gams, Pius Bonifacius, 158
Garampi, Giuseppe, 37
Gardiner, Samuel Rawson, 112-13, 149
Gatchina, 17
Gibbon, Edward, 11-12, 15, 98, 108
Giesebrecht, Wilhelm von, 110
Gindely, Anton, 156
Gladstone, William Ewart, 51, 72, 86, 100, 145, 147
Goethe, Johann Wolfgang von, 70
Goodwood, 146
Gordon, Sir Robert, 53
Görres, Josef von, 65
Gortchakoff, Prince Alexander, 81
Göttingen, 74, 76
Grace Dieu Manor, 41
Granard, George seventh Earl of, 36
Grant, Thomas, 119
Grant Duff, Sir Mountstuart, 53, 132
Granville, George second Earl, 46-53 *passim*
   Marie (de Dalberg) Countess, his wife, *see* Acton
   Henrietta (Cavendish), his mother, 51
Gratry, Auguste Joseph, 121
Green, John Richard, 149
Grenville, William Lord, 19
Greville, Charles, 142, 144, 146
Grey, Charles second Earl, 153
Guizot, François, 50, 64, 97, 145
Guthrie, Thomas, 143

Hafod, 108
Hallam, Henry, 127
Hamilton, Sir William, 16-17
   Emma Lady, 18
Hardwick, Charles, 125
Hardwicke, Philip second Earl of, 16
Harrington, James, 153
Harvington, 53
Hawarden, 53
Hegel, George William Friedrich, 74
Heine, Heinrich, 65, 147
Herbert, John, 52
Herder, Johann Gottfried
Herrnsheim, 26, 48, 51, 54

Hesleyside, 41
Hesse-Philippsthal, Landgravine of, 28
Hobbes, Thomas, 153
Holdford Farm, 33
Hontheim, Johann Niklaus von, 58
Hooton Hall, 41
Hope, James, 71-2
Husenbeth, Frederick, 45

Ince Blundell Hall, 41
Ironbridge, 39

Jerningham, Augustus, 52
Johnes, Thomas, 108
Joinville, Jean de, 108
Joseph II, Emperor, 59, 61

Kaunitz, Wenzel Anton Prince von, 59
Keble, John, 71
Kerr, Lord Henry, 71
Kidderminster, 44
Kimberley, John first Earl of, 81
Kingsley, Charles, 129
Kirchberger, Dr., 155
Knowsley, 138
Königsberg, 24

La Cloche, James, 111, 127
Ladykirk, 38
Lafayette, Marie-Joseph Marquis de, 91
La Ferronays, Albert de, 22-4
La Fontaine, Jean de, 160
Lamennais, Félicité de, 83-4
Lamoignon de Malesherbes, Chrétien de, 89
Landseer, Sir Edwin, 142
Landshut, 63
Langdale, Mrs., 18
Lanjuinais, Comte, 96
Lapoukhyn, Prince, 24
Lappenberg, Johann Martin, 156
La Salette, Notre Dame de, 118
Lasaulx, Ernst, 163
Leamington, 45
Leghorn, 11-13
   Annunciata dei Greci, 13
   Cisterone, 13
   English factory, 13
   Porto Mediceo, 13
Leibnitz, Gottfried Wilhelm von, 128
Letterfourie, 53
Leveson, Lord, see Granville, second Earl

Lewisham, Lord, see Dartmouth, third Earl of
Lichfield, Thomas second Earl of, 80
Lieven, Dorothea Princess, 83
Lincoln, Earl of, see Newcastle, sixth Duke of
Ligne, Eugene Prince de, 81
Lingard, John, 127
Lisle, Ambrose de, 41
Llanarth, 41, 52
Lobenstein, 69
Locke, John, 153
London—
   Athenaeum, 132, 150
   Bank of England, 139
   Bedford Row, 134
   Bethnal Green, 134
   British Museum, 143
   Bruton Street, 47, 51, 121
   Brompton Oratory, 121, 122, 148
   Bryanston Square, 134
   Cavendish Square, 30
   Coventry House, 80
   Devonshire House, 47
   Downing Street, 174
   Edgware Road, 142
   Euston Square, 141
   Exeter Hall, 143, 144
   Foley Place, 30
   George Street, 30
   Golder's Green, 80-1
   Holland House, 153
   Hoxton, 149
   Kensington Gardens, 143
   Lambeth, 149
   Lincoln's Inn, 150
   National Gallery, 143
   Portman Square, 134
   Reform Club, 137
   Southwark Bridge, 40
   Surrey Gardens, 142
   University, 31
   Westminster School, 27
   York Place, 148
Londonderry, Frances Anne Marchioness of, 142
Louis XIV, King of France, 63, 84, 103
Louis XV, 103
Louis XVI, 89
Louis XVIII, 27
Louis-Philippe, King of the French, 68, 89, 97
Louth, Randal thirteenth Lord, 36

INDEX

Loyola, St. Ignatius, 71
Lucca, Charles Louis Duke of, 21
Ludwig I, King of Bavaria, 63-4, 76
Ludwig II, 70
Lushington, Sir Henry, 21
Lynar, Roch Friedrich Count von, 159
Lyons, Richard Earl, 166
Lytton, Edward Bulwer-, 129

Macaulay, Thomas Babington Lord, 110-11, 125, 127, 145
Machiavelli, Nicolo, 98
Mackintosh, Sir James, 127
McKnight, Thomas, 138
MacMullen, Richard Gell, 117-18
Madeley, 106
Mainz, 55
Maistre, Joseph de, 63, 125
Malmesbury, James third Earl of, 171
Malta, 25
    Order of, 17
Manning, Henry Edward Cardinal, 118, 174
Marescalchi, Countess Anna, 28
Maret, Henri-Louis, 121
Maria Carolina, Queen of the Two Sicilies, 15-18
Maria Cristina, Queen of Spain, 23
Maria Theresa, Empress, 59, 164
Marie Louise, Empress, 27
Marie Nicolaievna, Grand Duchess, 82
Marini, Luigi Gaetano, 74
Marlborough, John Duke of, 56
Marshall, Sir James, 117-18
Martin, Henri, 95
Marx, Karl, 147
Masurian Lakes, 24
Mathew, Theobald, 35
Maximilian II, King of Bavaria, 69
Maynooth, 148
Mecklenburg-Strelitz, George Grand Duke of, 65
Melrose, 64
Mentmore, 142
Mentone, 28
Metternich-Winneburg, Clement Prince von, 82
Metz, 102
Michelet, Jules, 102
Migne, Jacques-Paul, 83
Mill, John Stuart, 87, 137
Millais, Sir John Everett, 142
Milner, John, 34

Milton, John, 67
Minton, 80
Miot de Mélito, André, 87
Mirabeau, Honoré Gabriel de Riqueti, Comte de, 84
Mivart, St. George, 36
Molland, 44
Moltke, Count Helmuth von, 70
Monaco, 28
Monaco, Charles III, Prince of, 53
Monstrelet, Enguerrand de, 108
Mont Blanc, 21
Montalembert, Charles Comte de, 23, 104, 125
Monte Cassino, 37
Monte Pellegrino, 37
Montes, Lola, 64
Montesquieu, Charles Baron de, 60
Moore, Thomas, 23, 67
Morny, Charles Louis Duc de, 81
Morville, 133
Moscow, 78-82
    Graziani Palace, 81
Mostyn, Frances Lady, 9
Mount Edgcumbe, Richard second Earl of, 71
Moyen Moutier, 162
Munich, 56-73
    Austrian Legation, 71
    English Garden, 68
    Old *Pinakothek*, 68
    Residenz, 56
    Royal Library, 69
Münster, 59
Muratori, Lodovico Antonio, 74

Nantes, Edict of, 103
Naples—
    Capo di Monte, 21
    Casa Margherita, 22
    Palazzo Acton alla Chiaja, 20, 22, 24
    Via della Chiaja, 21
Napoleon I, Emperor, 102
Napoleon III, 95-6
Nassau, Adolf Duke of, 65
Navestock, 149
Nelson, Horatio Viscount, 18
Newcastle, Henry sixth Duke of, 80
Newman, John Henry, Cardinal, 114-22
Newport Pagnell, 33
Nicholas I, Tsar of Russia, 65, 82
Niebuhr, Barthold Georg, 75, 77
Noble, Matthew, 48

Norfolk, Bernard twelfth Duke of, 39
   Henry thirteenth Duke of, 39
   Henry fourteenth Duke of, 115
Noris, Enrico, Cardinal, 74
Norwich, 43
Nottingham, 141

Oakeley, Frederick, 117-18
O'Connell, Daniel, 35
Oldfield, Mrs., 48
Orleans, 101
Orsay, Count Alfred d', 88
Orsi, Giuseppe Agostino, Cardinal, 74
Osborne, Ralph Bernal, 171
Oscott, 31-7, 45, 53
Ottobeuren, 60
Oxford—
   Balliol College, 120
   Christ Church, 71
   Merton College, 72
   Oriel College, 114, 118, 150
   Trinity College, 149

Pacca, Bartolomeo Cardinal, 169
Paget, Sir Arthur, 18-19
Palermo, 17, 18
   Monte Pellegrino, 17
Palmerston, Henry John third Viscount, 131, 137, 172
Paris—
   Faubourg St. Germain, 83-4, 102
   Faubourg St. Honoré, 27
   Port-Royal des Champs, 58
   Rue d'Anjou, 27
   Rue de Babylon, 87
   Rue de Bac, 87
   Rue de Castellane, 87
   Rue Saint-Florentin, 54
   Rue Saint-Guillaume, 53
   Saint-Nicolas du Chardonnet, 53
Parry, John Orlando, 20
Pascal, Blaise, 92
Pater, Walter, 187
Pauli, Reinhold, 159
Payne, James, 123
Peel, Sir Robert, 80
Pekin, 35
Persigny, Victor Comte de, 101
Petavius or Petau, Denis, 75
Pétigny, François Jules de, 102
Petre, Mary Teresa Lady, 123
Pisa, 11 ; San Giovanni al Gatano, 11
Platina, 163

Pollen, John Hungerford, 72
Ponsonby, Gerald Henry, 80
Popes—
   Benedict XI, 128
   Benedict XIV, 74
   Boniface VIII, 128
   Boniface IX, 128
   Clement VIII, 158
   Clement XIV, 59, 162
   Gregory XVI, 29, 34, 82
   Innocent XI, 162
   Julius II, 68, 169
   Leo X, 68
   Pius V, 157
   Pius VI, 162
   Pius VII, 162
   Pius IX, 23, 166, 168
Praslin, Duchesse de, 161
Preobajensky Guards, 25
Psara, 66
Pugin, Augustus Welby, 33, 40
Pusey, Edward Bouverie, 71-2
Putbus, Count, 24
Putz, Wilhelm, 151
Pym, John, 153

Quin, Dr., 27

Racine, Jean, 103
Radetzky, Johann Karl Count von, 76
Radowitz, Josef von, 65
Raleigh, Sir Walter, 98, 158
Ranke, Leopold von, 78, 104, 126
Reade, Charles, 129
Reeve, Henry, 91, 101, 173-5
Reichensperger, August, 63
Renan, Ernest, 53-4
Reumont, Alfred von, 156
Reuss, 69
Rhodes, 101
Ringseis, Dr., 63
Robertson, James Craigie, 125
Roebuck, John Arthur, 171
Rome, 13, 22
   Coliseum, 22
   German College, 64
   Gesu, the, 127
   Palazzo Barberini, 126
   Palazzo Simonetti, 48
   San Bernardo alle Terme, 29
   Santa Maria della Pace, 37
   SS. Trinità del Monte, 22
Roscher, Wilhelm, 157

INDEX

Roscoe, William, 109
Rossini, Gioacchino, 21
Rotherwas, 41
Round Acton, 11
Royer-Collard, Pierre-Paul, 91
Ruffo, Fabrizio, Cardinal, 18
Rugby, 153
Ruinart, Thierry, 157, 158
Rumford, Benjamin Count von, 19
Russell, John first Earl, 50, 153

St. John, Joseph, 27 ; Lady Isabella, 27
Saint-Laurent-du-Var, 87
Saint-Martin, Louis Claude de, 154-5
St. Petersburg, 8, 24-5, 82-3
   Catherine Canal, 182
   Leuchtenberg Palace, 82
   Winter Palace, 25
Saint-Simon, Louis Duc de, 154-5
Sankt Martin, 133
Savigny, Friedrich Karl von, 68
Schérer, Edmond, 98
Schiller, Friedrich, 69, 70, 98
Schlegel, Friedrich, 84
Schleiss, 69
Scott, James Hope, *see* Hope, James
Scott, Sir Walter, 64, 70
Selden, John, 152
Senft-Pilsach, Count, 84
Senior, Nassau, 87-91, 137
Shaftesbury, Anthony Ashley seventh Earl of, 144
Shakespeare, William, 70
Sheridan, Richard Brinsley, 51
Shaw-Lefevre, Sir John, 73
Shiffnal Manor, 39
Shrewsbury, 14
Shrewsbury, John sixteenth Earl of, 35, 39
Sidney, Algernon, 152, 153
Sigonius or Sigone, Carlo, 75
Simancas, 156
Simpson, Richard, 87, 106
Smythe, Sir Edward, 38-9
Solesmes, 61
Somerleaze, 149
Somers, John Lord, 152
Sorrento, 91
Spetchley, 41
Spurgeon, Charles Haddon, 49
Stafford, George eighth Lord, 39
Stafford, Marquess of, *see* Sutherland, third Duke of

Stair, John fifth Earl of, 159
Stamford, Harry fourth Earl of, 14
Stanhope, Philip Henry fifth Earl, 145
Stockholm, 25
Stolberg, Count Friedrich Leopold von, 84
Stralsund, 163
Strawberry Hill, 10
Strelitz, 65
Stubbs, William, 149
Surrey and Arundel, Earl of, *see* Norfolk, fourteenth Duke of
Sutherland, George third Duke of, 80
Swetchine, Madame, 83
Swynnerton, 41
Sybel, Heinrich von, 77

Talacre, 124
Talleyrand-Périgord, Charles Maurice de, 27
Tarrazona, 125
Taylor, Jeremy, 160
Tedder, Henry, 163
Tegernsee, 68
Terracina, 23
Tetschen, 71
Thackeray, William Makepeace, 129, 130
Thierry, Augustin, 102
Thiers, Adolphe, 50
Thorndon, 41, 123
Throckmorton, Sir Robert, 30, 31, 43
   Elizabeth (Acton), his wife, Lady, 19, 43
Thun und Hohenstein, Count Friedrich von, 71
Tichborne, Roger, 41
Tillemont, Sébastien Le Nain de, 158
Tilsit, 19
Tixall, 41
Tocqueville, Alexis de, 86-98, 137 ; château of, 88-9
Trafalgar, 19
Treitschke, Heinrich von, 77
Trent, 74
Trentham, 47
Trevelyan, Sir George Otto, 111
Trier, 55, 58
Trollope, Anthony, 129
Tübingen, 74
Tunbridge Wells, 43
Turin, 162

Ullathorne, William Bernard, 121
Urbino, 109
Ushaw, 122
Utrecht, Peace of, 5
Utterson, Edward, 107-8

Valognes, 88
Val Richer, 145
Vaughan, Henry Halford, 127
Vavasour, Sir Edward, 52, 70
Venice, 126, 136
Vere, Aubrey de, 122
Versailles, 86, 103
Veuillot, Louis, 87
Via Aurelia, 12
Vichy, 80
Viel-Castel, Louis de, 88
Vienna, 24
Villefranche, 28
Villiers, Hon. Mrs. George, 143
Viollet-le-Duc, Eugène, 92
Vitrolles, Eugène de, 84
Voltaire, François Arouet de, 42, 102

Wallenstein, Albrecht von, 157
Walpole, Sir Spencer, 50
Ward, Thomas Baron, 21
Ward, Wilfrid, 35
Ward, William George, 118, 120

Wardour Castle, 41, 43, 123, 127
Ware, St. Edmund's College, 70
Wareing, William, 34
Waterton, Charles, 41
Webbe, Samuel, 33
Weedall, Henry, 9, 44
Weld, Sir Frederick, 123
Wellington, Arthur first Duke of, 67
Wells, 149
Wenlock, 106
Wessenberg, Freiherr Ignaz von, 155
Westmorland, Francis twelfth Earl of, 80
Weston Underwood, 43
Whiteladies, 106
Wiesbaden, 65
Wilberforce, Henry, 118
Wimpole Hall, 16
Windischmann, Dr., 115-16
Winwood, Sir Ralph, 127
Wiseman, Nicholas Cardinal, 30-8, 123-124, 131
Wolverhampton, 134
Wooton Wawen, 39
Worcester, 106
Würzburg, 69, 162
Wynnstay, 146

Ximena, Martin de, 162

Zoroaster, 60

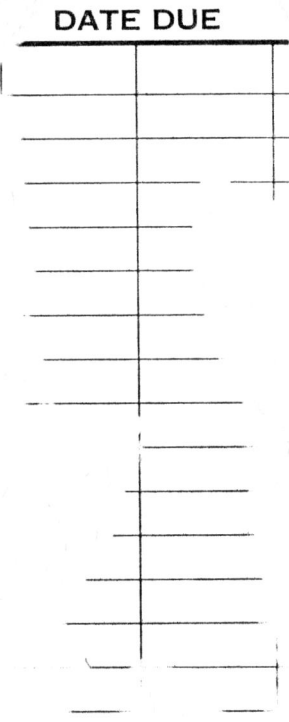